Library of
Davidson College

The Task of Universities in a Changing World. Stephen D. Kertesz, ed.

The Church and Social Change in Latin America. Henry A. Landsberger, ed.

Revolution and Church: The Early History of Christian Democracy, 1789–1901. Hans Maier.

The Overall Development of Chile. Mario Zañartu, S.J., and John J. Kennedy, eds.

The Catholic Church Today: Western Europe. M. A. Fitzsimons, ed.

Contemporary Catholicism in the United States. Philip Gleason, ed.

The Major Works of Peter Chaadaev. Raymond T. McNally.

A Russian European: Paul Miliukov in Russian Politics. Thomas Riha.

A Search for Stability: U. S. Diplomacy Toward Nicaragua, 1925–1933. William Kamman.

Freedom and Authority in the West. George N. Shuster, ed.

Theory and Practice: History of a Concept from Aristotle to Marx. Nicholas Lobkowicz.

Coexistence: Communism and Its Practice in Bologna, 1945–1965. Robert H. Evans.

Marx and the Western World. Nicholas Lobkowicz, ed.

Argentina's Foreign Policy 1930–1962. Alberto A. Conil Paz and Gustavo E. Ferrari.

Italy after Fascism, A Political History, 1943–1965. Giuseppe Mammarella.

The Volunteer Army and Allied Intervention in South Russia, 1917–1921. George A. Brinkley.

Peru and the United States, 1900–1962. James C. Carey.

INTERNATIONAL STUDIES OF THE COMMITTEE ON INTERNATIONAL RELATIONS UNIVERSITY OF NOTRE DAME

Empire by Treaty: Britain and the Middle East in the Twentieth Century. M. A. Fitzsimons.

The USSR and the UN's Economic and Social Activities. Harold Karan Jacobson.

Chile and the United States: 1880–1962. Fredrick B. Pike.

East Central Europe and the World: Developments in the Post-Stalin Era. Stephen D. Kertesz, ed.

Soviet Policy Toward International Control of Atomic Energy. Joseph L. Nogee.

The Russian Revolution and Religion, 1917–1925. Edited and translated by Bolesław Szcześniak.

Soviet Policy Toward the Baltic States, 1918–1940. Albert N. Tarulis.

Introduction to Modern Politics. Ferdinand Hermens.

Freedom and Reform in Latin America. Fredrick B. Pike, ed.

What America Stands For. Stephen D. Kertesz and M. A. Fitzsimons, eds.

Theoretical Aspects of International Relations. William T. R. Fox, ed.

Catholicism, Nationalism and Democracy in Argentina. John J. Kennedy.

The Fate of East Central Europe. Stephen D. Kertesz, ed.

German Protestants Face the Social Question. William O. Shanahan.

Soviet Imperialism: Its Origins and Tactics. Waldemar Gurian, ed.

The Foreign Policy of the British Labour Government, 1945–1951. M. A. Fitzsimons.

Bolshevism: An Introduction to Soviet Communism. Waldemar Gurian.

Democracy in Crisis:
New Challenges to Constitutional
Democracy in the Atlantic Area

Democracy in Crisis

New Challenges to Constitutional Democracy in the Atlantic Area

Edited by E. A. GOERNER

CONTRIBUTORS

Jean Blondel • Gerhart Niemeyer
Donald P. Kommers • Glenn Tinder • Robert H. Evans
Giovanni Bognetti • Douglas V. Verney • Anthony Hartley
Bastiaan van der Esch • E. A. Goerner

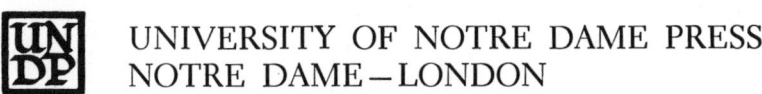 UNIVERSITY OF NOTRE DAME PRESS
NOTRE DAME – LONDON

Copyright © 1971 by
University of Notre Dame Press
Notre Dame, Indiana 46556

Library of Congress Catalog Card Number: 70-160487
Manufactured in the United States of America by
NAPCO Graphic Arts, Inc., Milwaukee, Wisconsin

CONTENTS

Introduction   E. A. Goerner   xi

1. Challenges to Democracy in Britain and France   1
   Jean Blondel
2. The "New Left"   19
   Gerhart Niemeyer
3. Judicial Power and Constitutional Democracy
   in Italy and West Germany   33
   Donald P. Kommers
4. Current Challenges to Democracy in the United States   65
   Glenn Tinder
5. The Changing Role of the Communist Party in Italy   89
   Robert H. Evans
6. The Crisis of Parliamentary Government in Italy   111
   Giovanni Bognetti
7. Challenges to Democracy in Canada   133
   Douglas V. Verney
8. The Withering Away of Western Liberal Democracy   153
   Anthony Hartley
9. The European Community and Constitutional Democracy   165
   Bastiaan van der Esch
10. Epimetheus   177
    E. A. Goerner

Notes on the Contributors   197

INTRODUCTION

The papers that compose this volume are the work of a conference that was conceived and organized by Professor Stephen Kertesz, Director of the West European Studies Program. Held in March of 1970 at the University of Notre Dame, the conference brought together a group of participants from diverse parts of Europe and North America. Of course, it is quite possible to bring together a group of scholars from various North Atlantic countries whose intellectual formations and points of view are virtually identical. But in this case, the diversity of the participants was, by design, rather wide and the papers reflect a wide range of intellectual tendencies and methods.

The papers express conservative and liberal views. There are elements of behavioral, philosophical, and legal method. Furthermore, the nature of the specific subject matters and nations about which the participants were asked to speak inescapably imposed a further diversification of the conference's papers. Nevertheless, there is a powerfully unifying thread that may not at first sight appear to the casual reader. The diversities are easier to see and so I will review them first.

Our participants were quite diverse in their views both as to what might be the appropriate methods of political inquiry, as the reader can easily see, and even as to what questions it might be appropriate to raise in pursuit of political science.

The material diversity of their contributions is quite as great as the formal. Their papers range over six countries and the European Community. And within those countries the foci of concern are various: problems connected with the political movement commonly called the "New Left," operations and problems of constitutional courts, defects in the American view of reality, problems of integrating a, perhaps, formerly revolutionary party into a bourgeois democracy, problems in bi-cultural democracies, developmental problems for democracy within a dynamic of international integration, the problems of superficially rooted democratic institutions burdened with the massive demands associated with major economic, social, and cultural change.

The obvious danger in such a conference is that it turn out to be no conference at all but merely an unrelated series of papers that happen to deal with matters in Europe or North America. But this conference had a common element.

The uniting thread was the sort of concern that citizens and scholars may share. In his letters of invitation to the conference, Professor Kertesz wrote that "the nations of the North Atlantic area, including the United States, have a common cultural heritage which is founded on the principles of democracy, individual liberty and the rule of law." Although they may have wished that one or another principle might be added to that triad, the participants did not object to that triad's being seen as central to the fundament of their common cultural heritage. Nor did they reject the other basic formulation in Professor Kertesz's letters of invitation: "The major issue of our time is whether these [free] institutions, along with political democracy itself, can survive the internal conflicts and social problems that currently afflict these nations."

The fact that those formulations were accepted by the participants[*] inevitably gave to the conference a broadly conservative character. The political institutions of the participants' states, all of them democratic, were not radically questioned by the participants. Even Professor Tinder's paper, which is radically critical of what he takes to be some root presuppositions of American public life, does not call into question the formulations that structured the invitation. Of course, that might not be too surprising given the fact that invitations in general are normally tendered and accepted by people who have something in common.

But reflection leads one to notice a more curious phenomenon: even had the most radical critics of the institutional structures and functioning of North Atlantic democracies participated in the conference one could not reasonably have expected to hear democracy

---

[*] For obvious reasons I exclude from discussion my own paper which, although it appears at the end of this volume, recounts a dialogue that preceded the conference.

INTRODUCTION

criticized in principle. One *could* have expected a variety of arguments showing that the constitutional democracy of the bourgeois states in question was sham democracy: that the constitutionalism in question was an obscurantist trick, typical of bourgeois formalism, used to conceal the really oligarchical character of political power in bourgeois society; that "the rule of law" carries a facade of formal equality over every sphere of social life where, in fact, the most grotesque inequalities actually prevail; that the "individual liberty" of the poor and the black in our societies is a hypothetical liberty hiding real bondage; that the freedom of speech and inquiry formally guaranteed by our institutions is actually available only to those few with the financial resources to employ the enormously expensive machinery of study and communication; and other charges of similar character and weight.

But is it reasonable to suppose that someone would have questioned the validity of democracy? Evidently, the partisans of the liberal establishments would not be expected to do that. But might one imagine a radical voice suggesting that rule of the people on the basis of liberty and equality is not altogether desirable? To be sure one might imagine a radical view that the way to assure such a goal is not, in a modern, technological, mass society where the forms of athenian, city-state democracy cannot suffice, the alternative offered by liberalism: multiple group membership and the politics of competing and countervailing groups. One can imagine a radical voice arguing that the masses have been so seduced by the manipulative techniques of bourgeois society that the masses in a formally free election would scarcely choose an authentically democratic economic, social, and political life since they would be unable even to envisage such a life. And one can imagine a "radical, revolutionary" voice arguing that democracy can only be achieved by traversing a transitional period during which a creative minority would hold the initiative in both the work of bringing down the bourgeois system and the work of educating and leading the masses to political, social, and economic maturity. But can one imagine a radical voice suggesting that political, social, and economic maturity would not be democratic in character, based on individual freedom and equality?

The papers in this volume do not include the voices of the revolutionary minorities directly. They are only represented by their opponents. But the literate reader will have no difficulty in articulating for himself the main thrust of the replies they would make to what is said of them here. But having done that, the literate and reflective reader will be struck by the fact that the most radical challenge to democracy has still not been raised and he will wonder what it is in our situation that keeps it out of sight, permitting it to appear only in corrupt and corrupting inversions. It is, at root, to raise the question whether a kind of mature political, social, and economic life is possible for us that would be integrally structured by human excellence yet compatible with the elements of equality and liberty inherent in our notions of justice. That question is infinitely more radical in its challenge to democratic dogma than any issue raised by contemporary revolutionary minorities because it questions the final congruity with the full range of human experience of a regime rooted exclusively in liberty and equality.

Contemporary radical, revolutionary minorities, like the Romans, view dictatorship as, by nature, a crisis measure, a temporary measure, a transitional measure, unfortunately necessary. It may be true, as their opponents charge—indeed it is almost surely true—that the transitions into decisively new phases of history are less easy and less clearly marked than revolutionaries imagine and, by consequence, that such dictatorships may not be very temporary. But the value of a society organized exclusively in terms of liberty and equality as the *telos* of revolutionary action is not questioned and, therefore, the substance of the democratic principle is not questioned. This is what gives the contemporary challenges to constitutional democracy their curiously conservative dimension, their developmental continuity with the democratic establishment.

Were an authentically radical challenge to democracy, one that went to the roots, to be posed it would consist in asking seriously what neither we nor the revolutionary minorities asked: Is it really as clear and sure as everyone thinks that authentic aristocracy is impossible? It is clear and sure enough that the rule of the best in terms of wealth, or birth, or status, or brains, or will, or their combinations is both possible and odious. But the radical question would be whether some few men can achieve or be blessed with a simple human excellence or virtue compatible with fraternity such that a polity might freely accept it in them as a standard or rule to struggle toward and be measured by.

Our conference was not directed to that question. It was directed to the far more frequently raised challenge to the "constitutional," liberal, procedural, formal-legal versions of democracy and to the related problem that such challenges to the adjectives and what they stand for may turn out to be challenges to democracy itself even though the challengers may not think so. Those are important matters to discuss and it seems to me that the papers in this volume throw valuable light on them. The conventions of large-scale, foundation-supported, public, academic conferences are particularly suited to the illumination of such critical problems and to the work of intellectual cross-fertilization produced by the confrontation of diverse views about such an issue as the nature and scope of challenges to constitutional democracy. If conferences such as ours were actually organized to discuss as a serious alternative to democracy the more radical issue of aristocracy, democracy would scarcely be the universal thought-form for political life that it evidently is in modern society. At such a time it is inevitable that only other, less representative contexts are likely to see raised and, given the peculiar dangers inherent in such a discussion, are likely to be well suited to discussing that radical question in relation to democracy: concerning the possibility and political relevance of comprehensive human virtue.

E. A. Goerner

1: CHALLENGES TO DEMOCRACY IN BRITAIN AND FRANCE
Jean Blondel

For the historian, the 1960s will probably constitute one of the most puzzling periods of the twentieth century. Having started in a very conservative atmosphere in most developed countries, the decade ended in a tone of widespread questioning of all established institutions, including those of the left. In 1959, Eisenhower and Adenauer were in power, de Gaulle had routed his opponents and his only fear was from the "fascist" right, while Macmillan was leading the Conservative Party to its greatest victory for a generation. There were no student troubles, workers seemed to demand higher wages to buy more consumer goods. The total "end of ideology" appeared to be in sight. Ten years later, Labour rule had brought disillusionment in Britain among many sections of the working class and the "intelligentsia." De Gaulle had barely survived one of the most traumatic episodes of French contemporary history and was eventually forced to resign on a referendum defeat, while French Communists were branded as defenders of the "system," like "mere Social-Democrats." The permissive society, first limited to dress and personal behavior, had extended to all aspects of political life. Brutally and suddenly, as in France in the spring of 1968, or very gently and insidiously, as in Britain, all Western democracies seemed to be attacked and undermined.

Attacks of this kind are not without precedent, of course. Indeed, there is much more anomy or instability in Western democracies than one is usually led to believe. In France, sudden collapses in the "will to work" occurred with strange regularity every fifteen years or so throughout the century (1909, 1920, 1936, 1953, 1968). Britain itself is not always placid: demonstrations and strikes were common in the thirties; in the last few years before 1914, the country seemed to border on civil war. It may be that periods during which the "system" is accepted without question are exceptional, but the end of the 1960s were peculiar in that discontent was not the direct consequence of major economic difficulties or did not focus on clashes between supporters and opponents of democracy. The closest parallel to the current form of direct action can be found in the wave of syndicalism of the early part of the century, a period during which the standard of living was comparatively high and parliamentary democracy was beginning to be accepted by the right. But social and political life was vastly different, since consumer goods were shared only by a small fraction of the population and socialism had not begun to look "respectable."

The challenge facing modern democracies at the end of the 1960s —Britain and France in particular—is thus in many ways paradoxical and in part the by-product of the success of the mixed economy. First, the challenge is not, ostensibly at least, a challenge to democracy. It is a challenge to contemporary democracies of the West, often made in the name of democracy, and in particular in the name of "fuller" participation. It is a challenge about a way of life, about cultural arrangements, more than about economics. It is a challenge about boredom more than about hunger. Second, it is a challenge without an institutional base, which uses art (or pseudo-art) more than parties and pressure groups and revives traditional feelings, such as nationalism, as much as it fosters new forms of "communal" living. Third, it occurs at the time when democracies have become readier than ever to accept forms of participation and decentralization; indeed it seems to increase as democracies become more open. Thus democracies have difficulties in both understanding and meeting the challenge. It seems to occur as a cataclysm which has to be weathered, and indeed has been weathered everywhere, even though the escape was narrow, or so it seems, in the case of France. It poses for the future, therefore, a very serious problem for Western democracies, as the dynamics of the growth and decrease of the "disease" are far from clear. While concentrating in this paper on two Western countries, Britain and France, in which unrest was, respectively, relatively low and very high, we should remember that this challenge extends, directly or by imitation, to all Western democracies and raises serious questions for the future stability of all of them.

A CHALLENGE TO DEMOCRACY?

This, of course, is not the place to examine in detail the various strands of opinion which characterize what has come to be known as the "radical left"; but it is important to note that one of the major difficulties for contemporary democracies arises from the fact that the opponents do not attack democracies because they are democratic, but because they are deemed to be not really democratic. Interestingly enough, one of the by-products of the current wave of left-wing discontent has been to silence almost completely, both in France and Britain, right-wing opponents of democracy. The contrast is particularly sharp in France with the late 1950s. At the time, first Poujadism and, later, some segments of Gaullism appeared to constitute real dangers for democracy; even under de Gaulle threats of military take-over, spurred by the discontent of the French settlers in Algeria, seemed very real indeed. A decade later, there was scarcely a move from the radical right to attack left-wing militants. 1968 was not characterized, as were the thirties, by clashes between right and left; only small groups of students, under the label of "Occident," made limited attempts to oppose the prevailing left-wing groups. Even the left, though usually prone to uncover conspiracies of the "fascist right," found it difficult to "stigmatize" more than isolated instances. Never, since World War II, and indeed probably never in contemporary France has the antidemocratic right been so insignificant.

Although the right-wing challenge always was much weaker in Britain than in France, it did lead to clashes in the 1930s and it seemed to be regaining strength in the early part of the 1960s, essentially over the issue of colored immigration. The Conservative party was affected; much speculation occurred at the time of the 1964 General Election in relation to the white backlash. In later years, however, the stand taken by Enoch Powell probably contributed, though somewhat paradoxically, to moderate the issue; moreover, the Labour government did take measures in relation to immigration which had the effect (though perhaps at the expense of natural justice, as in the context of the Kenya Indians) of reducing the explosive character of the issue. Meanwhile, the emergence of the radical left contributed to steer opinion away from the antidemocratic right and thus to reduce its potential membership.

The challenge faced by democracy in both Britain and France thus comes wholly from the left and it is wholly made in the name of democracy itself. But, as a further somewhat paradoxical by-product, the growth of the radical left also led to a decrease in the real strength of the Communist Party, which, in France at least, had undermined democracy since 1945 and even since the 1930s. Admittedly, the electoral strength of the French CP did not diminish during the 1960s (the decrease took place in 1958, when de Gaulle came to power) but the appeal of the radical left was probably sufficient in the second half of the 1960s to prevent the CP from recovering all the ground which it had lost ten years earlier (about 20 percent of the CP electors and 5 percent of the French electorate). Moreover, the CP was pushed on the defensive and lost its attractiveness in many intellectual quarters; it is unlikely to recover its prestige unless it becomes more open. Indeed, the pressure of the radical left may even force the party to become permanently less "Stalinist" in outlook, though the change will be only a slow one. The condemnation of Soviet intervention in Czechoslovakia was mild, half-hearted and almost taken back. But it did take place. The 1970 Congress of the Party did eventually dismiss Roger Garaudy from the Central Committee; but it allowed Garaudy to explain himself and even to attack the party leadership and Soviet policy from the platform.

Thus the increased challenge of the radical left may well have been compensated for in France by a gradual decline of the challenge of the CP. Indeed, overall, both in France and in Britain, the radical challenge has remained ambivalent about direct action: some liberal features may have accounted for its relative lack of success. Having started as critics of comtemporary society on the grounds that this society was culturally "repressive," members of the radical left became increasingly involved in concrete activities of mass participation, decentralization and institutional opening which did lead, in France at least, to a genuine democratization of many features of the polity. In trade unions, in farmers' organizations, in the universities, in the Roman Catholic church, the radical challenge has been in part directed at decreasing the hold which the traditional elite groups had on these organizations. As in relation to the CP, moves towards making groups more responsive to pressures contributed indirectly to a strengthening of the bases for democracy. Church-based organizations in France, for instance, do not constitute a potential base for the antidemocratic right; Communist-led unions have greater difficulties in organizing workers in favor of the purely political goals of the CP or of the Soviet Union, even though Communist unions have tried to regain some of the lost ground. In fact, Communist elements have even sometimes seemed to be the best supporters of law and order, particularly among students, and they have acquired some sympathies in middle class circles as a result. Thus the challenge of the radical left is both a challenge to democracy and a support for democracy. In Britain, where organizations have been relatively open and liberal, such developments have been less common, but some traces of the same phenomenon can be found in a variety of pressure groups and probably also in the universities.

Yet the radical left did mount a challenge to many political institutions, both in Britain and in France. The overall "plan" is somewhat romantic in character. It is literary and cultural as well as political and economic. Many literary figures occupied a prominent position in the British New Left of the late 1950s, which did constitute the starting point of the resurgence of the ideological left. Naturally enough, as a result, the theme of the cultural revolution preceded chronologically the participation theme, which was to characterize both the student protest in Britain and the May Revolution in France. From the theme of the cultural revolution stems the attack against the consumer society and the "insidious" influence of mass culture which is alleged to shape the tastes of individuals and thereby stop desire and ability for self-expression. The theme of the environment and of the necessity to create a society which can cater to the demands of men as creative individuals is closely associated to the cultural theme, but it also provides a link with the participation theme, which is more directly political and had, therefore, a greater immediate audience. (The masses are likely to be the "slaves" of mass culture and may, therefore, not respond easily to the anti-mass society themes.) The participation theme became increasingly dominant; it extended to local government (decentralization) and management (though workers' control was one of the early themes of the British New Left). It led to an analysis of rural life as well, at least in France, where the smallholder was being squeezed out of the land as a result of modernization. Thus the challenge of the radical left constitutes essentially a drive towards "fuller democracy"; it is idealistic rather than scientific, more Rousseauite than Leninist, more libertarian than authoritarian, rather unconcerned with the "transitional" phase to socialism and about possible difficulties relating to change in the attitudes of men.

A LIMITED ORGANIZATIONAL BASE

The "assault" on society conducted by the radical left, both in Britain and in France, is also somewhat romantic in that it did not aim at establishing a strong institutional base. Most of the activities of the radical left have taken place outside organizational structures. In Britain, no large organization, not even the National Union of Students, has been controlled by the radical left; a small breakaway organization, the Radical Students Association, had only limited support from the students' unions in universities and colleges. In France, the Union Nationale des Étudiants de France did appear at some time to be controlled by radicals, but this led to the gradual decline of the organization. In neither country was there a base as strong as even the American SDS, on which a campaign of national agitation could be started.

Admittedly, in France at least, one party, the Unified Socialist Party (PSU), did appear to support to some extent the views of the radical left. Particularly at the time of the May Revolution, the pronouncements of the PSU and the defense which it organized for the students seemed to suggest that the party might be gradually becoming a mouthpiece for the radical left. But the link was somewhat superficial and temporary. At the 1969 presidential election, the radicals supported their own candidate and did not rally to the PSU; the leadership of the party did not change during the 1968 Revolution or afterwards; the links between some of the radical student leaders and the national secretary of the party were episodic and the most radical student leaders never associated with the PSU. Moreover, since even in 1968, the electoral strength of the PSU was very small (2 percent of the electorate overall and 5 to 10 percent in the constituencies in which it was strong), the contrast between the apparent ability of the radicals to mobilize considerable anomic support and its inability or unwillingness to acquire a large organized base remained very marked indeed.

Both in France and in Britain, the challenge of the radical left thus depends on a combination of somewhat inchoate and unorganized support among sections of the electorate and on some infiltration among preexisting organizations. This mobilization of discontent on a nonorganized basis does therefore depend both on a capitalization on situations, which are unlikely to repeat themselves very often, and on the extent to which existing organizations are unable to deal with grievances. This, ultimately, explains why French political structures were more affected than British political structures, and why, in each country, student organizations were more affected than workers' or farmers' organizations, or why small farmers' organizations and national minority groups were more affected than workers' organizations.

Although the characteristics of student discontent and the role which students played in the development of left-wing radicalism is well documented, it is important to note that the climate of student opinion (as distinct from behavior) was not, and still is not very different in the two countries. Similar categories of students tend to be affected to a similar degree: scientists and engineers remain immune to radicalism, while social scientists and students of literature have been at the forefront of demonstrations. One is apt to minimize student troubles in the UK in comparison with the wild antics of French students during the period of the May Revolution, in particular at the beginning of the revolt, but the traditions of student behavior in France are such that it is difficult to give an adequate comparative measure of the *variation* in behavior as a result of the current wave of unrest. French students have always taken to the streets, whether for fun or politics, and clashes with the police are part of the folklore of French students' attitudes, particularly in Paris. The importance of the May revolt lies in what took place within university buildings, not in what took place around them; and what took place within French university buildings was echoed, somewhat faintly admittedly, within the buildings of many British universities. Large numbers of uncommitted or moderate students were suddenly mobilized into action (which often meant debating resolutions for long hours in buildings which had been occupied) by small minorities of radicals who denounced universities, the government, and the social system. This link between radicals and moderates was provoked by situations which the radicals were very eager to create. In most cases, the link was of short duration; but it did exist for a while, without an organizational base, indeed often against the existing organizations, as if anomic behavior was suddenly replacing the interest group characteristics of the society.

British farmers, and in particular British small farmers, are so few that any radical development on the land is very unlikely; the French peasantry is much larger and its antigovernmental attitudes are so ingrained that it became in part a ground for radical action. Radicals did succeed in holding some considerable influence in the CJA (Confédération des Jeunes Agriculteurs) in which left-wing Roman Catholics have always been relatively strong and even, for awhile, in the main farmers' organization, the FNSEA (Fédération Nationale des Syndicats d'Exploitants Agricoles). Ideas of cooperative organization of the land began to spread as a countermeasure to the changes which economic rejuvenation were bringing to rural France. French peasants had often adopted direct action tactics in the past; they became naturally prone to direct action under radical guidance. Indeed, the border between right-wing Poujadism and left-wing "cooperativism" is sometimes thin, and the attitudes of the peasantry at large were probably very mixed. Yet considerable successes were gained in some traditionally Catholic areas, such as Brittany and even the East, though these were rarely linked with workers' or students' protests and, surprisingly enough, rural France was calm at the time of the May revolt.

Peasant unrest has tended to be associated with the complaints that began to be expressed with increasing loudness in relation to national minorities in the course of the 1960s. Thus French peasant unrest can be linked to some extent to the current wave of nationalism which spread to the whole of the Celtic fringe in the UK, mainly in Northern Ireland of course, but also in Scotland, Wales, and, for the folklore, Cornwall. Current forms of nationalism have a left-wing flavor: anticapitalism, participation, decentralization are all associated and linked to the ideology of defense of the national culture. The original ideas of the New Left are being adopted, and, not surprisingly, students—at least from these areas—become identified with the protest. Symbolically perhaps, the only British MP who can be labeled as belonging to the radical left is Miss Bernadette Devlin, who precisely combines a youthful student appeal with Irish nationalism (Roman Catholicism is not given much importance, presumably because, for the radical left, such a "cultural" element is not a relic of the past which should be fostered). The example of Miss Devlin and of the current Northern Irish wave of nationalism shows the reluctance of the radical movement to agree to the creation of permanent organizations. French Breton peasants and Irish Roman Catholics are brought to the barricades by leaders who do occasionally go to jail; but the logic of antisystem attitudes presumably forces these leaders to refuse to fight the Establishment through organizations which would quickly become oligarchical.

The extent of infiltration of the radical right in working class unions is difficult to measure, possibly because even in France, workers' organizations have always been better structured than other groups and permeation is thus both more limited and/or more easily concealed. Much speculation about radical influence occurred in Britain in connection with some of the strikes of the late 1960s, and in particular the Ford strike of 1969, as it was alleged that efforts were made to undermine the political system as a whole and the government in particular. Such speculation often took place in the past in relation to Communists and these rumors are difficult to substantiate, in part because the workers themselves are unlikely to be as clear about the conditions under which strikes occur at a particular moment and even the aims of the stoppage as is sometimes assumed. In France, some infiltration did take place, mainly within the Christian union, the CFDT (Confédération Française Démocratique du Travail), but much of it was directed to or connected with attacks against the rigid Stalinism of the Communist CGT (Confédération Générale du Travail). The idea of workers' participation began to spread, and the CFDT placed great stress on the necessity to improve not just working conditions and wages, but the overall relationship between worker and employer. Ideas of a syndicalist character developed somewhat. They seemed to spread to a number of factories in the Paris area (such as Renault) and, significantly, to a number of plants in Brittany (particularly in Nantes) and in the East (Peugeot, near the Swiss border). The anomic character of the 1968 strikes has of course been emphasized: the "situation" seemed ripe for radical leaders to attempt to go to the workers and to organize them on the basis of the ideas of participation that students had adopted. The success was limited, though the exact dimensions, both in time and space, of the influence will probably never be known; the much publicized clashes between students and workers may have been somewhat exaggerated. More fundamentally, it is equally difficult to ascribe to genuine radicalism some of the anomic characteristics of French workers, as well as those of French peasants. French workers have been prone to down tools fairly suddenly over grievances which did not move them for long periods; they then return to work equally abruptly without clear-cut victories. In 1968 left-wing radicalism in France and even in Britain was surely more than an occasional outburst of anger, but the long-term strength of the radical left remains difficult to deduce from this series of large, or minor, skirmishes.

Measured in terms of column inches of reports in the newspapers of the two countries, the activities of the opponents of the system do not appear insignificant, though they are localized, somewhat sporadic, and based on a volatile broader support which never concurs with more than a fraction of the views of the radical leaders. It is therefore not surprising that judgments passed on the current importance and future influence of the challengers should vary considerably. At one extreme, it is not unreasonable to suggest that the challenge is of limited moment, and that the people at large, in both countries, have enough common sense to realize the bizarre or utopian attitudes of the radicals. At the other extreme, it is possible to analyze the current situation as one in which major political change can be created and attitudes of the population modified. At the root of the debate are two opposite views of man, that which believes that man cannot be changed and that which believes that the culture, attitudes, and behavior of men can be radically altered. It would be a great triumph for political science if it were able to solve the problem and answer the question with precision. This cannot be done, at least at present. What we can do is merely to examine, in the light of the response to the challenge, how liberal democracies have been reacting and to extrapolate what consequences are most likely to ensue.

THE RESPONSE TO THE CHALLENGE

One of the paradoxes of political life in Britain and France has been that many reforms proposed by governments have gone in the direction of the challenge of the left-wing radicals and indeed seemed to anticipate this challenge. Yet the discontent did grow, though it might have grown faster or more strongly if changes had not occurred.

But it seems at least true that both governmental action and radical reaction have often curiously been both very markedly apart and closely linked together, while radicals accused governments of irrelevance or cynicism and governments saw in the radicals either ineffective adolescents or sometimes sinister conspirators.

Whether chronologically a response to the challenge or a natural development of contemporary democracies, the ideas of participation and of decentralization came increasingly to be one of the main *leitmotivs* of speeches and meetings of governments and public officials. While Britain was traditionally more decentralized than France, a change in attitudes, and indeed also in behavior, marked French ministers and civil servants in the 1950s and increasingly in the 1960s. Modern democratic participation can be traced back to the development of interest group activities which, from relatively low levels before the war in the two countries, reached considerable importance by the mid-1960s. Even if such contacts are deemed by radicals to constitute forms of establishment behavior which they try to combat, they have unquestionably opened the society: where contacts used to be on a personal basis and somewhat haphazard, organizations have become established channels of participation. The development of group action was relatively smooth in Britain and the legitimacy of groups grew gradually through the 1940s and 1950s. In France, the streamlining of the executive under de Gaulle and the decrease in the role of Parliament led to a more massive and more recognized level of group intervention, even though earlier legislation did recognize the part that employers' and workers' organizations were to play in many aspects of society. The French plans of the 1960s incorporated and institutionalized committees representing all sectors of production. While these committees were justly criticized for not being truly representative of the various shades of the public, their very creation did constitute a major transformation of the attitudes of the government in relation to participation.

The 1960s were perhaps more specifically characterized in both countries by various efforts at local decentralization, ranging from regionalism in the broadest sense to detailed economic and social planning. Here, too, criticisms have been leveled at the performance of governments: neither country has come close to adopting federalism. There have been more efforts towards consultation, mainly on economic matters, than towards genuine decentralization of the powers of decision to locally elected bodies. Indeed, the French regional reform of 1969 was rejected by the electorate after a campaign in which it was claimed that the proposed plan would not give much power to the regions and that regional prefects would be in charge of decisions. In Britain, the reforms proposed by the Maud Commission have not been implemented as yet and even these remain some distance from full regionalism. Yet in both countries, governments have discussed and come to accept change. Indeed, while the radical left did demand greater decentralization, in particular in France, the mass of the political public seemed to remain relatively indifferent. If, in the field of interest group participation, governments have involved organizations in decision-making because they demanded to be involved, governments did try more actively to develop forms of local decentralization and the response has been sometimes limited and in part contradictory.

More recently, and for different reasons in the two countries, some limited forms of participation have been extended to new sectors, including even worker-employer cooperation. Admittedly, it is in relation to students that participation of "users" in decision-making has been allowed to go furthest. But the idea of workers' participation has begun to gain ground—in Britain as a result of the policy of wage restraint and of the thorny problem of productivity; in France, because of the ideology of the government party and its leader. De Gaulle did little to implement the idea of copartnership in most of his period of office, but towards the end of the 1960s some form of profit sharing was introduced, though without the support of organized workers. Participation of workers went somewhat further after de Gaulle's departure, though the opposition of the unions, and in particular of the Communist union, is likely to remain strong and the suspicions of the workers will probably be maintained.

Thus, except in relation to students, efforts to introduce participation in society have remained very limited, but opposition has come precisely from those who were asked to participate as much as from the governments. The response to the radical challenge may have been limited—it did take place in the direction of accommodation and acceptance, not in that of rejection. Similarly, though less unsuccessfully, the history of geographical decentralization has encountered considerable criticism from those who might have benefited: in France in particular, and possibly also in Britain, a kind of *politique du pire* practiced by local representatives tended to reduce the scope of reforms and thus to justify more limited reforms on the part of the government. Similar tactics can be found in other fields. While little was done in Britain to integrate youth in the political system—possibly because the need was less great—the creation in France of the *Maisons de Jeunes et de la Culture* constituted an attempt (which took place before the radical upsurge) to inject a measure of participation and responsibility among the teenagers. Their partial failure was described as the consequence of the limited character of the reform by some of the radicals who had been involved in them. But such arguments can be put forward in relation to the creation of any organization which purports to reform a situation which was held to be unsatisfactory. Moreover, whatever their merits, these moves did constitute attempts to encourage and to develop participation. Thus the response of governments can scarcely be held to have been negative. The problem of participation did occupy the minds of members of governments, of civil servants, of the Establishment at large: there was some response to the challenge.

Compared to earlier periods, the 1960s were perhaps characterized more by the eagerness of the Establishment to meet demands than by the forcefulness with which it tried, at least in Britain and France, to maintain the status quo. This may be due in part to the fact that many members of the Establishment saw their sons and daughters involved in radical activities. This may also be because, though the language (and dress) of the radicals might have offended the Establishment, their political behavior was, as we noted earlier, much more liberal than they are sometimes given credit for, at least in these two countries. But the result of this somewhat paradoxical situation has probably been that, while the system as a whole was maintained, the belief in the validity of the system was significantly shaken: levels of legitimacy declined in both countries. The problem is therefore to attempt to assess whether this decline is likely to continue and whether the radical left, despite its lack of organization and its romantic, rather than scientific appeal, will gradually be able to undermine the "good conscience" of the society to the level at which it might be altered, as the saying goes, "radically."

THE BELIEF IN DEMOCRACY AND THE
NEED FOR "COMPETITIVE MOBILIZATION"

Despite this drop in confidence, the scars of the 1968 May Revolution were healed fairly rapidly in France. In Britain, the Labour government continued in office, relatively little perturbed not only by the troubles in the universities, but by problems of Irish nationalism. Workers' discontent was attributed to economic difficulties, in turn explained by the legacy of overspending which had characterized the previous period. The political setbacks of the Labour Party helped to restore the chances of the Conservative Party and the game of politics appeared to follow traditional rules. Thus the 1960s ended on a paradox both in Britain and in France. While many cracks appeared in the political structures, the political system withstood the challenge without having either to break or to integrate the radicals. By and large, democratic processes functioned adequately; the challenge took place outside the system. By and large, the people as a whole showed little inclination to follow the radicals for more than short periods or in isolated pockets of the country. If no major economic or international crisis comes to upset the equilibrium, the impact of the challenge may diminish. Britain may remain scarcely touched by the challenge and France itself may return to normalcy.

Yet, more profoundly, the current challenge does appear serious in that a major problem faces modern democracies, which contemporary Britain helps to exemplify. Student troubles occurred in Britain as everywhere throughout Western democracies. The overall amount of disruption was even relatively low in the United Kingdom. At the same time, however, public opinion seemed to show some disaffection towards the political system. This coincided with a period when, after great expectations, the government in power had displayed little ability to "deliver new goods." It is not possible to prove that Labour's policies in the 1960s were responsible for greater British cynicism or discontent. But it does seem at least reasonable to suggest that disenchantment with Labour has been in part at the root of the problems of British democracy. The Labour Party benefited both from its reputation of the 1940s and from the general failings of the last years of Conservative rule: it was *the* alternative; but the alternative failed or did not materialize. Even though such ideas may have not been conscious in the minds of the electorate at large, they probably affected many sections of the population and they did affect parts of the political public and the students especially. Support for Labour—and an enthusiastic support for Labour—was widespread in 1964. Whatever difficulties may have justified Labour's policies or rendered them inevitable, enthusiasm declined and had indeed vanished by the end of the 1960s. Thus radicalism can be seen as an indirect consequence of some general, though somewhat inchoate, discontent with the workings of the political system.

In the course of the twentieth century, two broad conceptions of liberal democracy came to be adopted successively in Western societies. In the first conception, which was widely shared in Britain, democracy was related to policy choices, embodied in political parties competing for votes on the basis of different views of the future of society. However disheartened supporters of these broad views may be by the state of society at any given moment, their enthusiasm was maintained through hope in the future. Once their party achieved power, the views in which they believed would, at least in part, be tried and implemented. This was a conception of democracy as "competitive mobilization" in which large bands of supporters fought for policies held to be opposed, though with enough tolerance to allow opponents to manifest their views, by equally large bands committed to a different future for the polity. Whether this conception was a good approximation of past realities is admittedly doubtful, but with the development of socialism, it spread gradually throughout many political circles. As a myth, it was valuable. It contributed to integrate activists within the political system by maintaining their enthusiasm while keeping levels of tension in society to a tolerable level.

Meanwhile, however, another concept of democracy began to prevail, though it was not sufficiently noted that this second conception did in fact contradict the basic premises of "competitive mobilization." This was the model of "interest group democracy" in which governments and parties slowly integrated, through incremental change, many divergent views, on an "instantaneous" basis. Competition remained, but through daily compromises and limited adjustments, competition became detailed and based on discussion, rather than mobilization, on constant revisions, rather than enthusiasm. First developed in the United States, this model extended to Western Europe in the course of the postwar period and by the 1960s few European political parties hoped to achieve more in their years of office than some marginal moves in a continuing process. Increasingly, leaders became convinced that modern societies were so complex, and the number of groups so great, that only in this way could any change be achieved. But while leaders may have come to be reconciled with—or indeed genuinely to believe in—interest group democracy, much of their electoral language remained based on radical change and much of the electoral process was based on global competition. Thus party leaderships appeared somewhat ambivalent, at best; hypocritical, at worst, to the broad electorate or its most active elements. The gaps between views (as expressed in party programs) and policies appeared increasingly large. Parties appeared "irrelevant," as they lost their prior function and were unclear about their new role. And liberal democracy could be blamed by some for its inability to bring to the fore leaders and institutions which implemented policies and styles corresponding to the old language.

Present difficulties, and the radical upsurge in particular, do thus constitute a symptom of a genuinely fundamental problem facing democracies. At best the problem is one of a transition; it might, at worst, lead to a crisis in institutions—at least in party institutions—and to a need to develop somewhat different forms of popular representation. To add to the paradox, the emphasis placed by radicals on participation tends to confuse issues, in that participation, if it takes place in detail, pulls democracies away from competitive mobilization and pushes further towards interest group action. The aim of the radicals may have been to increase the control which the people at large would exercise on leaders. But the radicals' utopia is based on the assumption that the people will be consistent, rational in their scale of values, and more concerned about broad issues than about selfish and limited aims. If, on the contrary, the people happen to be sectional, inconsistent, and emotional, participation will lead to interest groups and democracy will zigzag through details and not stride along broad aims. The "defense of apathy" which characterized much of political science in the 1950s may have been an oversimplification; but it is also an oversimplification to believe that increased participation will automatically lead to a more streamlined and purer democracy. Democracy in detail may be the end product.

Yet, whether interest group democracy will necessarily follow or not, and as long as competitive mobilization remains a powerful myth in the politicized public of modern democracies, the problem of the challenge will remain a serious one. In a bizarre fashion, the French political system of the 1970s may be more immune to the challenge of despair than the British political system because, as long as France is led from the right and as long as the divided left is unable to achieve office, the myth of competitive mobilization may remain unimpaired as it will not come to the test. In the Britain of the 1970s, the myth of competitive mobilization will probably be strong enough to reduce substantially the support for the system. Only if some way is eventually found to reconcile the idea of competitive mobilization with that of interest group democracy and if this compromise does not wholly dampen the enthusiasm of the young and of those who benefit relatively less from the social system can this crisis of confidence be gradually reduced and the future of democracy assured.

In the short run, the challenge to democracy is thus probably more limited than it might have appeared in the late 1960s. In 1970, France seems to have begun to forget student demands and regionalism, let alone farmers' cooperatives and workers' participation. But the long-term prospects for the strength of democracy in the West, and in particular in Europe where the tradition of ideological parties has been strong and long, do depend on the ability of these polities to meet at least some of the requirements of competitive mobilization. Thus the problem is more to integrate within the party system standpoints and ideologies relating to the future of society than to increase at a constant and very small rate the percentage of participation, though the problem is also to educate leaders and the political public to the idea of the "possible." Interest group democracy, as it has been discussed here, is still not wholly satisfactory for the European public, whether in Britain, in France, or in other democracies; and politicians also feel this lack of attractiveness. Behind the idea of "cultural repression" lies the idea of impotent challenge. Leaders of Western democracies should not exacerbate this feeling of impotence, even if some dramatic postures are difficult to tolerate or are plainly infantile. The integration of enthusiasm remains one of the major problems for developed societies if they are, in the long run, to meet the challenge and not merely reduce it.

2: THE "NEW LEFT"
Gerhart Niemeyer

By the end of the fifties it seemed—did it not?—that the leftist ideologies of the nineteenth century had run their course. Germany's Social Democrats had foresworn Marxism, the anarchist movement expired in a violent death during the Spanish Civil War, even Leninism appeared to have reached a kind of plateau and run out of new ideas and methods. One of America's noted social scientists published a book proclaiming *The End of Ideology*. But then a new ideological upsurge made itself felt in a number of Western countries. Its first spectacular outbreak occurred at Berkeley in 1964, the Free Speech Movement with Mario Savio and Bettina Aptheker. The latter being a Communist suggested a novel tactic of the Communist Party as the probable cause. Subsequent developments, however, made clear that the situation was not that simple. In Germany the former student organization of the SPD had broken away from the mother party and set itself up as a more radical autonomous group (SDS). In the United States, another SDS had been founded at Port Huron in 1962. A left-wing student group within the civil rights movement, SNCC, turned into an exclusively black radical organization. A still more radical group, the Black Panthers, emerged on the West Coast. Among white students there was formed the Youth International Party (Yippies), while the SDS recently split into a number of different groups, one of them Trotskyist. German students rioted repeatedly in 1966 to 1967, French students in 1966 and the spring of 1968, during which latter time they succeeded in pushing the French workers to a revolutionary general strike and some occupations of factories. Italian students, with a long background of radicalism particularly at Bologna, occupied Rome University, and Spanish students followed suit in Madrid.

The first salient feature of the New Left, then, is its character as a movement of radicalized students and professors, except in the United States where there is also a black New Left. Secondly, the movement cannot be said to operate under the effective command and discipline of the Communist Party and has not produced anything like the tightly knit centralized organization of Communism or even democratic socialism. Third, it puts revolutionary action as such above carefully planned revolutionary strategy and will engage in riots, demonstrations, occupations, and confrontations even when the Marxist parties want to avoid such spectaculars. Fourth, the ideology of the New Left is complex, eclectic, and, by derivation, one step removed from that of the Old Left. Fifth, besides and behind the New Left there is also a broader rebellious culture, something of which the Old Left could never boast. On the other hand, Old Left and New Left both are aware that they are moving toward the same ultimate goal. The New Left has focused frequently on university issues, but has also mobilized its cadres on the more general issues of Vietnam and military armaments, occasionally picking special events like the visit of the Shah of Iran and a merger enlarging the press empire of Axel Springer, for their symbolic value. However, all of these issues, as numerous New Left leaders have openly admitted, are secondary and merely serve to advance toward the real goal which is the destruction of the entire social order and the reversal of all values in Western countries. In this sense the New Left knows it is pulling in the same direction as the Communists, Trotskyists, Maoists, Castroists, with all of whom it seeks to combine efforts.

In the past, many intellectuals sought to understand the Old Left in terms of alleged underlying material causes. This kind of approach cannot get us very far with regard to a movement composed of the sons and daughters of affluence. Their radicalism must be understood as rooting in ideologized ideas, irrational thinking about history, society, and the human condition. The New Left will remain enigmatic unless we can secure a critical grasp on its ideology. Its ideological manifestations are of two kinds: unsystematic, spontaneous outbursts of ideological language, imagery, prejudices from the rank and file of the movement, and, on the other hand, coherent and systematic ideological writings of the intellectual leaders. This situation differs from the Old Left, the ideology of which was invariably first created in writing before it began to shape the consciousness of rank-and-file members to whom the teaching was mediated by the organizations. The New Left, then, is a second growth, as it were, on ideologically contaminated soil. A phenomenon like ideological spontaneity would not be possible had not the teachings of Marx, Lenin, Bakunin and others spread through our culture so that they were absorbed by youth from their parents, teachers, newspapers, and communication media. With regard to particular influences, however, one can go further than the apostles of the revolutionary left: the revolutionary student movement of our time has also derived its concepts, slogans, imagery, expectations, and prejudices from Nietzsche, Freud and Jung, Heidegger and Sartre, Blake and Breton, and ideas for its tactics from Sorel and McLuhan. One might say that it constitutes a potpourri of all major ideological currents of the past century and a half, not all of which one can place on the left. It might be better, then, if we could think of another name for the new movement, possibly: the "New Emancipation."

Emancipation is the main accent through most of the ideological writings, by contrast with the nineteenth century, which produced something like apparently scientific analyses of society's structure and dynamics. That kind of semirationality is now gone: "The Revolution" is taken for granted; no elaborate argument is needed to establish it; rather, it appears as a "self-evident" truth around which one can build not only various conclusions but also a variety of premises. Herbert Marcuse, who has contributed more books to the new movement than anyone else, begins with Marx's assertion of total revolution as an axiom from which he himself has removed Marx's supporting evidence. For Marx, the Revolution followed from the instability inherent in the proletariat's ever deepening misery from where indignation and growing class consciousness would arouse it to the final triumphant battle against its capitalist masters. Marcuse admits that the proletariat has not sunk and will not sink into misery, that its consciousness is not revolutionary, that capitalism has bestowed considerable wealth on all classes, and that its economic crises are not likely to intensify toward a wholesale collapse. He admits that the capitalist economy satisfies human needs on an unprecedented scale. Such abandonment of Marx's analysis, however, causes him not to abandon Marx's conclusion but rather to think of a substitute set of supporting reasons for the central concept of total revolution. The Revolution turns out to be the absolute, its explanations merely relative.

Marx assumed that the evolution of economic forces followed from the pressure of human needs in which he saw a kind of rock-bottom driving energy. Marcuse, by contrast, looks on human needs as artificial contrivances of the capitalist system, invisible threads by which the system enslaves men and falsifies human existence. Marx accepted the value of industrialization and confined his critique to the system of appropriation. Marcuse rejects the industrial system to which he attributes what he regards as an entire false system of values and men's "false" contentment in the present society. Hence everything is to him suspect and must be turned into its opposite: the tolerance in our country is actually a powerful means of oppression, our freedoms are nothing but chains of enslavement, our ideas mere mental perversions. The Revolution and its radical negation, on the other hand, are man's creative expression, intolerance is a moral duty, physical uncleanliness an "unsoiled" condition of the body, obscenity the mark of the emancipated human being. What matters is total newness, which will spring from total rejection and destruction of all that exists. There is a dialectic relation between total newness and the alleged total evil that is supposed to prevail in the present. The road to newness then goes through an intellectual destruction of the present order in one's mind to an eventual practical destruction in the political and social sense. In dialectic opposition, since the present is depicted as total evil, the new world is postulated as wholly good. Marcuse's radical indictment of the present-day society comes as a kind of one-upmanship on Marx. Marx boasted of having discovered grounds for a critique of society far deeper and more basic than political oppression and social injustice. Marcuse piles Freud on Marx and depicts alienation in psychic terms, thus discovering cause for profound discontent even in the midst of affluence and security. He has no need of Marx's proletarian misery; in the heart of contentment he finds slavery, oppression, and indignity. Unlike Marx, Marcuse is not forced to play down any positive features of present-day society: every one of them serves him to prove man's dehumanization.

Marcuse uses Marx minus his historical materialism. Similarly, Norman Brown, having discovered Freud in the mid-fifties, derives from him a message of emancipation that does away with Freud's own pessimistic analysis of civilization. To this end, Norman Brown adds to Freud the nineteenth century visionary Blake, as well as Nietzsche. "Freud is the great emancipator from the reality principle." Norman

Brown wants to join Freud, Marx, and Pope John XXIII for the "unification of mankind"; unity is of bodies, thus social organization is ultimately sexual. "The endless task; to achieve the impossible, to find a male female (vaginal father) or a female male (phallic mother). It is to square the circle; the desire and pursuit of the whole in the form of dual unity or the combined object; the Satanic hermaphroditism of Antichrist." In these terms Norman Brown proclaims the emancipation from "this world of generation and death," which we "must cast off" in its entirety. Again, such condemnation of present reality far exceeds Marx's rather instrumentalist critique. All morality and religion, being itself is called before the bar and rejected out of hand. An emancipation is postulated that will liberate bodies and passions from frustration, separateness, and any sense of guilt or imperfection. On a far lower intellectual level Abbie Hoffman bears witness to the new emancipation by writing books in the language of absurdity and by using obscenity as the mark of the new freedom. Hoffman, like Brown and others, celebrates his escape both from normativity and rationality which to him appears as a cultural prison. Demonstrative madness is the form this celebration takes, the display of mind unchained from logic, reason and structure, language gleefully splashing in nonsense. Similarly, among the French students, Sartre is worshiped as the bringer of absolute freedom, for he has shown that being is nothingness and thereby taken from man the most fundamental limitation his mind has to acknowledge, that of reality itself.

We have already moved from the politically revolutionary movement to what Theodore Roszak calls the "counter-culture," patterns of living chosen in pointed opposition to the customary, moral, aesthetic, religious traditions of our civilization. The Old Left never knew anything like this: neither Socialists nor Communists could draw support from any culture other than that of the society which they sought to combat, and even to this day the Soviet Union has not produced a specifically Soviet culture, for even the vaunted Soviet realism merely imitates art forms well developed long before the Communist revolution. Behind and besides the student revolutionary organizations, however, young people on both sides of the Atlantic are clustering together under the slogan "turn on, tune in, drop out." "Turn on" refers to the antirational state of mind produced by hallucinogenic drugs; "tune in" to rock music and the life style that goes with it; "drop out" to the extant order of society and culture. Rock, sex, drugs, and unbounded subjectivism characterize the varieties of "life styles" and their manifestation in the absence of norms for dress, hairdo, and cleanliness acceptable to these youths. Certain cultural productions complete the picture: besides rock music, also absurdist poetry and absurdist art. Finally, there is a pervading preoccupation with exotic religiosity, borrowing freely from a diversity of Oriental religions as well as from shamanism, magic, and astrology.

What is the significance of this "counter-cultural" phenomenon? First, it provides the political activists with a broad substratum of support, sympathy, and supply of recruits. More important, however, it maintains a public impression that something new is actually growing, something that serves as conclusive proof for another coming society to succeed after the destruction of the present one. The counter-culture seems to substantiate the claim that we are in the presence of cultural creation and that the new freedom can already be discerned at least in dim outline. If it were not for this impression generated by the counter-culture, the New Left would appear to everyone somewhat like the emperor without his new clothes, a rebellion bare in its nihilistic refusal. The counter-culture thus provides an apparent justification for the political revolutionaries, it nourishes their self-righteous confidence and optimistic resort to total destruction. In its confrontation with democracy, the New Left feels entitled to claim rights in the name of human creativity, demanding freedom to express its ideas and "do its thing," justified by a cultural promise vaguely identified by the god-words "peace" and "love."

Alas, the claim is false. What we witness is not the creation of a new culture but merely the reversal, or withdrawal syndromes of nihilism. The counter-culture consists of nothing but the principle of negation of which it has made a cult. It deeply distrusts any form, any norm, any kind of structured present. It seeks perpetual restlessness, dynamism without pause, destination, or fulfillment. Rebellious youth "drops out" not merely from a political, economic, or cultural system, but from goodness, reason, and being as such. LSD has been embraced as an instrument of antibeing, a vehicle for phantasmic flight from reality and all its structures. For an acknowledgement of reality implies all kinds of limitations, but "dropping out" means escape into the boundless freedom of undefined nonreality. Similarly, the metaphysical enhancement of subjectivity amounts to a thrust into a dreamlike nothingness. All alone, the subject feels capable of creating worlds. moralities, societies, because he finds himself freed from otherness, the otherness of God, nature, or fellow men, having risen from the *esse cum* to a freedom that has no qualities, where he feels like God.

The one aspect of the counter-culture that might seem to contain some germs of a new growth is youth's pervading interest in religion, its discovery of depths of life that were ignored by their liberal and positivist parents. Alas again, the appearance is deceptive. In the indiscriminate invocations of Hindu or Buddhist deities, the mixing of Christian, pagan, shamanist or magic rites one can find little evidence that the human condition of creatureliness in a divinely created world is taken seriously, or even that there is anything like serious worship. Rather such practices indicate a disposition to flirt with any kind of myth or ritual in playful combinations of religions high and primitive, thereby incidentally annihilating the past with its leaps from compact to more differentiated orders. The apparent culture of new religiosity thrives largely on the excitement or fascination with whatever is strange as well as on its shock value, even though behind it there may well lurk a genuine yearning. The genuineness, however, turns to counterfeit when religious symbols are perverted mainly for rebellious purposes. Thus no norm of human conduct, no ordering orientation, no moral obligation, no structure of society flows from the counter-culture. Roszak's designation seems to be a misnomer: one should rather speak of an anticulture. The only believable claim of the anticulture is youth's desire to do, feel, think in any way that negates Greco-Judaeo-Christian morality, aesthetics, and understanding of reality. There is in it no power to bring forth a higher or even alternative order of existence. One possibility remains: the widespread fascination with the culture of primitives, including shamanism, archetypal myths, also the absence of dress and shoes, the possession of amulets, and the practice of ritually painting the body suggests something like Vico's *ricorso*: after the "barbarism of reflection" which in our time would be the same as the wasteland of positivism, men might return to a barbarism pure and simple, a life below civilization which, however, might imply the chance of a genuine turning to God.

Short of such speculations, however, our immediate interest bids us focus on the relation between anticulture and student revolutionary movements. One cannot assume that one is necessarily a function of the other: witness England where the anticulture has flourished long and vigorously while political student movements have remained relatively unexplosive. The reverse can be observed in France, where the student movement brought the nation to the brink of civil war but the anticulture is not as noticeable as in the United States. In France as well as Germany, revolutionary students seem to draw slogans and motives more from Marxist-Leninist Communism and Bakunist and Kropotkinist anarchism, while new ideological writings have been produced mostly in the United States.

At this point, one may venture some generalizations about the New Emancipation in both its revolutionary and culture aspects:

1. The ideological crux of all student revolutionary movements is the total condemnation of their own community, be it university, the society, or the civilization as a whole. Even though such indictment usually comes replete with particular illustrations, the underlying intention is not to change for the better this or that practice, institution, or norm; rather, the condemnation is its own end. Thus whatever concrete demands the students present do not adequately express their limitless discontent but rather are instruments to attain further power positions. The French students coined the slogan: "Be realistic —demand the impossible!" German student leaders desired something they called "protest in permanence." All student movements reject the rather strict discipline of strategy and tactics observed, in different ways, by both trade unions and the Communist Party; instead they all desire revolutionary action as such, for its own sake. One group of students talked about a mystical "revolutionary synthesis of food and dispute" and wanted to destroy all comfortable homes which merely bar "total man" from "space opening on him." In May 1968, the Parisian students wrote on the walls: "It is forbidden to forbid!" The limitless character of the total critique is evidenced also by the multitude of sweeping descriptions of society's evil which seem to be interchangeable. Thus our society is simultaneously defined as a "world of death," a "world of violence," of materialism, racism, constraint, a system of exploitative capitalism, oppressive imperialism, a culture of repressive tolerance, oppressive consciousness, mindless power. Every one of these terms of indictment can replace another. Thus the French student leader Lefèvre formulated: "Capitalism equals fascism." No detailed analysis of society's evils is required any more. The equation of society with evil is an a priori

one, not to be proved but simply to be evidenced in any one of many examples one may choose to pick up. Society in their eyes amounts to instituted evil. This obsession with the totality and positivity of evil and the corresponding negativity of good has been manifested in many utterances of radical leaders on both sides of the Atlantic who have conceded that the reasons they stated for particular confrontations were but expedient contrivances. On another level it may be quite possible that a student group formulate complaints and demands which they sincerely believe to be the motive for their revolt. When their complaints and demands are met in good will it usually turns out, though, that their unrest was after all not confined to such narrow limits and moves on to other complaints and demands, none of them wholly representative of their metaphysical discontent.

2. Defining the Establishment as the totality of evil establishes the innocence of all revolutionary action. As all conceivable evil has been attributed to the Establishment, such a sweeping *j'àccuse* implies ultimate self-justification: he who pronounces such global judgements denouncing an entire society rather than particular actions can speak only from Beyond Good and Evil, which position provides a metaphysical warranty of his innocence. It is the a priori innocence of total condemnation and total destruction that dispenses the revolutionary students from any requirement to define their goal even in terms of a utopia. While they admit that they cannot see what will come after the destruction of the present society, they are supremely confident that the destruction will be good in its results. An effort to spell out their anticipation of good more precisely seems to them both constraining and superfluous.

Whence there results a kind of ontological and moral division between two kinds of people: *they*—the supporters and beneficiaries of the Establishment who are all guilty; and *we*—the radical revolutionaries who have "dropped out" from the instituted evil. "IBM, Mobil, and GT &T are enemies of all life," ran the message of those who planted bombs in the New York offices of the three firms, implying that the planting of bombs in such places was the cleaning and righteous work of the avenger of life itself. When men make such fundamental distinctions between themselves and others, it amounts to a refusal to share a common civic life, even more, a refusal to share the human condition as such (The "Great Refusal"). The revolutionary students, by charging the totality of evil to extant society, to "them," have moved out, as it were, from "being in the same boat" with their fellow men and consequently cannot be reconciled to any human order. As a consequence, they feel that they should affirm their solidarity with the enemies of order, the heroes of total revolution and destructive activism: Che Guevara, Mao Tse-tung, Fidel Castro, Ho Chi Minh.

3. From the sense of the implicit innocence of their own action flows a notion of limitless power, limitless both in the normative and factual senses. The students cannot conceive that revolutionary power should be subject to any limiting norm, principle, or objective, or that it could be conceived as a mere means to an end. On the other hand, they are convinced that revolutionary power and power of the Establishment are just not in the same class, since the power of revolutionary action is innocent while that of the Establishment is guilty. Even in a purely factual sense, the two powers are incommensurable. Hence the revolutionary students have really no sense of defeat, even when the other side is stronger than theirs. An acknowledgement of defeat is always a mental process implying an acknowledgement of the other side as a human being like oneself who can be powerful in the same way as oneself, which is tantamount to perceiving power limitations. When one begins by denying that the other side shares the same condition of existence as oneself, however, one cannot see one's own power limited by that of the others, and cannot accept a settlement in terms of power relativity. The only moments when the relativity of power seems to have become real to revolutionary students is when the doors of jail closed behind them. Otherwise their inability to assess power relations soberly has manifested itself both in a reckless lack of inhibition and a quixotic overestimation of gestures, slogans, and resolutions. It is precisely on this point that the revolutionary students have most sharply diverged from the Communist Party which, obedient to Lenin's teaching, has always maintained a clear eye for power realities. All the same, the Communists' ultimate goal also consists in limitless power of the dictatorial Party, a goal which again comes close to the student revolutionary spirit.

A critical analysis of the revolutionary student movement by one of its former members (Jens Litten, *Eine verpasste Revolution?*, 1969) predicts that the movement will die from internal emotional exhaustion. That may well be; what is sure, however, is that it cannot be satisfied by appeasement, concessions, or reforms. Even if some student leaders might settle for this or that concrete change, others would replace them, and the ante would be raised. The fact is that a late and hybrid ideology has been spawned in the soil of Western civilization and will be a source for disorder for considerable time. Many people are confused by the appearance of the revolution as one of youth as such; the anticulture appears to have become the way of life for people under thirty. This, of course, is very far from the truth. The impression is created by the fact that the anticulture is widely scattered and seems to have taken hold in practically every town and most schools, and that between the anticulture and revolutionary movements there are many affinities. In the face of this appearance, it is important for us to remind ourselves again and again that the cause of disorder is not youth as such but a radical ideology, a body of irrational ideas, notions, slogans, and the ensuing attitudes. All this forms a cult the adepts of which range from seventeen to seventy, and the cult is more characteristic of uprooted Western intelligentsia, Julien Benda's clercs, than of youth.

The activist part of the movement must be considered as bent on destruction rather than reform in our society. In view of its small numbers, that assessment may seem exaggerated to many; one should remember, though, that both Lenin and Hitler began with less than a dozen. Unlike Lenin and Hitler, the radical students are not well organized; they are poorly armed, and they have had scant success in breaking out of the gilded ghetto of social privilege. In any kind of frontal assault, they could be no match for the forces that preserve the order of society. If they could attract the urban masses, as seemed possible for a moment in the Paris of May, 1968, their power might loom more formidable, but the possibility still seems remote. Two other courses are left to them: urban guerilla warfare, and provocative confrontations. The first would result in much material damage and some loss of life, but it would tend to consolidate the moral and political force of society, and to isolate the revolutionists. Provocative confrontation has been the chosen technique of revolutionary students on both sides of the Atlantic until now, and it presents democracy with its greatest challenge. The technique relies on the myth of an abstractly perfect democracy, a myth frequently invoked by the slogan "participatory democracy," which myth is used as an ideal yardstick to measure the historical legal guarantees of the democratic citizen: freedom of speech and assembly, freedom of the press, protections of the defendant in court, freedom of using the street for demonstrations. The technique consists in demonstrating *ad oculos*, i.e., on TV, that the present society not only falls far short of a perfect democracy but actually is a regime of oppressive power, thus confirming the revolutionists' contention that it ought to be destroyed. The means to attain this result consist in misuses of various civil liberties: freedom of speech is misused for obscenity, irrationality, and subversive appeals; defendants in court misuse their rights to disrupt and discredit the judiciary process; street demonstrations are conducted so as to provoke the police into clashes with the demonstrators; the freedom of gathering is misused to the end of physical obstruction of others.

Such practices hit democracy in its weakest spot. Under the influence of positivism, democracy in the last hundred years has defined itself more and more in terms of mere procedure, progressively neglecting or even banning the problem of moral and intellectual substance. By 1970, this has gone so far that a recent article by Paul Eidelberg (*Review of Politics*, January 1970) could make the documented assertion that "intellectual and moral anarchy" prevails in American society, resulting from the unwillingness or inability of the nation's leaders to make significant distinctions. "No society can endure unless its members are capable of feeling disgust or indignation, hence of being intolerant of certain kinds of behavior and sometimes of the ideas which encourage such behavior." The situation is characteristic not merely of the United States but prevails as far as the influence of Western positivism reaches. Much earlier, the Weimar Republic stood committed to the idea that democracy existed in the quantitatively widest possible extension of the sameness of procedure; it therefore permitted exactly the same security to the destroyers of the Republic as to its defenders. Some political scientists, it is true, insisted that freedom of speech made sense and was effective only within a community of values and rationality. Others pointed out that civil rights were meaningful only within a continuum of political obligation. There were some warnings that free elections as such could not guarantee a free government. The courts, however, on both sides of the Atlantic took the strictly positivistic line. For a long while they refused to make substantive distinctions between bona fide and perverted uses of civil rights. By now a significant number of leaders in our society are actually incapable of making such distinctions. Eidelberg pointedly quotes Justice Douglas in the Ginzberg case, where the Justice put the words "good," "bad," and "truth" in quotation marks, thereby indicating that he no longer could make any rational statements regarding pornography. A similar inability seems to have befallen academic administrators who confess impotence to distinguish between academic freedom and student license, freedom of expression and the use of words for destruction, rational dialogue and the clash of irrationalities, speakers who communicate ideas and others who speak to incite rebellious action. Where such deep uncertainty and confusion manifests itself, weakness spreads from society's leaders to all citizens, and strength accrues to the forces bent on ending it all.

The real challenge to democracy in our time lies therefore not in the streets or on some battlefield, but in the hearts and minds of those on whom it is incumbent to make decisions in the name of the whole. Too long have they allowed the substance of order to atrophy within their souls. Now they are confronted with tests which threaten to expose the hollow shell of what was once a rational public understanding on right and wrong, high and low, real and unreal, decent and indecent. Too many of our leaders look back on the course of the past thirty years with complacency, feeling that if only it went on a little longer everything would be all right. The truth is that during the last thirty years we have allowed the basis of public rationality to erode, and unless we succeed in stopping and reversing that course, and in recovering some knowledge of "the things that belong to our peace," our "intellectual and moral anarchy" may well end in a scene strewn with corpses, waiting for a Fortinbras in full armor to enter and take over.

3: JUDICIAL POWER AND CONSTITUTIONAL DEMOCRACY IN ITALY AND WEST GERMANY*

Donald P. Kommers

This paper is a comparative study of the constitutional courts of West Germany and Italy. Authorized to review the constitutionality of legislation and to define the boundaries of governmental power, these institutions, established in the 1950s, have settled a very large number of constitutional disputes. The contemporary constitutional law of Italy currently fills fifteen hefty volumes; that of West Germany twenty-five volumes. And annual case loads keep getting heavier. The time is ripe, therefore, to review the work of these tribunals and to relate this work to the growth and condition of constitutional democracy in the two polities. The record of these courts and their impact upon the political processes of Italy and West Germany will also give us an opportunity to explore some of the underlying conditions for the effective exercise of judicial review.[1]

I. HISTORICAL BACKGROUND

At the end of World War I, Western political leaders sought to make the world safe for democracy. Their constitution-making efforts mirrored large faith in the twin principles of parliamentary government and popular sovereignty. The ensuing two decades, which saw democratic governments crumble before dictators and voting publics succumb to totalitarian appeals, brutally exposed this faith as an act

* This research was supported by grants from the American Philosophical Society, the Social Science Research Council, and the Program of West European Studies, University of Notre Dame. The author is grateful for their support. Thanks are also due the *Jahrbuch des öffentlichen Rechts* in whose 1971 edition this paper was first published.

of gross self-deception. The net result was a loss of faith in popular democracy, together with a marked decline in esteem for written constitutions. Yet, after World War II, a freshet of such documents seemed to reflect the determination of Western leaders now to make the world safe for constitutionalism.

Reacting to the violence and despotism of the last two decades European constitution-makers tried to engineer limited government. In doing so they simply modified the liberal democratic constitutions of the previous generation in an effort to avoid past pitfalls. This meant tinkering with political institutions and tightening governmental machinery to mend cracks through which dictators had thrust their ugly heads and to plug holes that permitted popular majorities to get out of hand. The patchwork included all kinds of procedural and institutional devices to circumscribe majority rule.[2]

Among the most important of these devices, and relatively new to Europe, was judicial review. Drawn from American political experience, judicial review is simply the authority of a court to invalidate laws and to nullify acts of governmental officials on *constitutional* grounds. In the United States all courts traditionally have exercised this authority. As adapted to West Germany and Italy, judicial review is less broad in scope and is lodged exclusively in separately organized tribunals independent of the ordinary law courts. Nevertheless this represents a significant expansion of judicial power in both nations. For the first time in modern history the "founding fathers" consciously opted to place the constitutions of both regimes squarely under the protection of a judicial authority separate from the political branches of government.

This development was not looked upon with universal favor. To some observers judicial review was wholly incompatible with parliamentary democracy. To others a judicial power regarded as indigenous to the United States simply could not be adapted to the conditions of Europe's legal environment. This did seem to be a likely possibility. Karl Lowenstein, for example, writing in 1951, frankly doubted that judicial review would "integrate itself into [European] political life as the unique regulatory force it is in the United States."[3]

All this of course begs the question whether judicial review was intended to work in Europe as it does in the United States. About all the debates of the Italian and West German constituent assemblies show is that the "founding fathers" themselves were unable to agree on how judicial review would really work in practice. They exhibited no greater clairvoyance in this respect than did the framers of the American Constitution. The future uses of judicial review would depend as much as anything upon experience and the character of constitutional court judges. (Awareness of this fact probably accounted for the imposition of limited terms of office for the judges and parliamentary controls over their selection.) It would depend also upon the structure and decision-making processes of these tribunals. It is pertinent to observe here that even the institutional forms which the constitutional courts of Italy and West Germany ultimately assumed were themselves a bundle of compromises forged from a cauldron of hot argument over the desirable range and extent of judicial review.

While judicial review, for Italy, was a brand new experience, West Germany was not writing on a wholly clean slate when the Federal Constitutional Court was created. The origins of much of its authority can be traced to the Frankfurt Constitution of 27 March 1849 (Article 126), to Article 76 of the Constitution of 1871, to the jurisdiction of the *Staatsgerichtshof* together with the review powers of the *Reichsgericht* during the Weimar Republic, and to the constitutional courts of the German states set up during the occupation period immediately following World War II. While it is true that the mainstream of German jurisprudence is unfavorable to judicial review, there are rivulets in Germany's recent history congenial to judicial supremacy. But frequent political uprootings—six fundamental regime changes in the last century—blocked seepage of these waters into Germany's constitutional topsoil. What makes this study of Italy and West Germany so interesting is that both nations have historical records largely at variance with Western concepts of constitutional democracy. Would judicial review take root? That was the question.

II. JURISDICTION OF CONSTITUTIONAL COURTS

It was noted above that judicial review is broader in the United States than in Italy or West Germany. The reason is that any ordinary lawsuit originating in an American state or federal court may involve a federal constitutional question that the Supreme Court has the authority ultimately to decide. The Supreme Court's opportunity to settle constitutional conflicts is further broadened by the right of any person to invoke its authority in a proper judicial proceeding. These procedural rules give to the Supreme Court a voice enormously influential in the articulation of constitutional values.

In Italy and West Germany the gates of the constitutional court are not quite so open. Access to the Italian Constitutional Court is limited to central and regional governments and ordinary courts of law. Private citizens are barred from taking appeals directly to the Constitutional Court. But a judge of an ordinary court may certify a constitutional question to the high tribunal if, in his view, a statute under which a case arises is of doubtful constitutionality. The Italians refer to this as "indirect judicial review." A similar procedure, called "concrete judicial review," is followed in West Germany. Review is concrete because it pertains to a constitutional question arising out of an actual case before a regular court. The judge, on his own discretion, certifies the question to the Federal Constitutional Court. As in Italy the pending case is stayed until the court renders its decision. Unlike Italians, however, German citizens have also been permitted, by statute, to file constitutional complaints with the Federal Constitutional Court, but only afrer the exhaustion of all other judicial remedies. In January 1969, the Basic Law was amended to turn this statutory privilege into a constitutional right. As before, this included the right to file such complaints against court decisions.

It is of interest to note here that in the United States judicial review invariably is justified as essential to the protection of individual rights. This was also one justification for the establishment of judicial review in Italy and West Germany. Yet, it may seem strange that the vindication of constitutional rights rests on so slim a foundation as the willingness of ordinary judges to forward constitutional questions in an indirect or concrete review proceeding. Even in West Germany it was only after long parliamentary debate that the individual citizen won the right to file a constitutional complaint directly with the Federal Constitutional Court. On the other hand, the historic role of special administrative courts in protecting Italian and German citizens against arbitrary encroachments of government may have obviated the need for constitutional courts of general appellate review so long as the integrity of the political system ordained by the constitution was retained.

The constitutional courts of Italy and West Germany seem mainly to have been designed to police the *political system* by preventing any constituent unit or branch of government from violating the precepts of liberal democracy or from transcending the limits of power imposed by the constitution. The jurisdictional provisions outlining the authority of these tribunals seem also to have been premised on the belief that, ultimately, the liberty of individual citizens could best be preserved by the judicial resolution of *direct* conflicts between political units and branches of government. Hence all routes to both courts—except for the constitutional complaint in West Germany—are reserved to certain public officials, official political groups, and governmental organs. In Germany these include federal and state governments together with principal organs of the federal government such as the Federal President, the Bundestag, the Bundesrat, and the Chancellor. In certain cases one-third of the members of the Bundestag may invoke the court's jurisdiction. Political parties, candidates for public office and individual members of the Bundestag may also submit cases involving their rights as public officials or electoral agencies. In Italy, as noted earlier, only the highest governing authorities of state and region may submit cases to the Constitutional Court.

Cases which may be submitted to the Italian Constitutional Court are (1) state-regional conflicts, (2) conflicts between regions, (3) conflicts between major organs of the central government, (4) impeachments of ministers and the president of the republic, and (5) conflicts over the validity of referenda. The German Federal Constitutional Court has much more authority. In addition to hearing conflicts of this nature, along with constitutional complaints by individual citizens and by local governments, the Court is empowered to decide cases involving (1) the forfeiture of a person's basic rights, (2) the prohibition of unconstitutional parties, and (3) election disputes. Of equal political importance and unknown to American law, is the so-called abstract judicial review proceeding which can be initiated by politicians to secure a decision on the validity of any federal or state law. Review is available either to the federal or a state government solely in the event of genuine differences of opinion or serious doubts concerning the "formal and material compatibility of federal or land law with [the] Basic Law or the compatibility of land law with other federal law."[4] This is not an adversary proceeding in the American sense. But neither is it an advisory opinion, for the question of the law's validity is squarely before the Court. The political importance of these cases stems partly from the rule that allows 100 members of the Bundestag (a minority) to petition the Court for a review of a statute immediately after its passage and before it has become the object of litigation in the courts.

III. JUDICIAL REVIEW IN OPERATION

In the following analysis of the actual output of the Italian and West German constitutional courts it will be useful to treat each country separately and to divide the work of each court into its principal jurisdictional categories. In the case of Germany the period covered by this treatment is from 1951 to 1967; in the case of Italy from 1956 to 1969. The earlier years indicate when the courts were established; the latter are the terminal years for which official records were available at the time of this writing. The figures represented in Table 1 do not include all the dispositions of the West German Court, only the cases disposed of on their merits. Nearly 19,000 constitutional complaints have been filed with the Federal Constitutional Court since its founding in 1951. Most have been dismissed as frivolous or rejected for not meeting threshold procedural or jurisdictional requirements. Around 1,000 cases involving the Court's concrete review jurisdiction were not decided on the merits for similar reasons.

A. WEST GERMANY

Federal-State Conflicts

The West German Federal Constitutional Court is divided into two senates with separate judges and mutually exclusive jurisdiction. This observation is important because the original division of authority between the senates was the product of gross miscalculation regarding the frequency with which federal-state conflicts would come before the Court. Jurisdiction over these disputes, together with conflicts between the high organs of the Federal Government, was originally allocated to the second senate; nearly all other matters were to he handled by the first senate. The first five years of the Court's existence—from 1951 to 1956—yielded an incredible imbalance between the work of the second senate, which decided 26 cases, and that

TABLE 1

Decisions of the West German and Italian Constitutional Courts

Type of Case	West Germany (1951–1967)	Italy (1956–1969)
Indirect (or concrete) judicial review	454	2576
Conflicts between high federal organs	14	1
Federal-state (or state-regional) conflicts	9	398
Abstract judicial review	32	
Unconstitutionality of political parties	3	
Election disputes	25	
Constitutional Complaints	2527	
Other	78	
TOTAL	3142	2975

Source: For Germany see Gerhard Leibholz and Reinhard Rupprecht, Bundesverfassungs-gerichtsgesetz (Koln-Marienburg: Verlag Dr. Otto Schmidt KG, 1968), p. 463. For Italy, up to 1966, see Il Primo Decennio de Giurisprudenza della Corte Costituzionale 1956–1965 (Roma: Corte Costituzionale, Ufficio Studi, 1968), pp. 727–742. The figures for 1966–1969 were generously provided by Dr. Alberto Marradi, Center for the Study of Comparative Politics, University of Florence, who recently completed a very detailed study of the Court's work. The results of that study were presented in a preliminary report given before an informal group of comparative law scholars at the 1970 meeting of the International Political Science Association in Munich.

of the first, which decided over 2,000. Uncertainty over the future of German federalism along with doubts about the coming stability of the Bonn Republic may have accounted for the decision to reserve one of the court's chambers for the determination of federal-state relations.

By 1 January 1968 the Court had actually decided only nine cases involving direct conflicts between federal and state governments arising under Article 93 of the Basic Law. Two of these cases are of critical importance to federal-state relations in Germany. On 28 February 1961, in the well-known Television Case, the Constitutional Court nullified Chancellor Adenauer's attempt to establish a national television station.[5] The decision is still regarded as the boldest assertion of judicial authority against the Federal Government. The Court viewed Adenauer's scheme both as a violation of free speech and of the constitutional provision that reserves to state governments authority over cultural affairs. Several years prior to the Television Case the Constitutional Court also ruled that certain provisions of the Concordat of 20 July 1933 pertaining to the education of children do not bind the states of the Federal Republic.[6] Thus, contrary to the American precedent of *Missouri* v. *Holland*,[7] a foreign treaty may not violate a reserved right of the state. Even in the area of defense policy the Court gave Adenauer's government a scare in the early 1950s when it seemed as though it was prepared to nullify West Germany's decision to join the European Defense Community. The Federal Government had to go through the cumbersome process of amending the Basic Law to obviate that possibility.[8]

In recent years, probably because of the "Grand Coalition" of 1966–1969 between Christian Democrats (CDU/CSU) and Social Democrats (SPD), hardly any federal-state cases have been brought to the Court. But Professor Ulrich Scheuner of Bonn University, who has represented the Federal Government in several court cases, adds that the two levels of government "prefer now to settle their questions by amiable (or less amiable) agreement within the . . . constitutional twilight [zone] than in Court."[9]

Thus the Federal Constitutional Court has not played a wholly unimportant role as a protector of German federalism. It was precisely this role that the Bavarian delegation and many Christian Democrats defended so ardently in the constitutional convention (Parliamentary Council) of 1948, whereas Social Democrats, being largely antifederal, hoped that the Court would become—much as the early American Supreme Court—an agency for the consolidation of national power. It is one of the ironies of German politics that Social Democrats over the years have become the defenders of both federalism and the Court, while Christian Democrats, whose plans for augmenting federal power have been dashed by judicial vetoes, number among themselves many of the Court's harshest critics. This anomolous situation was one by-product of two decades of Christian Democratic control of the Federal Government along with Social Democratic control of several state governments. But now that the

Social Democrats have obtained power in Bonn, and seem to be striking out in new policy directions, federal-state conflicts may well return to the Court. It only remains to be seen whether the Christian Democrats will now switch roles with the Social Democrats and become the defenders of federalism and the Court from their own bastions of power in the states.

"Separation of Powers" Conflicts

What must be noted concerning the cases involving conflicts between high organs of the federal government—*Organstreit* proceedings as they are called—is that in no case decided by the Court has the Chancellor, the Bundesrat, or Bundestag been involved as the initiating party. Nearly every case was brought by a minor party outside parliament or the major opposition party inside parliament, usually the Social Democratic Party, for the purpose of challenging some procedural rule or law alleged to impinge on the party's rights.[10] In only three cases did the moving party win. Two cases decided on 10 July 1966 were brought respectively by the Bavarian Party (BP) and the National Democratic Party (NPD) against the Bundestag and Bundesrat to challenge a party finance law that excluded nonparliamentary parties from its benefits. The court nullified the statute partially on the basis of Article 21 of the Basic Law which defines the role of political parties in the federal republic.[11] The other case involved simply the nullification of a rule of parliamentary procedure that discriminated against the Social Democratic Party.[12] All remaining cases originally taken to the Court appear to have been dropped. Thus the Federal Constitutional Court appears not to have played any meaningful role in mediating conflicts between traditional organs or branches of government. Such controversies apparently are resolved in nonjudicial ways.

Abstract Judicial Review and Political Process Cases

The ability of the federal or a state government, or 100 members of the Bundestag, to test the validity of a federal or state law in the event simply of serious *doubts* about its constitutionality has led some people to deplore what they regard as the "judicialization" of West German politics and the consequent blunting of the edge of the democratic process.[13] Arnold Heidenheimer has observed that the "German legislature is frequently regarded not as the final arbiter whose decisions can only be changed by the voters, but as a trial arena for arguments which may eventually be submitted to the Constitutional Court."[14]

Experience has shown this to be an overstatement. By 1 January 1968 only forty-nine abstract review cases had been brought to the Court. Actually the Court exercised this jurisdiction with considerable discretion. In an early ruling the Court restricted its scope of review by declaring that it had no authority to rule on the constitutionality of a policy not yet embodied in a formal law.[15] The Court has also very deftly employed the tactic of delay to drain cases of their political urgency. Several cases, pending for years, have been dropped because of the Court's deliberate use of time and the tactic of nondecision.

In the thirty-five cases actually decided, twenty-nine of the original petitions were filed by state governments, two by the Federal Government, and only three by the relevant number of representatives in the Bundestag. Thus the states, not the Federal Government or disaffected members of the legislature, have made the most use of the Court's abstract jurisdiction, ordinarily to challenge a federal law, but occasionally to secure a review of one of their own laws. Seven provisions of federal law and three of state law have been struck down. The most important case involving state law was the Federal Government's challenge to referenda in Bremen and Hamburg, both controlled by Social Democrats, on whether West Germany should be armed with atomic weapons. The Court held that popular referenda on a matter of national defense policy constituted a violation of the principle of comity between levels of government; the state did not show the proper respect for the Federal Government's prerogatives in military affairs.[16]

Two decisions of the Court arising under its abstract review jurisdiction have been of major political consequence. The first is the decision of 4 June 1958 invalidating provisions of the Federal Income and Corporation Tax Law which allowed taxpayers to deduct contributions to political parties.[17] The second is the Decision of 19 July 1966 nullifying the appropriation of federal funds for the maintenance and general support of political parties with representation in the Bundestag.[18] The party finance cases, together with decisions affecting the electoral process, have done much to maintain an open system of political competition in the Federal Republic. Instead of blunting the democratic process the Court here seems actually to have invigorated it. The German Court's role in policing the electoral process actually rivals the Supreme Court's determination to secure equal legislative representation for American citizens.

The one provision of the Basic Law which hurls the Constitutional Court into the very center of the political process is Article 21. It empowers the Court to declare political parties unconstitutional. The Court has done so twice, pursuant to motions filed by the Federal Government. In 1952 the Neo-Nazi Socialist Reichs Party was declared unconstitutional. In 1956 the Communist Party was also banned on the grounds that it was totalitarian in character and dedicated to the eventual defeat of the liberal democratic order created by the Basic Law.[19]

Constitutional Complaints and Concrete Judicial Review

The decisions discussed so far constitute a very small segment of the Federal Constitutional Court's output. Almost 95 percent of the cases are constitutional complaints of ordinary citizens, together with those cases arising under the Court's concrete review jurisdiction. Since 1951 the Court has received nearly 19,000 complaints, as mentioned earlier, averaging over 1,000 per year. Only a handful, however, are accepted for full court deliberation. Most complaints are dismissed as readily as *certiorari* petitions are denied by the United States Supreme Court. A high percentage involve defendants claiming a violation of procedural rights. Nevertheless, the volume of complaints shows at least the willingness of Germans to go to court when they feel that their constitutional rights have been violated. Eighty percent of all the Court's published opinions are in response to constitutional complaints. That approximately 35 percent of these opinions sided with the complainant is one measure of the Court's solicitude for the basic rights of German citizens.

Yet few of these complaints challenge laws for the violation of basic liberties such as the freedoms of speech, association, and religion. The most important exception to this observation is the *Spiegel* Case. There the Court was asked to invalidate the Federal Government's nighttime raid on 26 October 1962 of the offices and records of West Germany's leading news magazine *Der Spiegel*, as violative of free speech. *Der Spiegel* editors were subsequently charged with treason for having published military secrets. The case resulted in the first major postwar crisis for the German government when members of the Free Democratic Party (FDP) walked out of the government coalition. Four years later the Constitutional Court handed down the first split decision in its brief history.[20] Because of a four-to-four tie the Government's original action against *Der Spiegel* was upheld, but not without a ringing defense of a free press by the four justices who were in "dissent."[21]

Except for criminal defendant cases, which make up the largest category of constitutional complaints, most Germans have gone to Court to vindicate social and property rights. In this respect the work of the Federal Constitutional Court largely mirrors the primacy of the economy in the life of postwar Germany, much as American constitutional jurisprudence reflected the dominance of economic values in the nineteenth century. Finally, pursuant to its concrete review jurisdiction, the Court has decided nearly 500 cases in approximately 250 written opinions. Considerably more than half of the statutes involved in these proceedings were federal laws, the remainder state laws. In most cases the constitutional doubt of the judge below was resolved in favor of the law's validity. Yet, in nearly seventy cases a provision of federal or state law was found unconstitutional. These nullifications, when combined with other cases in which laws have been struck down, make the Supreme Court of the United States look like a paragon of judicial restraint. A large number of these laws, like judicial rulings, administrative decrees, and statutory provisions challenged in constitutional complaints, have to do with regulations pertaining to social security, welfare, taxation, and the practice of a trade or a profession. A balanced view, however, should include the observation that these nullifications of federal and state laws have not been very significant politically. They have not precipitated strong negative reactions on the part of federal or state authorities.

B. Italy

It should be noted at the outset that the Italian Constitutional Court was implemented with considerable difficulty. Though the Court was the major institutional innovation of the 1948 Constitution, it did not open its doors for business until 23 April 1956. The eight-year delay in the establishment of the Court is attributable partly to emergent doubts concerning the wisdom of such a tribunal within Italy's scheme of government. Parliamentary inertia and procrastination by the ruling Christian Democratic Party was the main reason for the delay, however, along with a thirty-month battle among parliamentary parties over the selection of justices.[22] The refusal of Christian Democrats initially to compromise with the Communist Party in choosing justices made it impossible for Parliament to select its quota of five justices. It was not until Christian Democrats agreed to seat a Communist on the Court that this quota was actually filled.

Despite its late start, the Court's decisional output has been substantial, exceeding the expectations of its creators. By the end of 1969 the Court had handed down a total of 1,107 full opinions. The one separation of powers dispute that came before the Court in all that time was dismissed on procedural grounds. There have been no cases involving impeachments or the validity of referenda. The Court has served primarily, it seems, as a forum for the resolution of state-regional conflicts and for hearing cases, mostly involving defendants' rights, on indirect judicial review.

State-Regional Conflicts

Direct federal-state conflicts in Germany have been negligible when compared to regional-state conflicts in Italy. Regarding the latter it is important to distinguish between two classes of cases. The first, resembling the abstract judicial review proceeding in the German Court, are disputes in which the central government or a reigon petitions the Court for a decision on the constitutionality of legislation passed by the other unit of government. The second are jurisdictional conflicts between the central government and a region not ordinarily involving statutory review. Of the 295 cases decided as of 1965, 205 were conflicts of law between state and region, while 90 were jurisdictional conflicts arising out of opposing claims to competency in certain areas of public administration.

In sharp contrast to a German Court, the Italian tribunal shows a strong bias in favor of the central government. The Court ruled against the region over 80 percent of the time. Trentino-Alto Adige, for example, brought fifty-eight cases against the central government. The region won two, whereas the central government won eight of the ten cases it brought against the region.[23] The antiregional bias of the Constitutional Court seems congruent with the general reluctance of Italian political leaders to grant any real measure of autonomy to the regions.

Most of these conflicts have their origin in the five regions of Sicily, Sardinia, Valle d'Aosta, Trentino-Alto Adige, and Fruiuli-Venezia Giulia. (Italy has only recently moved to establish governments in the remaining fourteen autonomous regions created by the 1948 Constitution.) The extremely high incidence of these conflicts is rooted largely in the unique territorial and linguistic characteristics that prompted the establishment of these regional governments in the first place. Sicily, described by Kogan as a "sink-hole of corruption and misgovernment,"[24] and noted for its record of resistance to Rome, has been one of the principal sources of these cases. The central government has successfully enlisted the aid of the Constitutional Court to forestall the emergence of a genuine Sicilian autonomy, and thus to keep the separatists within Sicily at bay. For example, the region's autonomy was drastically curtailed when the Constitutional Court claimed exclusive jurisdiction to review the constitutionality of Sicilian laws and the applicability of national laws within Sicily.[25]

The Court has made clear on a number of occasions that regions have no authority over matters not expressly assigned to them in the Constitution. It has ruled that they are barred from exercising legislative authority in the area of criminal law or in private law matters covered by the Civil Code since these are areas preempted by the central government.[26] In a few instances, however, the court has affirmed concurrent legislative authority for both levels of government. Thus Sicily's right to set transportation rates of carriers licensed by the Sicilian government was sustained.[27] In one very important decision the Court also held that the central government may not nullify an administrative act or regulation sanctioned by communal or provincial law by appealing simply to its general authority; it ruled rather that the central government must initiate a proceeding in the Constitutional Court if it wishes to void an administrative act promulgated by a region.[28] However, in seeking to mark off some zone of regional independence, the Court has declared that the principle of regional autonomy is violated when the central government impinges upon local administrative functions under exclusive regional jurisdiction.[29]

Indirect Judicial Review

The remaining decisions of the Italian Court range over a wide area. Many of them, reflecting judicial sensitivity to the undemocratic procedures of Fascist Italy, are decisions that seek to bind legislators, administrators, judges, and police to the procedural standards set forth in the Constitution. The Court has even sought to make Parliament observe the principles of fiscal responsibility outlined in Article 81, insisting, for example, that legislators follow the requirement that all statutes appropriating funds include corresponding tax measures.[30] But the Court's greatest vigilance is over the administration of criminal justice. Nearly one-half of all cases before the Court deal with defendants' rights, along with actions involving constitutional objections to certain procedures employed in committing persons to state institutions, such as mental hospitals.[31] Scores of police regulations and penal statutes enacted under Mussolini, and applied after the ratification of the 1948 Constitution, have been struck down as violative of constitutional standards.[32]

Other dispositions before the Court deal with laws regulating aspects of the economy and the use of property. A considerable number of these have applied the equal protection clause of Article 3 to social and welfare legislation containing discriminations against certain classes of people. On balance these decisions have sought to eliminate arbitrary encroachments on the right to run a business, to receive welfare benefits, and to choose a trade or join labor unions;[33] yet the Court maintains that these are also rights subject to reasonable regulation in furtherance of constitutional norms like "social utility," "security," "health," and the "interest of society." These values are important in assessing the validity of legislation in Italy and often prevail against countervailing claims based on infringement of individual rights.[34]

Less than 5 percent of the Constitutional Court's decisions involve the classical freedoms of speech, association, religion, and assembly. Nevertheless, the Court's record here may fairly be described as moderately progressive: It has nullified restrictions on the right of association; it has defended the right to vote, the right of equal access to public office, and the equal right of political parties to be heard on state-owned radio and television; it has supported the right of a legislator to vote in parliament against party directives; it has supported the right of protestant sects to proselitize; and it has imposed the general requirement that all limitations on free speech be clearly justified by the principles and provisions of the Constitution.[35] The liberalism of this record is no mean achievement within a system lacking consensus on political fundamentals and torn by ideological conflict.

Yet the Italian Penal Code includes dozens of provisions against libel, slander, and subversion, all of which have been carried over from the Fascist regime, that bracket speech in such a way as to leave dissenters and dissident minorities virtually at the mercy of the state. Some of these laws the court has tended to justify largely on the ground of an overriding state interest in maintaining security. For example, speech may constitutionally be suppressed if it tends to debase political institutions, disturb the public peace, subvert the existing legal order, or undermine the democratic process.[36] This is a long way from American free-speech theory which rejects the notion of institutional slander and requires speech to be bracketed with action before it can validly be suppressed.[37]

An even wider gulf separates American and Italian constitutional law in the area of religious liberty. The School Prayer Case,[38] for example, would be unthinkable in the religious and cultural environment of Italy. More important is the problem of equal protection of religion under Italian law. A major difficulty confronting the Court here is that the Constitution itself offends the principle of equal protection of religion, for Article 7 accords to the Catholic Church independence and sovereignty in the area of its jurisdiction, and requires a constitutional amendment to alter any provision of the Lateran Pacts. On the other hand, while Article 8 declares that all religious confessions are equal before the law, the state may regulate religions other than Catholic by law. Under the authority of the 1929 Concordat the Italian government has also enacted far-reaching criminal laws protecting both the Catholic religion and the person of the pope against derision and ridicule. This was one justification for banning Hochhuth's play, *The Deputy*, in Rome. In a recent decision the Constitutional Court sustained one of these laws on the ground that derision of Catholicism would elicit a stronger public reaction than derision aimed at other religious groups.[39] Yet the Court went on to diminish the inequality of the statute by construing it to punish derision of all religions. The Court's decision, of course, is not likely to comfort those whose conception of free speech includes the right to make sport of any institution of society, including organized religion. Yet it is important to remember that the Court is deciding these cases and many others in the free-speech field largely in accordance with the predominant value orientation of the Italian community.

IV. THE IMPACT OF JUDICIAL REVIEW
IN ITALY AND WEST GERMANY

To study the impact of any court is a hazardous undertaking. It is hazardous because no seismographic research instrument is available at the present time to carefully measure the vibrations caused by court decisions. The political scientist writing on such matters has to depend for the most part on newspaper reports, interviews with knowledgeable people, and his own informed impressions. Systematic public opinion surveys, some of which will be used below in connection with Germany, are helpful in tracing impact, but are hardly conclusive. In Italy no systematic public opinion surveys of attitudes toward the Constitutional Court are available. Hence this study has had to rely on inferences from other kinds of public opinion data.

These caveats should be kept in mind in the following analysis of impact. This paper will seek to measure impact by the pattern of (a) *compliance* with judicial rulings, (b) *support* of the constitutional court among the public and critical political elites, and (c) *awareness* of the court among the general public.

1. COMPLIANCE

The West German record of compliance with the decisions of the Federal Constitutional Court seems fairly widespread. Germany has yet to experience the resistance to decisions that has characterized the American response to the Supreme Court School Desegregation Case or to the School Prayer Case.[40] While no German case packs the emotional wallop of American decisions obliterating long-standing racial or religious practices the German Court has handed down many decisions reversing critically important governmental policies. Examples of such cases, as noted earlier, are the Decision of 26 March 1957 holding that the German states are not bound in their educational policies to the terms of the Concordat; the Decision of 28 February 1961 nullifying a federal plan to create a national television station; the Decision of 30 July 1958 forbidding the states to hold referenda on the question of atomic rearmament; the Decision of 8 August 1966 voiding a law appropriating federal funds in support of political parties represented in the Bundestag; or even the Decision of 19 July

1966 which the editors of *Der Spiegel* could claim as a moral victory against the Adenauer government in support of a free press.

But what about decisions which require the implementation of policy changes at the level of a police department, administrative agency, or a district court? Even here, if newspaper reports and the views of informed officials are trustworthy sources of information, there appears to have been little open or brazen defiance of Constitutional Court rulings by lower public officials charged with their implementation. This observation does not imply that the Court has not been threatened or that its decisions have not been circumvented by agencies of government. A massive and expensive research effort would be required to determine whether German judges and prosecuting attorneys, for example, are following Federal Constitutional Court decisions governing fair hearings for criminal defendants.

By contrast, Italian policemen and prosecutors systematically appear to ignore constitutional decisions, especially in the area of defendants' rights.[41] Given the nature and attitudes of these officials, as reported by students of Italian government, it is unlikely that the situation has measurably improved. The most dramatic case of noncompliance was the refusal of a cabinet minister to follow a Constitutional Court decision voiding the provisions of a public security law.[42] In this instance noncompliance actually occasioned the resignation of the Constitutional Court's first President, Enrico de Nicola. His successor, Gaetano Azzariti, also complained about official lassitude in executing the high court's mandates.[43] Even parliament has been a principal offender in this regard for not having instituted reforms in the penal code that appear to have been necessitated by court decisions. Indeed Parliament has resolutely refused to change provisions of the penal code that the Court has invalidated.[44]

It would not be remiss here to take "judicial notice" of the well-known fact that Italian public officials have manifested considerable laxity in upholding the principles and provisions of the 1948 Constitution. According to Adams and Barile the Italian bureaucracy is not only spotted with corruption, but is also "imbued with the negative aspects of Fascist mentality."[45] Prefects are known to exercise arbitrary authority in their bailiwicks, suspending civil liberties when it suits their purposes, slapping down vetoes on the acts of provincial and communal councils, and manipulating the electoral process, often against left-wing parties and occasionally in collusion with local church officials and right-wing political leaders. No less than Luigi Einaudi, Republican Italy's first president, condemned the prefectural system of public administration as being wholly incompatible with liberal democracy.[46] Noncompliance with Constitutional Court decisions would seem related to this general crisis of constitutional government in Italy.

2. Support

Support of a constitutional court may be measured partly by determining whether judicial review is accepted as legitimate by critical elite groups in the society and whether attitudes toward the court as an institution are generally favorable. At best this would measure the relative amount of diffuse support for the court within the political system. Diffuse public support has value in that it contributes to the survival of an institution in times of stress, when a court, for example, hands down unpopular decisions which generate attempts to limit its powers.

Empirical data from West Germany are available for getting a handle on this general question. In the spring of 1968 the author mailed a questionnaire to seven elite groups in West Germany whose attitudes were regarded as critical to the effective exercise of judicial review. These groups included federal judges, state judges, civil servants, professors of public law, party leaders, interest group leaders, together with journalists and television commentators who write and report on law and judicial matters. The sample included 500 respondents; members of some groups were selected by position, members of other groups at random. The questionnaire was designed to elicit their views on judicial review and the Federal Constitutional Court.

TABLE 2

German Elite Attitudes Toward Judicial Review

Question	Absolutely necessary	Somewhat necessary	Not very necessary	Unnecessary
In your view, how necessary is judicial review to the stability and continuity of German democracy?	44%	49%	3%	1%

TABLE 3

Elite Attitudes Toward the Federal Constitutional Court

Question	Good	Satisfactory	Unsatisfactory	No Answer
How would you evaluate the general performance of the Constitutional Court during the first 17 years of its activity?	68%	27%	5%	—
	Too Much	Just Right	Too Little	No Answer
How much influence do you think the Federal Constitutional Court has had on German politics?	10%	74%	9%	7%

The reliability of the results is in need of some qualification since only 34 percent of the respondents returned completed questionnaires. Yet 14 percent of the respondents who chose not to fill out the questionnaire wrote letters instead. The letters were largely in support of judicial review and the Court, confirming the general findings of Tables 2 and 3. These data tend to be confirmed by another study conducted in 1968 by the Social Science Research Institute of Mannheim University under the direction of Professor Rudolf Wildenmann. The attitudes revealed in Table 4 are an expression of what importance the respondents think the Federal Constitutional Court *should* have in the political system. The findings also confirm the widely held impression that law professors, party officials, and civil servants are least sanguine about judicial review, though here too the level of support is high.

Since comparable data are not available for Italy, one is able to map the pattern of opposition to the Constitutional Court more clearly than the pattern of support. But even here the lines on the opposition map are hazy. It is almost impossible to determine the strength or intensity of opposition among Italian elite groups. Yet it is not possible to overlook extremely harsh attacks on the Constitutional Court by regional governments, by Parliament, and by the Vatican. The only groups really conspicuous for their defense of the Constitutional

TABLE 4

Elite Assessment of the Federal Constitutional Court's
Influence Upon the West German Federal Republic

Elite Groups N = 400+	Very Important	Important	Unimportant
Party Functionaries	14%	41%	45%
Federal Legislative Leaders	37	42	21
State Legislative Leaders	10	66	24
Federal Ministerial Leaders	24	35	41
State Ministerial Leaders	7	63	30
Publishers	31	44	25
Editors	24	48	28
Labor Leaders	23	40	33
Industrial Leaders	18	52	23
Professors	27	31	42

Source: Rudolf Wildenmann, Eliten in der Bundesrepublik: eine sozialwissenschaftliche Untersuchung über Einstellungen führender Positionsträger zur Politik und Demokratie (Mannheim University, August, 1968), pp. 61–62.

Court are the justices themselves and a small but influential group of law professors.

Yet there is little evidence for concluding that the Constitutional Court does not enjoy latent support among many Italian political leaders. Negotiations incident to the recruitment of the justices would seem to indicate the seriousness with which the Court is taken in Italy. That the pretore and tribunale have certified more than 1,400 questions for judicial review suggests also some support for the constitutional role of the high court among lower court judges. But too much should not be made of this point. Italian constitutional law scholars have frequently upbraided the regular judiciary for its general tendency to reject as "patently unfounded" constitutional objections that are raised in the course of an ordinary lawsuit. It appears, too, that the overwhelming majority of questions that are certified to the Constitutional Court are raised originally by litigants and not by judges.[47] The latter simply let them pass.

This is not surprising behavior on the part of the Italian judiciary. Judges, along with civil servants and the clergy, have not been conspicuous for their defense of the 1948 Constitution. One reason, actually, why the framers of Italy's Constitution did not confer the power of judicial review upon the ordinary courts was the fear that Italian judges, trained under the Fascist system, would not interpret the Constitution in a democratic spirit.[48]

3. AWARENESS

While general public awareness of a judicial institution is no necessary indication of public support, still the visibility of a court would seem to be related to the public support that it is likely to receive. Walter Murphy and Joseph Tanenhaus point out that one condition of public support for a judicial tribunal is that it be regarded "as carrying out its responsibilities in an impartial and competent manner."[49] Quite obviously this condition cannot be met if people are unaware of the tribunal's activities. In any case there appear to be notable differences in the visibility of the Italian and German tribunals.

The activities of the West German Court are very well reported, perhaps because the Court is equipped with its own press office. Press releases, originating inside the Court, are automatically distributed to wire services and reporters as each decision is handed down. The appointment of justices is normally accompanied by wide newspaper and television coverage, along with formal celebrations and interviews. And as the burgeoning clipping files in the archives of the Federal Constitutional Court bear witness, newspaper coverage, especially of the "great cases"—such as the Spiegel, Television, Party Finance, and Communist Party Cases—has been very extensive.

Insight into the degree of the public's awareness of the Federal Constitutional Court is provided once again by the Mannheim Research Institute. The following question was put to a random sample of West Germans in 1968: "Do you by chance know what are the functions of the Federal Constitutional Court in Karlsruhe?" The results, presented in Table 5, indicate, rather surprisingly, a high degree of awareness, even rivaling the visibility of the Supreme Court among the American public.[50] The result is consistent with Almond and Verba's finding that Germans follow accounts of political and governmental affairs almost as much as do Americans.[51] But the further Almond-Verba finding that Germans, despite their knowledge of governmental affairs, are not highly committed to their political institutions should caution us once again to differentiate between awareness and support of an institution.

TABLE 5

Public Awareness of the Federal Constitutional Court and Its Roles*

Awareness	Percent
A. General	
1. No answer or knowledge	58
2. Aware	42
B. Roles mentioned by those aware	
1. Protects Basic Law	17
2. Decides constitutional complaints	8
3. Serves as general court of last resort	5
4. Tries cases involving espionage, treason, and other offenses against state security	3
5. Reviews legislation and acts of parliament, government, and the police	1
6. Safeguards the democratic order	1
7. Other	7

N = 2016

* The author is indebted to Professor Rudolf Wildenmann and Dr. Max Kaase for their generosity in supplying these figures.

Although no empirical data is available for determining the visibility of the Italian Court, certain well-known aspects of Italy's civic culture may assist this analysis. It is probably because of West Germany's highly developed communications system and literacy rate that the average German is considerably more informed about his political institutions than his Italian counterpart. Almond-Verba findings on political cognition show that Italians are highly uninterested in and largely uninformed about their political institutions.[52]

Another important feature of Italy's civic culture, which actually has more to do with support than awareness, is the profound distrust that Italians have for their political officials and official agencies. This is in sharp contrast to the relative respect for authority that typifies the average German's attitude. A recent survey by the Italian Institute of Public Opinion (Doxa) reported that 41 percent of Italians feel that their civil servants are dishonest while 61 percent believe that they can be bought off by offers of money.[53] Attitudes towards the judiciary seem similarly infected. The Italian Judiciary, says Kogan, "must operate in an atmosphere . . . without the support of a broad public sense of constitutionality or legality, in the absence of a widespread feeling of confidence in the courts themselves."[54] It is doubtful that the Constitutional Court has entirely escaped the impact of this civic malaise.

Another reason Italy's Court may be less visible than Germany's is the inability of Italian citizens to directly appeal to the Constitutional Court. This may also be a reason why public interest groups dedicated to the promotion of constitutional litigation have not developed in Italy. One is reminded here of the impact that American groups such as the Legal Defense Education Fund of the National Association for the Advancement of Colored People, the American Civil Liberties Union, and the American Jewish Congress have had on the Supreme Court.[55] While it is true that no such groups as prominent as these have sprung up in West Germany either, still over 19,000' German citizens have filed 19,000 constitutional complaints to date. This has notably sharpened the salience of the Federal Constitutional Court in the German system.

V. JUDICIAL REVIEW: SOME CONTRASTS BETWEEN ITALY AND WEST GERMANY

This paper does not suggest that judicial review will succeed in West Germany or will fail in Italy. What it may suggest is that judicial review has survived its first test in the Federal Republic but is still largely on trial in Italy. Nor does this paper suggest that judicial review is a necessary condition of constitutional democracy. Because judicial review is an important principle of American constitutional government some people have concluded that it is a principal cause of constitutionalism in America, and that its importation into foreign legal systems will also insure the existence of constitutional government there. In actuality, judicial review would probably rank toward the bottom of a list of institutional devices known for their effectiveness in limiting the power of majorities. Moreover, the ability of constitutional court judges to influence the course of constitutional development depends largely on the political and legal environment in which judicial review operates.

It is important to note that in both Italy and Germany the constitutional court has functioned mainly as an agency for the "ratification" of the policies of the political branches of government. When these courts "ratify" the policies of political decision-makers, they make an impact upon the political system which is marginal at best. They do not make policy in quite the same way as the American Supreme Court, which combines the functions of a constitutional court with those of an appellate tribunal with general jurisdiction over all controversies arising under the public laws of the United States. However, it is tempting to suggest that the constitutional courts of Italy and West Germany, precisely because of their role as "ratifiers" of public policy, are performing an important legitimizing function within the political system, although it would be extremely difficult to show empirically that this is the case. For one thing, most public laws are not submitted for constitutional review. For another, it is probable that in *parliamentary* democracies like Italy and West Germany the legitimacy of a public policy is ultimately equated with its embodiment in a law passed by a legislative majority.

Yet each decision that legitimizes a public law does so—indeed must do so—against constitutional objections that have to be overcome with reasoned arguments. Through their decisions, the justices interpret the Constitution, specify the meaning of its provisions, and sketch the outer limits of governmental power. In so doing they are creating a body of constitutional jurisprudence which political decision-makers will find increasingly difficult to ignore in defining their own authority.

If Tocqueville could travel through Italy and West Germany today he would never be driven to observe, as he was with reference to the United States, that all major political questions tend invariably to resolve themselves into constitutional issues. However, he would be conscious of the role these constitutional courts have played in the public life of each country. He would certainly be conscious of their important educational role. He would also observe the increasing tendency of politicians, political groups, and individuals to use the constitutional law created by these courts as a tool in their quarrels with government. But he would find this tendency considerably more pronounced in West Germany than in Italy.

In West Germany, as we have seen, the Constitutional Court has disallowed major policies of federal and state governments and gotten away with it; that is, its decisions have been accepted by political leaders as authoritative and binding upon all other units of government. The Federal Constitutional Court has contributed to the development of German constitutional democracy in three notable ways: first, the Court has slowed down the gravitation of power to the central government; second, it has kept vigilant watch over the system of political parties and elections, thus helping to maintain a regime of free and open political competition; third, it has provided a means by which citizens may vindicate constitutional rights allegedly infringed by the state. Each of these roles the Court has played with the dexterity and restraint necessary to consolidate and solidify its support among critical elite groups. One may surmise also that traditional German respect for law and authority has constituted reserve strength that has enabled the Court to buttress its authority within the political system.

The Italian Constitutional Court, on the other hand, seems not to have made as deep an imprint upon the political system of Italy. It has "ratified" the policies of the central vis-à-vis the regional governments as well as the general socioeconomic policies of the former. The general direction of the Court's decisions, particularly its frequent nullification of Italian laws, has been to uphold constitutional government, especially in the area of defendant's rights. Yet the Court's authority tends to be resisted and frequently ignored by civil servants, judges, and occasionally by Parliament itself. Nevertheless, the Constitutional Court is one of the few genuine beacons of constitutional democracy capable of guiding Italy into a more serene era of constitutional government.

It was suggested earlier that the success of judicial review in any country depends largely on the politico-legal environment in which it operates. Once again it seems necessary to add that though judicial review is not an essential condition for the existence of constitutional democracy, certain conditions do seem required for the effective exercise of judicial review. In this regard we can learn much from the West German and Italian experiences.

In Germany the Federal Constitutional Court has a power base which the Italian Court does not enjoy. That power base is provided in part by the federal nature of the Bonn Republic, together with the relative stability of West Germany's party system, a stability to which the Court itself has contributed. Because Germany is basically a two-party system the main opposition party—until 1967 the Social Democratic Party—has managed to secure a foothold in several state governments, giving it considerable, if not disproportionate, influence in the upper house—the Bundesrat—of the national legislature where the states are corporately represented. (Recall, too, that the Bundesrat elects one-half the members of the Constitutional Court). This particular diffusion and division of power partially accounts for the leverage of the Federal Constitutional Court in the German system. For the system is sufficiently bipartisan, federal, and pluralistic in character to enable the Court to win support among power centers and important political groupings in and out of government. Perhaps these are some of the reasons why judicial review seems to work best in federal systems.

The Constitutional Court has not found similar shelter on the Italian political landscape. Italy's political and institutional topology is notably different from that of Germany. Its principal features are (1) a multi-party system heavily weighted with nondemocratic elements at both poles of the political sphere; (2) a society torn by ideological and religious cleavage; and (3) a basic system instability that has caused thirty-one governments to collapse since 1948. This is not an environment in which judicial review is likely to flourish.

Legal climate is equally important for the effective exercise of judicial review. First, the constitutional court must be accepted as the final interpreter of the constitution. But this involves the prior assumption that the constitution itself is universally accepted, for a vibrant judicial review assumes a framework of shared constitutional values, norms, or goals. No one has to be reminded of the Dred Scott Case[56] to appreciate that judicial authority is weakest in times of constitutional crises. And Italy, unlike West Germany, is saddled with several unresolved constitutional crises one of the most important of which is the critical relationship between church and state. Though the Constitutional Court so far has been able to withstand ecclesiastical criticism it can only do so much to achieve religious liberty in a society where clerical influence is so pervasive and where the Lateran Pacts hang like an albatross around the neck of Italian constitutionalism.

Even at the level of Italian political and legal theory, the Constitutional Court is still an object of controversy. First, there seems to be some difficulty in fitting the decisions of the Constitutional Court into the orthodox Italian tradition of law. Italy is heir to a very long and proud tradition of systematic jurisprudence that is foreign to a decisional process that must often strike a political balance between competing interests and values. Second, Italian legal scholars, unable to reconcile judicial review with the traditional tripartite division of governmental authority, seem to view the Court as a fourth branch of government, positioned midway between the legislative and judicial branches. The Court is not exclusively a judicial institution, according to this reasoning, because it is a sovereign body with power to "unmake" laws. On the other hand, it is not a genuine legislative body since it does not make law *ab initio* and uses judicial forms and norms to resolve controversies. By contrast, German legal scholars seem to have fairly well made a place for the Federal Constitutional Court in the German scheme of parliamentary government.

These contrasts, sharp as they are, furnish little basis for predicting the future of constitutional democracy in either Italy or West Germany. This essay has focused on a single institution in each country, and one that operates, at most, on the edge of the political system. A constitutional court's capacity both to support and maintain constitutionalism is severely limited, even in politico-legal environments most favorable to judicial review. At the same time the public record or output of a constitutional tribunal is relevant to any assessment of the condition of a constitutional democracy. One may note with lament, sharp resistance against judicial review in Italy. But more impressive, actually, is the stubborn persistence of the Court in the face of so much resistance.

Let us recall, as we conclude this essay, that against the backdrop of history the last twenty years have represented heroic efforts on the part of Italy and West Germany to install and to institutionalize regimes of liberty constrained by law. That is the meaning of constitutional government. Constitutional courts are important symbols and agencies of constitutionalism. They would be the first institutions to be crushed under the heel of a dictatorship. Their persistence is, therefore, an important measure of the willingness of governors to submit to a government based on law.

NOTES

1. The material on the Italian Constitutional Court was drawn from my paper, "Cross-National Comparisons of Constitutional Courts: Toward a Theory of Judicial Review," presented at the American Political Science Association meeting, Los Angeles, California (September 8–12, 1970). For a more extended treatment of the West German Federal Constitu-

tional Court see my chapter, "The Federal Constitutional Court in the West German Political System" in *Frontiers of Judicial Research*, ed. Joel B. Grossman and Joseph Tanenhaus (New York: John Wiley and Sons, 1969), pp. 73–132.

2. See *Constitutions and Constitutional Trends since World War II*, ed. Arnold J. Zurcher (New York: New York University Press, 1951), pp. 4–6.

3. Karl Loewenstein, "The Value of Constitutions in our Revolutionary Age" in Zurcher, p. 217.

4. The Basic Law of the Federal Republic of Germany (May 23, 1949), Article 93 (2).

5. *Entscheidungen des Bundesverfassungsgericht* (Tübingen: J.C.B. Mohr [Paul Siebeck], 1962), vol. 12, p. 205. (Hereafter cited as BVerfGE)

6. 6 BVerfGE 309 (1957).

7. 252 U.S. 416 (1920).

8. See Edward McWhinney, *Constitutionalism in Germany and the Federal Constitutional Court* (Leyden: A.W. Sythoff, 1962), pp. 34–50.

9. Letter from Professor Ulrich Scheuner to author, July 28, 1968.

10. These cases are listed in chronological order in Gerhard Leibholz and Reinhard Rupprecht, *Bundesverfassungsgerichtsgesetz* (Cologne-Marienburg: Verlag Dr. Otto Schmidt KG, 1968), pp. 466–468.

11. 20 BVerfGE 119 (1967) and 20 BVerfGE 134 (1967).

12. 1 BVerfGE 144 (1952).

13. See, for example, *Governing Postwar Germany*, ed. Edmund H. Litchfield (Ithaca: Cornell University Press, 1953), p. 262.

14. Arnold Heidenheimer, *The Governments of Germany* (London: Methuen & Co., 1965), p. 151.

15. 1 BVerfGE 396 (1952).

16. 8 BVerfGE 104 (1958) and 8 BVerfGE 183 (1958).

17. See 8 BVerfGE 51 (1958).

18. 20 BVerfGE 56 (1967). A detailed analysis of the party finance cases appears in my article, "Politics and Jurisprudence in West Germany: State Financing of Political Parties," *American Journal of Jurisprudence* (Forthcoming, 1971).

19. 2 BVerfGE 1 (1953) and 5 BVerfGE 85 (1956).

20. 20 BVerfGE 162 (1966).

21. For a general discussion of the *Spiegel* affair and the *Spiegel* case see my chapter, "The Spiegel Affair: A Case Study in Judicial Politics" in *The Political Trial*, ed. Theodore Becker (Indianapolis: Bobbs-Merrill, 1971).

22. With respect to the general composition of the Court, Constitutional Act No. 1 of March 11, 1953 provided for a Court of fifteen mem-

bers, a third to be elected by the highest courts (three by the Court of Cassation, one by the Council of State, and one by the Court of Accounts), a third by the President of the Republic, and a third by the two houses of Parliament meeting together. See Constitution of the Italian Republic (1947), Articles 134 to 137.

23. *Il Primo Decennio di Giurisprudenza della Corte Costituzionale 1956–1965* (Roma: Corte Costituzionale, Ufficio Studi, 1968), p. 733. These cases are also discussed in John Clarke Adams and Paolo Barile, "The Italian Constitutional Court and its First Two Years of Activity," 7 *Buffalo Law Review* 251 (Winter 1958), and Gaspare Ambrosini, "Der Italienische Verfassungsgerichtshof in den Ersten Sieben Jahren Seiner Tätigkeit," 14 *Jahrbuch des Öffentlichen Rechts* 300 (1965).

24. Norman Kogan, *The Government of Italy* (New York: Thomas Y. Crowell Co., 1962), p. 162.

25. Decision of 9 March 1957 (Nr. 38), *Giurisprudenza Costituzionale*, p. 463 (Hereafter cited as GC). See also John Clarke Adams and Paolo Barile, *The Government of Republican Italy*, 2nd ed. (Boston: Houghton Mifflin Co., 1966), p. 141.

26. See Decision of 5 November 1957 (Nr. 124), GC, p. 1128; Decision of 26 June 1956 (No. 6), GC, p. 586; and Decision of 8 July 1957 (No. 109), GC, p. 1016.

27. Decision of 27 June 1958 (No. 43), GC, p. 548.

28. Decision of 26 June 1956 (No. 5), GC, p. 586 and Decision of 8 July 1957 (No. 109), GC, p. 1016.

29. Decision of 26 January 1957 (No. 15), GC, p. 305.

30. See Decision of 15 July 1959 (No. 47), GC, p. 759.

31. See Aldo Sandulli, "The Constitutional Court in 1968," *Italy: Documents and Notes* (May–June 1969), p. 205.

32. Adams and Barile, p. 132.

33. See Decision of 28 December 1962 (No. 123), GC, p. 1506 and Decision of 19 December 1962 (No. 106), GC, p. 1408.

34. It is important to observe here that the Italian Constitution, reflecting an admixture of Marxist and Catholic social thought, perceives the individual as a member of "social groups through which his personality develops." And while the Constitution guarantees the inviolable rights of man without distinction as to sex, race, language, religion, political affiliation, or social background, it does "require the fulfillment of inalienable duties of political, economic, and social solidarity." Personal freedom is, accordingly, limited by the social context in which the individual functions. See Dante Germino and Stefano Passigli, *The Government and Politics of Contemporary Italy* (New York: Harper & Row, 1968), pp. 46–47. One such social context or group is the family; it is

accorded special protection under Title II of the Italian Constitution dealing with the "ethical-social relations" of society (Articles 29–34). A community norm that ranks high on the scale of ethical-social values is the belief in the centricity of the father as the mainstay of family unity. Both constitutional and community norms have been used to justify legislative distinctions based on sex. The wife is far from her husband's equal in Italian law as it relates to the care and education of children or to the disposition of property. Until recently it was even constitutionally permissible to impose a heavier penalty on the wife than on the husband for adulterous behavior (Decision of 28 November 1961 [No. 64], GC, p. 1224). The Court has also upheld the withholding of special benefit payments to orphaned children who are illegitimate, on the ground that such laws are in accord with the "conscience of the community" (Decision of 6 July 1966 [No. 92], GC, p. 1153). Recently, however, the Court has begun to reverse some of these decisions. In December 1969, for example, the Court finally voided the penal statute on adultery (*New York Times*, 5 December 1969, p. 11).

35. See Decisions of 15 May 1963 (No. 71), GC (Supplement), p. 235; 11 July 1961 (No. 43), GC, p. 968; 10 June 1963 (No. 60), GC, p. 194; 14 April 1965 (No. 26), GC, p. 252; 29 March 1960 (No. 15), GC, p. 147; 18 May 1960 (No. 33), GC, p. 563; 11 July 1961 (No. 42), GC, p. 951; 8 June 1963 (No. 86), GC (Supplement), p. 309; 18 June 1963 (No. 92), GC (Supplement), p. 345; 7 July 1964 (No. 72), GC, p. 736 and 19 February 1965 (No. 9), p. 61.

36. See Decisions of 16 March 1962 (No. 19), GC, p. 189; 11 July 1966 (No. 100), p. 1216; and 6 July 1966 (No. 87), p. 1096.

37. See, for example, *New York Times Co. v. Sullivan*, 376 U.S. 255 (1964).

38. See *Engel v. Vitale*, 370 U.S. 421 (1962).

39. Decision of 31 May 1965 (No. 39), GC., p. 602.

40. See, for example, William Beaney and N. Edward Beiser, "Prayer and Politics: The Impact of Engel and Schempp on the Political Process," 13 *Journal of Public Law* 475–503 (1964); Richard Johnson, *The Dynamics of Compliance* (Evanston: Northwestern University Press, 1967); and Walter Murphy, "The South Counterattacks: The Anti-NAACP Laws," 12 *Western Political Quarterly* 371-90 (June 1959).

41. See Adams and Barile, *Buffalo Law Review*, p. 251, note 30.

42. See generally Adams and Barile, *Republican Italy*, pp. 146–149.

43. Kogan, *The Government of Italy*, p. 130.

44. Adams and Barile, *Republican Italy*, p. 65.

45. Ibid., p. 55.

46. Ibid., p. 119.

47. *Ibid.*, p. 133. Empirical support for this statement comes from Dr. Alberto Marradi of the Center for the Study of Comparative Politics, University of Florence. Dr. Marradi, a close student of the Constitutional Court, informed the author that in a recent sample of 310 questions certified to the Constitutional Court under its indirect review jurisdiction, only 10 were forwarded on the initiative of the judges themselves. The rest were submitted by the judges pursuant to a request by one of the parties before the lower tribunal.

48. M. Cappelletti, J. H. Merryman, and J. M. Perillo, *The Italian Legal System* (Stanford: Stanford University Press, 1967), pp. 76–77.

49. See Walter F. Murphy and Joseph Tanenhaus, "Public opinion and the United States Supreme Court" in Grossman and Tanenhaus, *Frontiers*, p. 275.

50. *Ibid.*, pp. 282–283.

51. See Gabriel A. Almond and Sidney Verba, *The Civic Culture* (Princeton: Princeton University Press, 1963), p. 89.

52. *Ibid.*, pp. 90–100.

53. *Neue Züricher Zeitung*, October 9, 1965.

54. Kogan, *The Government of Italy*, p. 127.

55. See Nathan Hakman, "The Supreme Court's Political Environment: The Processing of Noncommercial Litigation" in Grossman and Tanenhaus, *Frontiers*, pp. 199–246.

56. On this general subject see Giuseppi Treves, "Judicial Review of Legislation in Italy," 7 *Journal of Public Law* 348 (Fall 1958); Gaetano Azzariti, "Die Stellung des Verfassungsgerichtshof in der Italienischen Staatsordnung," 8 *Jahrbuch des Öffentlichen Rechts* 13–24 (1959); Giovanni Cassandra, "The Constitutional Court of Italy," 8 *American Journal of Comparative Law* 1–14 (1959); Norberto Bobbio, "Trends in Italian Legal Theory," 8 *American Journal of Comparative Law* 329–40 (1959); and Mauro Cappelletti, John Henry Merryman, and Joseph M. Perillo, *The Italian Legal System* (Stanford: Stanford University Press, 1967), pp. 76–77.

4: CURRENT CHALLENGES TO DEMOCRACY IN THE UNITED STATES
Glenn Tinder

The main problem in appraising the present situation and prospects of American democracy is not that of discovering whether there are conditions that challenge it. Informed people not only agree that there are; they agree broadly on the nature of the conditions. Thus it is not difficult to set down the challenges to American democracy in a list which, setting aside all questions concerning moral priority, causal interconnection, and remedial action, would receive general assent among intellectuals. Let me suggest such a list.

1. Economic challenges: American democracy is weakened by the persistence of poverty and unemployment, by unjust privileges such as those embodied in present tax laws, and by inflation. All such conditions undermine the allegiance of important groups of citizens.
2. The racial situation: adamant discrimination against a large segment of the population expresses attitudes and incites emotions that are imcompatible with the readiness to communicate and compromise on which democracy depends.
3. The war in Vietnam: war is likely to weaken a nation's fidelity to liberal and democratic canons of order even when it is uncontroversial, short, and victoriously concluded; when it offends large groups, lasts for many years, and leads to no final victory, democratic order must be seriously imperiled.
4. Alienation: a number of well-known conditions, such as urban disintegration, a ravaged natural environment, and cultural vulgarity in the mass media, divide men in various ways from reality and thus give rise to alienation. A political order is jeopardized, as indicated by the example of the Weimar Republic, when those within it come to lack stable and satisfying relationships.

5. Political challenges: the French Fourth Republic fell in large part due to governmental immobility and popular dissension which became fatal with France's involvement in the Algerian War. Recent American political history provides little ground for confidence that our government can adequately meet any of the challenges listed above. Further, even in what it does, it is doubtful whether the government receives the kind of informed and critical assent which the standard of democracy demands.

This is admittedly a somewhat random list: it indicates no moral or causal order, and it is phrased with deliberate vagueness. But it does delineate the boundary-lines of an intellectual consensus and, moreover, it indicates the direction that must be taken in a discussion of current challenges to American democracy. Either the consensus must be called into question, or else the problem becomes that of interpreting conditions that already are well known. This paper follows the second alternative. I believe that the challenges we face have been widely and correctly identified but that there is little understanding of our relationship to these challenges. The problem then is one of interpretation. How should this task be undertaken? With what question do we begin?

The initial question for most Americans is one which expresses the traditional pragmatic temper of the nation: What should we do? Americans are not inclined to look for a philosophy of history or a metaphysics to shed light on their troubles; rather, they want to know which of the troubles are most urgent and how they should be attacked. It is easy to admire this attitude for its exclusion of discouragement and mystification. I suggest, nevertheless, that it misleads us. To concentrate on the question as to what we should do is to ignore the fact that we have for some time known of many things we should do and yet have not done them. Few if any of the conditions listed above are recent discoveries; they have for some time been matters of public knowledge. Anyone can think of a number of conditions, such as hunger and unfair tax privileges, which no one denies or defends but which we do not effectively attack. This realization explains the mounting fury of many American blacks; they are obsessed with the clear fact that, merely if they wanted to, whites could do much more than they have to improve the lives of blacks.

For another reason, as well, it is inappropriate to dwell on the question as to what should be done. To do so presupposes that one particular course of action, if only it can be discovered and followed, will definitely solve the problem which occasioned it. The most sensible undertaking, however, is subject to being invalidated by unforeseen consequences. These are not merely disadvantages such as those which attend any human undertaking and which, if plans have been well laid, are counterbalanced by advantages. They are due to unpredictable human responses, and they may falsify all reasonable forecasts and turn well-intended plans to evil ends. Ten years ago most liberals were horrified by John Foster Dulles' policy of "massive retaliation." That policy was discarded by President Kennedy, and the armed forces were expanded and equipped to fit them for waging limited war. The sequel was the tragedy in Vietnam.

The typical American insistence on knowing what we should do arises from what may be called the "liberal" view of man. It presupposes that man is free to do what is right—that his actions are chosen and not determined. It presupposes also that if he knows what is right he will generally do it. It presupposes finally that once the action is accomplished the ensuing state of affairs will not be perversely upset or misused. If this view of man were valid, meeting the challenges to democracy would require simply discovering, and making known, an appropriate course of action. A paper of this kind would properly be devoted to arguing what must be done. If the liberal view of man were valid, however, democracy would not be challenged so seriously as it is. Effective action would have been taken long before a crisis of such magnitude as the one in which we are now involved ever took shape. It seems clear that we must do more than merely try to devise a way out of our troubles. We must reconsider liberal assumptions concerning the relationship of man to historical troubles.

This has been done by some Americans, who have been led thereby to embrace the one major alternative (as most intellectuals see it) to the typical pragmatic liberalism of Americans, that is, Marxism. According to the Marxist view, men are not free to discern the good and to choose it, but are, so to speak, moral prisoners of their society. The conditions that challenge American democracy, as Marxists see them, are not historical accidents which we might choose to eliminate. They are structural features of the society; and they form, rather than being formed by, men and their choices. Changes do occur, but they originate in historical forces that are normally outside of human understanding and control. Obviously, then, a Marxist would not ask—at least not first of all—what should be done. He would ask instead what is occurring. He would inquire concerning the nature of the existing social system and the direction of historical evolution.

The Marxist view seems to me more plausible in present circumstances than the liberal view. It takes more fully into account our apparent inability to master our troubles. I do not adopt it in the present inquiry for several reasons which are widely shared and which I can in this context indicate only summarily. First, it contradicts the inner conviction (which Marx apparently shared, judging from the intensity of his indignation, but did not fully take into philosophical account) that men are personally responsible for the things they do; second, it requires a faith in historical teleology which seems to me implicitly idolatrous and is, furthermore, without sufficient empirical support; third, it precludes dialogue, for one's opponents cannot be regarded as fellow inquirers but only as objective historical forces.

In sum, neither liberalism nor Marxism—the two major methods that suggest themselves today—seem to offer an adequate approach to the crisis of American democracy. One of the challenges before us, then, is that of discovering how our plight is to be understood. The present paper is an experiment directed to this end.

I propose to assume, like the liberal but contrary to the Marxist, that persons are free, in that the choices they make cannot be reduced to historical conditions and laws. Unlike the liberal, however, I propose to assume that men are inclined to make the wrong choices. In short, the postulates of this inquiry will be that men are free to do good but disposed to do evil. These may seem to be ungenerous assumptions. But they accord with a far older tradition than liberalism or Marxism—that of Pauline and Augustinian Christianity. They accord also with much historical evidence. Further, I do not lay them down as unchallengeable principles but only as tentative premises of inquiry.

What questions arise from this position? Above all, probably, the question as to what hope there is for man on earth. Liberalism found in human goodness, and Marxism in historical destiny, grounds for looking ahead with confidence. But if men are not good in themselves, and are not controlled by benign historical forces, the future is forbidding. We must undoubtedly be capable of facing a future which is something less than an assured intensification of happiness.

But we are fully justified in recoiling before a threat of historical despair. For several hundred years, Western man's whole relationship to being has been increasingly structured in accordance with an attitude of hope. For this hope to be suddenly lost would mark a fundamental spiritual disorientation. Not only determined secularists, but important religious thinkers as well, believe that however shallow and heedless typical doctrines of progress may have been, the attitude of historical expectancy should not be forsaken. Thus an effort to explain the challenges to democracy as evils voluntarily done by men presents above all the question of hope.

Before that question can be confronted, however, the challenges to American democracy must be construed in accordance with the suggested postulates concerning human nature. And the first question that arises is how it is that these challenges can be presented as widespread and enduring uniformities of thought and behavior. The notion that men are free, but disposed to do evil, suggests that men would create chaos rather than patterns that can be studied by social scientists and historians. Marxism involves no such difficulty for it assumes that human behavior is determined by historical conditions. But freedom is presumably manifest in actions that are individual and unique. Hence, in order to interpret the challenges to American democracy in accordance with the postulates I have suggested it is necessary first to consider the nature of moral failure and to understand how that which is essentially personal—an evil choice—becomes the kind of phenomenon that is subject to sociological generalization.

St. Luke reports that when Jesus was crucified, he said, "Father, forgive them; for they know not what they do."[1] These words suggest a rough typology of moral failure which may prove useful in understanding the situation of the United States today.

Speaking very generally, there seem to be two basic types of moral failure. One may be called "conscious immorality." This is the immorality of those who do know what they are doing, or at least could know but consciously refuse to confront the consequences of their actions. Conscious immorality is deliberate choice either of evil actions or of the blindness out of which evil actions arise.

The other basic type of moral failure may be called "moral unconsciousness." It is the kind of moral failure Jesus seemed to recognize. Evil is done not so much by choosing as by failing to choose. Undoubtedly we encounter here a paradoxical spiritual state. In some sense one who is guilty of moral unconsciousness *chooses* not to choose; otherwise, he would not be guilty and his failure would not be moral. Nevertheless, it seems that whenever we recognize extenuating circumstances, such as youth, or passion, or extreme provocation, we recognize the distinction between moral unconsciousness and conscious immorality.

The reason this distinction is useful in the present context is that it makes it possible to explain how evil can be freely chosen and yet be uniform and even institutional. A person in a state of moral unconsciousness allows his behavior to be determined from without. He thoughtlessly does what his environment prompts him to do. It seems likely that many wartime atrocities are due to this moral state; the atmosphere of combat prompts men to commit acts which in most circumstances they would never even consider. Many of the crimes committed in the slums are probably acts of this nature. Through moral unconsciousness beings who have the power of free choice allow themselves to live on a level of causal determinism. They become appropriate objects for psychological analysis, and their behavior falls into patterns which social scientists and historians can study. The chaos one would expect if men are free but disposed to do evil arises from conscious immorality. Moral unconsciousness gives rise to uniformity.

But has not radical evil sometimes been uniform and institutional? The example of Nazi Germany would indicate that it has. It does seem that in framing a full typology of moral failure it would be necessary to recognize that conscious immorality may give rise either to chaos or to uniformity. There is a kind of conscious immorality that is a deliberate commitment to the level of causal determinism. A cynic in degenerate times who, from motives of ambition and sensuality, decides to live as the world lives, has placed himself in this moral state. He has decided to allow his behavior to be determined from without.

I recognize this potentiality in conscious immorality, however, merely in order to meet a possible objection. Little notice will be taken of it in the following analysis of the American situation because I do not believe that in dealing with present-day America we are dealing with the kind of radical evil exemplified by Nazi Germany. What is crucial for understanding our situation today is the distinction between moral unconsciousness, leading to uniform and institutional evils, and conscious immorality, in which there is the potentiality, even though not the certainty, of chaos. Two further points concerning this distinction must be made before returning to the American situation.

First, it should be noted that a whole people might fall into a state of moral unconsciousness. Indeed, the idea that peoples are normally in such a state is not wholly implausible. It is not necessary in the present context either to accept or reject such an hypothesis. It is sufficient to recognize that, at least occasionally, circumstances might lure an entire society away from its moral awareness, as apparently occurred in Athens during the Peloponnesian War. Obviously this is not to say that every individual in such a society would be morally unconscious; some would be morally conscious, and protesting, and others consciously immoral. Both Socrates and Alcibiades were Athenian citizens during the Peloponnesian War. Exceptions of this kind do not invalidate the principle that a certain moral mood may predominate in a whole society.

Second, let us take note of a borderline state between moral unconsciousness and conscious immorality. It may be termed "moral awakening," without meaning thus to indicate that what follows must necessarily be a moral advance. In moral awakening the determinism of unconsciousness dissolves and man realizes that he is responsible for what he does. There may follow some kind of moral renewal, such as that which comes about through repentance; but there may follow instead a conscious commitment to evil. Actual moral life of course is complex and ambiguous. No moral awakening would be likely to be altogether lucid, and the aftermath of a moral awakening might in some way combine the two basic moral states I have distinguished. Still, in the lives both of individuals and of peoples there are moments when awareness of responsibility dawns. These moments may come through remorse or through sudden realization of an obligation. In most cases the way back to full moral unconsciousness is barred. A new moral condition becomes unavoidable.

Let us turn back to the problems of American democracy.

These can now be viewed from an altered vantage point. To begin with, it appears that for the society as a whole, they are not conditions *suffered* so much as they are conditions *chosen*. This is indicated by the postulate that human choice is not determined by external circumstance but is disposed in the direction of evil. The nature of the challenges to democracy tends to confirm this hypothesis. There is, for example, no manifest necessity dictating the continuance of poverty or of racial injustice. Far poorer nations, such as Great Britain and Sweden, have less poverty than America, and in the first few decades after the Civil War, racial discrimination was less harsh and deliberate than it is at the present time.

Looking at America from the standpoint of the suggested moral typology, however, readily leads one to conclude that these evil choices are due less to deliberate malice than to moral unconsciousness. Not everyone, of course, would agree. It seems to me, however, that very few Americans are consciously willing to accept the various conditions cited above; nor does it seem to me that many have reached the point of deliberately refusing to see them. A great many people explicitly repudiate them and almost everyone else maintains merely that while they may be indefensible they cannot be immediately rectified. These attitudes do not excuse grave moral and political failures. They do suggest, however, that these failures can best be interpreted in terms of some peculiarly distracting circumstances.

It is not difficult to discern such circumstances. While the moral awareness of the ancient Athenians was dimmed by war, and that of Romans under the Republic by the acquisition of an empire, the moral self-forgetfulness of Americans, I suggest, has come about due to circumstances apparently much less sinister; namely, having at hand an incomparably broad and exciting field of action. There has been no other time or place in history in which men have had opportunities such as those available in America for changing and possessing the material world. The result has been an unusually pragmatic and impatient people. These qualities are often useful and attractive. However, they are also spiritually debilitating. In order to see why this is so it may help, before considering the moral state of America, to examine briefly the circumstances which have occasioned it.

First of all one thinks of a nearly uninhabited and unused continent. Millions of square miles of land, most of it neither cultivated nor owned, was the physical field of action. Its opportunities and demands shaped Americans from the time of the first settlements.

But the field of action cannot be understood merely as a vast, rich physical area. The establishment of the United States as an independent, stable political body coincided roughly with the beginning of the industrial revolution. This has been an enthralling event for every society where it has occurred—an event that has both fascinated and enslaved. It has meant an intoxicating enhancement of human power; and whether it has come about under the aegis of capitalists or communists it has prompted sweeping rearrangements of society, bringing new kinds of coldness, instability, and oppression into human relations.

In America there was less to inhibit the full unfolding of the industrial revolution than in any other country where it occurred. An unparalleled stock of natural resources, a greater number of workers and consumers than in most other nations, and a lack of the traditions and class systems that in varying degrees held sway all over Europe, made of America a setting in which the meaning of pure industrialism, unchecked by adverse circumstances or by the ideals and institutions of earlier ages, could be brought forth in action. If the industrial revolution has always been enthralling, it has been unusually so in America.

The ensuing state of mind—the American form of moral unconsciousness—may be called "omnisecularism." Mere secularism distinguishes the secular from the sacred and establishes the world as a legitimate field of activity in its own right; the sacred, however, is not denied. Omnisecularism, in contrast, means the inclusion of everything within the world. The world becomes the only field of activity, and the sacred disappears. (By "world" I mean the realm of objective and controllable realities.) Even if America had never experienced the industrial revolution, it would have been tempted by omnisecularism. All of being would have seemed spread out as a store of unused, unowned wealth. But industrialization, as a process of technological rationalization, gives action vastly greater assurance and scope than it otherwise would have. It both suppresses inner checks, such as awe of nature, and pushes back external limits. In sum, a combination of geographical and historical circumstances caused reality to be put before Americans as purely and totally a field of action, and Americans accepted it as such.

Is this not, however, to exaggerate? There seems to be much in America that does not readily fit into an omnisecular universe. Daniel Boorstin, for example, has stressed a national characteristic which seems at odds with the hard realism which would bring everything under deliberate control, that is, our preoccupation with images rather than with realities; both commercial and political life seem largely formed by this preoccupation. Other characteristics similar to this come readily to mind. Have not Americans for a long time gilded their world with sentimentality like that exemplified in the paintings of Norman Rockwell? And do they not at present spend several hours daily in the distorted universe of the television melodrama?

My response to these objections is that the prevalence of various kinds of unrealism does not contradict the hypothesis of omnisecularism but rather is explained by it. Omnisecularism does not make for a warm and livable world. It is a world that needs to be decorated and concealed, and this is what is done with images, sentimentality, and melodrama. Here I appeal to a verdict that is so widely accepted as to be trite; i.e., that television is "escapist." What people are trying to escape, through television and other means, is a universe that has been construed altogether according to the demands of action and has in this way been made frigid and uninhabitable.

Other grounds for questioning the present interpretation relate to more attractive features of the United States. Surely there is an old American idealism, for example, which is not omnisecular. Its spirit is compassionate and humanitarian, its aims liberal and democratic. Again and again it has expressed itself in movements of reform which have curbed the omnisecular drives of businessmen and have bettered the lives of many Americans. This objection must in some measure be accepted. Yet to admit that American democracy is threatened by economic inequities, by racial injustice, by a brutal war, by alienation, and by political immobility is to admit that American idealism has been seriously ineffective. It has often been defeated by war: World War I swallowed the New Freedom, World War II the New Deal, and the Vietnamese War the Great Society. And it has not been invulnerable to omnisecular reformulations. Thus in both world wars our idealism was summoned to combat with visions of a reconstructed world; and some support for the war policy in Vietnam has come from idealists who have assumed, in omnisecular fashion, that if we are merely rational and determined we can turn Vietnam into a prosperous, democratic society. Graham Greene, in his bitter novel *The Quiet American*, tried to show the violence inherent in our idealism. Thus one may admit a definite humanitarian proclivity in Americans. This does not negate the problem we are concerned with, however, but rather gives it another form: How can American idealism be made wise and effective?

Let us consider a final objection to the concept of omnisecularism. It is implicit in some of the most astringent criticisms of American society. The challenges to American democracy are not seen as originating in a national state of mind, but in the deliberate actions of ruling groups. *The Power Elite*, of C. Wright Mills, is probably the best-known expression of this point of view. According to Mills and most other contemporary radicals, the crisis of democracy is owing to the conscious immorality of a few rather than to the moral unconsciousness of all.

Obviously an issue of this kind cannot be definitively settled in a few lines. Two considerations, however, cast doubt on the power-elite thesis. One is that the men of power give every indication, through their spoken and written words as well as through their style of life, of being enthralled by the same omnisecular conception of national power and purpose that prevails throughout the society. This conception, according to radicals, is cynically instilled in the popular mind by the power elite. But are the people so readily manipulated? And are the dominant groups so cynical? Judgments may differ, but it is possible to argue that the American "power-elite" is naive and common to a degree that renders dubious both the term "elite" and the suspicions of sinister intent to which they are subject. I cannot, for example, see the men who manufacture the noxious and unsafe automobiles that fill American cities and highways as cold-blooded criminals; they seem rather to be men who "know not what they do."

A second consideration that tells against the charges of C. Wright Mills and the radicals is that America's moral failures by no means uniformly serve the interests of the dominant groups. The war in Vietnam, for example, certainly serves the interests of military men; but it is not altogether in the interests of businessmen and, as the retirement of President Johnson shows, it seriously threatens the interests of political leaders. The state of American cities is a like example. It is hard to see that urban disintegration is in the interest of anyone. It seems like the product more of monumental inattention than of conspiracy.

But assuming it is true that America, under the temptations inherent in vast empty lands and unrestrained industrialization, has fallen into an omnisecular moral unconsciousness, how does this help us to understand the present crisis of democracy?

Omnisecularism means insensibility to persons. The individual cannot be sacred in an omnisecular society because omnisecularism is essentially the denial of sacredness. All reality, including human reality, is brought under the authority of a pragmatic, and often technological, rationality. Noam Chomsky's argument that there is a link between social science and the military policy in Vietnam is plausible; both represent a depersonalizing worldliness. If all realities, including persons, are seen primarily as subject to rational comprehension and control, then the dignity of the individual, as anything but a cliché surviving from a vanished spiritual state, is forgotten. People become—in the constructive phases of omnisecularism—"human resources"; in the destructive phases, the generalization which finally disposes of them is a "body count."

Every one of the challenges to democracy listed above can be traced back to this kind of insensibility. It is not at all surprising that severe poverty and other unjust economic conditions persist within the most productive and prosperous society in history. The same omnisecular preoccupations which have enabled Americans to achieve their unparalleled prosperity have blinded them to the sufferings of those who do not share it and lack the organizational skill to translate their discontent into political pressure. Thus the continuance of poverty along with unexampled prosperity is ironic in accordance with Reinhold Niebuhr's definition of irony as consisting in "apparently fortuitous incongruities in life which are discovered, upon closer examination, to be not merely fortuitous."[2] From a like perspective, the persistence of racial discrimination is understandable. Blacks are surely right in charging that most white people do not wish to accord them justice; if they did wish to, they would. But it seems to me that white acquiescence in racial injustice is due to something less conscious and vicious than "racism." I suggest that for most white Americans blackness does not so much inspire hatred as it does reinforce human insensibility; it conceals the person.

The war in Vietnam is a tragic expression of omnisecular insensibility. One of the major conditions of this war is that most Americans, distracted by the power and pleasures of their industrial might, have had scarcely the slightest feeling for the lives and desires of Asian peasants. Those that were revolutionary seemed to be completely explained once they were classified as Communists—a notably omnisecular delusion. Blind to the peasants as persons, we were blind to their courage and tenacity and skill; it was easy for us to assume that our advanced weaponry would swiftly bring them under our control. It is no wonder that we find it hard to withdraw from Vietnam, for doing so requires much more than a vast military operation or even than a humiliating admission of defeat; it requires, in some form, a recognition of our past insensibility.

Economic injustice, racial discrimination, and the war in Vietnam all exemplify brutality toward minorities. Alienation is due to a kind of brutality toward all. But the underlying cause is the same. Personal insensitivity is bound to express itself not only in mistreatment of minorities but also in negligence of all personal relationships and of the conditions that encourage them. Owing to various conditions, some pertaining to habit and culture and some to physical environment, personal relations are less easy, graceful, and stable in America than in many, if not most, other countries. These conditions are not products of accident but of attitudes. Most American suburbs, for example, are clear physical expressions not only of human unrelatedness but of a society which, in all of its dynamic power, acquiesces in human unrelatedness. This is only one example of many that could be cited and it is unnecessary here to discuss circumstances that have been exhaustively analyzed in the recent literature of social criticism. But it does seem worth noting that America is not only the self-confident and hopeful land which seems usually to emerge from the studies of American scholars. It is also a lonely and tragic land; this is nearly a unanimous judgment among great American writers. And the loneliness and tragedy have not been simply human fate; they have been in part, however blindly, self-imposed.

It seems reasonable to attribute the immobility of the government and the lassitude of the people to the same insensibility which lies behind injustice, war, and alienation. Political imagination depends on a sense of what people need. Thus the impersonalism of an omnisecular society necessarily entails a failure of political imagination. This failure must mean, in turn, both governmental ineffectiveness and popular apathy. Of course, both might be overcome by some malignant national passion such as that which swept Germany under Hitler; but this would ordinarily presuppose entry into a state of conscious immorality. The normal political state of an omnisecular society is probably characterized by the spasmodic, and often irrelevant, activity, and the prolonged periods of somnolence, which have marked American political history for a century or more.

Perhaps the most adequate way of characterizing the general effect of omnisecularism on democracy is to say that it erodes its spiritual ground. Democracy is often held to be more practical or efficient than other forms of government; Thucydides, for example, suggested that it allowed for a uniquely effective mobilization of popular energies. But all such arguments are highly debatable. It is possible to argue that in its slowness and its dependence on the uncertainties of popular resolve, democracy presents more difficulties than other forms of government. The firmest defense of democracy is moral—that it accords full recognition to the principle that every person is sacred. Only democracy provides every person with equal protection and with the opportunity to take part in political decisions. But in an omnisecular society, the democratic vision of human dignity fades into a preoccupation with appraisal and action. Thus, for example, the manipulative goals of much American commercial life amount to an unstated rejection of the democratic conception of man.

We do not fully understand our situation, however, merely by perceiving the antithesis between omnisecularism and democracy. Employing the schema of moral states proposed above, I suggest that the past few years have been a time of moral awakening. The new self-consciousness and resolution of blacks, the rebelliousness of college youth, and the critical attitudes of intellectuals all seem to signalize an emergence from moral unconsciousness. President Nixon appeals to a silent, and presumably still morally unconscious, majority. But it is very doubtful whether such a majority, even if it is a present reality, will continue long to exist. It is the aim of vocal minorities, and the probable consequence of the president's own appeals, to awaken it. It is obvious that changes in national mood cannot be predicted with much assurance. But the troubled character of the world, the bitterness of various American minorities, the aridity and loneliness of American life, and, beyond all of these historical conditions, the very instability of human moods, render unlikely the indefinite endurance of our omnisecular distraction.

This, however, is not an altogether hopeful prospect. If man in his freedom is likely to choose evil, then a moral awakening may be only a passage into conscious immorality. This would probably be a passage into an era of authoritarian politics. As pointed out above, chaos is implicit in moral awakening; and chaos calls forth authoritarianism. Further, contrary to an old American prejudice, political immobility is not political safety. A democracy that cannot act invites its own replacement. Authoritarianism might come in behalf either of the right or of the left: to continue the war or to end it, to solidify economic inequalities or to erase them, to force the blacks into a position of permanent and legal inferiority or to force whites to accord them full equality; to drown the anguish of alienation in a flood of patriotic fervor or to forget loneliness in a frenzy of dictatorial reconstruction.

But have we not had earlier moral awakenings—Populism, the New Freedom, the New Deal, the Great Society—that did not involve any such dangers? Have we not had—and survived—our moral awakening long ago?

I suggest not. The various movements of reform in American history have been beneficial and have been signs of health in the American conscience. But it seems to me that they have lacked the depth of doubt that would make them real awakenings. They were hardly spiritual events. The basic principles of the society were not, for the most part, seriously questioned; liberal confidence in man's power and benevolence was undisturbed; reformers were less inclined to invoke visions of a new society, or of the grandeur of the moral law, than they were to dissolve all moral distinctions in a temporarily convenient morass of relativism and pragmatism; the results achieved were on the whole conservative; and the movements themselves were ephemeral. Perhaps the one event in American history of sufficient magnitude to shake and alter the national consciousness was the Civil War. But part of the tragedy of that event was that instead of leading into the kind of moral self-examination called for by the bloody termination of slavery, it initiated a period of furious industrialization and thus marked the onset of omnisecularism. The periods of self-criticism and reform have been relatively shallow experiences. Even the troubled state of mind induced by the depression of 1929 occasioned only the ebullient pragmatism of the New Deal and finally was displaced completely by wartime unity and determination.

But is the present any different? It is obvious that it is. The blacks have never been so resentful, nor college youth so insurgent; no war in national history has prompted misgivings so pronounced as those aroused by the conflict in Vietnam. It is still possible, of course, that the present period of self-doubt, like earlier ones, will prove to be merely episodic. If it does, however, we will only have postponed and intensified the trauma of awakening before us.

Thus no historical considerations can justify postponing the effort to come to terms with the implications of moral awakening. What do we face as we move toward this event?

The answer greatly sharpens the question of hope which was posed near the beginning of this inquiry. Given our postulates concerning human nature, the most unsettling experience involved inescapably in coming to moral consciousness is the realization of what may be called "moral insecurity." We are free but we are far from wholly good. Hence we must fear ourselves. Everything depends on the nature of our choices, and, not being reliably virtuous, those choices constitute a grave and irremovable danger. Both remorse for the past and anxiety for the future derive in large part from realizing this insecurity. If we were free and wholly good then we could cut ourselves off from an evil past by becoming new creatures; and in doing this we would lay the basis for a righteous and happy future. But remorse is regret concerning what one now is, and anxiety for the future stems in part from what one seems bound to be. Thus as the clouds of omnisecularism vanish, we will find ourselves on a narrow ledge over a steep precipice.

Probably most Americans can apprehend this situation only by realizing the unreliability of all programs of action. It is our instinct in times of crisis to tell ourselves that we have nothing to fear, beyond fear itself, and then with good conscience indulge to the full our activist inclinations. The scholar does this in a manner conforming to his profession; he conceives his duty as that of finding out through careful analysis what lines of action should be followed, and rarely does he examine critically the activist premises which underlie his scholarly activities. This liberal optimism is undoubtedly better than despair. Nevertheless, it involves moral forgetfulness. Since we are free and imperfect, to know what should be done is very far from the same as doing it. It is not surprising that activist America suffers from a kind of paralysis in the face of some of its great social and political problems. And further, since evil is ingenious and unpredictable, even when the most promising course of action is followed this may be done in a way that perverts its intent. The defeat of American isolationism, for example, threatens to bring us into an era of American imperialism.

Let us turn back to the set of challenges to democracy listed at the beginning of this paper and note the radical insecurity attending the major programs of actions which these suggest to the liberal mind.

1. The economic challenges have prompted among most informed and responsible people the conclusion that in some way poverty and economic insecurity must be ended, and unusual wealth and special privileges retained only so far as they demonstrably contribute to the public good. But these standards have been commonplaces of social idealism in America for at least a generation and it would be impossible at this point in our history to claim that there is even a prospect of enacting them. Moreover, it is easy to see that economic equalization, as morally imperative as it seems, might well be a decisive stage in the extension and consolidation of omnisecular society. To consign some people to poverty and insecurity in a society as wealthy as ours can hardly be justified; but it is not merely possible, it is perhaps easy, to provide wealth and security for everyone in a way that is suffocating to the spirit.

2. The racial situation has to be regarded in the same way. Certainly whites have no right to deny blacks equal access to the comforts and distractions of middle-class life; and to do so endangers democracy, both by expressing an undemocratic bias based on race and by encouraging violence among those suffering from discrimination. However, if blacks are accorded equal rights in a social order in which nothing is splendid or sacred, and justice means simply that all races have equal access to all-pervasive trivia, it will be difficult to say either that the blacks are really better off or that the whites finally have acted justly.

3. Ending the war in Vietnam has become nearly an obsession on the part of many humane people—and with much justification, in view of the dreadful consequences it has had both in Vietnam and in America. But peace, as well as war, can be deadly. Victorian England is to me a less inspiring society, even though it engaged in little warfare, than Renaissance Florence, where warfare was almost continuous. Just as the world of the future might be egalitarian but inhuman, it might be peaceful but spiritually cold and empty.

4. Alienation is undoubtedly one of the gravest evils of our time, but there are more wrong ways than right ways of responding to it. In the past, there have been many despotic and ignorant societies in which the cities were splendid, the villages beautiful, the water and air unpolluted, and organic social groupings highly developed and stable.

5. Many people today hold that the central problem is that government is in the hands of privileged minorities who have neither the capacity nor the will to do what is needed; thus the crucial step we must take is that of placing power in the hands of the people. Yet if all "power elites" were destroyed, their places might be taken by abjectly submissive politicians and by demagogues. Socrates was condemned by one of the great popular juries of the Athenian democracy; and, according to Thucydides, one of the decisive factors in the decline of Athens was the folly of the Athenian people. Today in America it is not clear that any of the conditions listed above—poverty, racial injustice, war, or alienation—are opposed by the people.

A program of action is no more than a perceived possibility; the actuality can be counted on only in the same measure as can man himself. If man is radically unreliable, then insecurity is inherent in historical existence. America has presented so vast a field of action that, in the past, our activism has probably been harmless if not beneficent; in the future, however, it may become increasingly a way of veiling historical dangers and perplexities.

It is not only liberalism, however, that has contributed to our moral forgetfulness. The Marxist faith in history, for example, has had effects similar to those of liberalism. In America, a Marxist is often one who has deliberately rejected liberalism as a result of realizing the infirmity of liberal good intentions. However, as Dostoevsky remarks, man must bow down to something. A Marxist who is disillusioned with liberalism has transferred his confidence from man to history. He realizes that men, as agents of political renewal, are highly unreliable; he believes, however, that natural forces of history are carrying mankind toward the free and democratic order which they are powerless, at any historical moment they might choose, to create. That human decision has its time and necessity is of course not denied by Marxists. Men finally will create just societies, but only when history empowers them to do so; and when history so empowers them, they cannot fail. The sense of moral security which the liberal draws from his view of man, the Marxist finds in a concept of history.

Seen from the perspective adopted at the beginning of this paper, however, the Marxist's sense of security is no better founded than the liberal's. To begin with, it is impossible to assume that history has any predetermined direction. If man is free, one set of circumstances never entails another as a necessary consequence; it is a basis for improvisation. Further, if there is evil in man's disposition, no rational confidence can be placed in the results of such improvisation. There is no need here to emphasize the widely recognized fact that the history of industrial societies during this century casts much doubt on the Marxist vision. It is sufficient to say that the evidence permits us to adopt the postulates suggested above and that if we do so we are deprived of the kind of reassurance Marxism has provided for many conscientious and courageous men. Democracy is no more underwritten by the logic of history than it is by the nature of man.

In one school of contemporary political thought, that of conservatism, these criticisms of the reigning ideologies seem to be recognized. Followers of Edmund Burke repudiate both liberalism and Marxism, and they do so commonly on the ground that they represent an overly optimistic appraisal of man and of history. I maintain, however, that Burkean conservatives have not really overcome the moral complacency of liberalism and Marxism. They have rather restated it and thus, often unconsciously, disguised it. If liberals place their trust in what man can do, and Marxists in what he is bound to do, conservatives place their trust in what he has done. Burke's vision of the old and established institutions of England was, at least after the French Revolution, hardly less romantic and uncritical than Marx's vision of the Communist society yet to come. It is doubtful that mistrust of man is any more conservative, in its logical implications, than it is radical. St. Augustine was not a conservative, nor, in our own day, is Reinhold Niebuhr. We can expect human malice to be as forceful and ingenious where tradition is strong as where revolution is being effected. A revolution undoubtedly constitutes a morally perilous situation. But so does the fixity and long endurance of a social order; the latter situation usually disguises a host of inequities and encourages an all-pervasive moral unconsciousness.

These criticisms of the conservative position tend to be validated by our present circumstances. The conditions that challenge American democracy are old and habitual. This is true of the economic and racial injustices, of the attitudes which led to the tragedy of Vietnam, of the circumstances giving rise to alienation, and of our political immobility. The main present problem is not to conserve but to change. Conservatives often admit this, of course, but insist that the change incumbent on us is that of recovering a traditional order which we have allowed to be weakened. But it would require a highly romantic rendering of the past to find a model for the humane industrial order we are seeking. While omnisecular society is technological in its forms and attitudes, it did not succeed a society without serious injustice. For example, while the situation of the blacks today is primarily determined by an industrial setting and by the omnisecular callousness of the whites, this situation is not without a preindustrial history—that of slavery—and the inhumanity occasioned now by industrial affluence and power was not without other occasions prior to the industrial revolution. In short, there is no grand tradition in which we can find moral security. Deprived of liberal and Marxist hope, we are bound to see democracy as imperiled not only now but in every conceivable future. The past offers no refuge.

Liberalism, Marxism, and conservatism have, of course, often been criticized. The concept of moral insecurity, however, implies more than the untenability of traditional views. It implies the untenability of every ideology.

An ideology is a political doctrine purporting to explain comprehensively and apodictically what is and what must be done. In any form, ideology is incompatible with awareness of moral insecurity. If one adheres to the postulate that man is free, but is disposed to do evil, he cannot be a liberal, a Marxist, a conservative, or an adherant of any other doctrine that claims to provide reliable programs of action. One may adhere to a set of standards, to a political philosophy. An ideology, however, relates standards to existing realities in a single world-view and in doing this contradicts the concept of moral insecurity. If human behavior is neither determined by causal laws nor governed by benevolence, then the relation between standards and reality is indeterminate. While one can accept the moral superiority of democracy, he has no right to assume that the present period of political instability is connected, through man's nature, through the laws of history, or through the glory of a tradition, with a future in which democracy will be secure. Our postulate concerning man implies historical vulnerability.

In America, such an outlook is peculiarly unwelcome, despite the disappointments and the tragedies of recent history. The American proclivity toward self-criticism has been often noted and is doubtless strong; and our problems are so serious and so obvious that no sophisticated writer would dream of denying them. It is remarkable, however, how seldom American essayists and scholars seriously confront the possibility that the nation will fail historically and that democracy will fade into a prolonged and sterile era of despotic, or merely bureaucratic, rule. Max Lerner's *America as a Civilization* strikes me as typical. Professor Lerner has a sharp and polished mind and is in command of an awesome quantity of information. There are few, if any, common criticisms of America with which he does not demonstrate an old and easy acquaintance. His work is far from being a simple nationalistic panegyric. Yet the mood he creates belies the criticisms he acknowledges. America, he seems to say throughout the work (although never would he be so crude as to do so in a single statement), is so dynamic and various that the problems of the nation always are finally solved and the sufferings of individuals are insignificant in comparison with the glory of the whole historical panorama. Lerner's mood is spontaneously and ebulliently Hegelian; but it is a surprisingly common mood in the literature of American self-examination. Americans clearly are able to blame themselves, and even love to do so. But there are definite limits to their strictures; they rarely face the possibility that their faults will be ruinous.

But does this not mean simply that they refuse to despair? Further, how could a man or a people believe in "moral insecurity" without sinking into despondency? This brings us finally to the question stated at the outset: If man is free and evil, what hope is there?

In preparation for considering this question let me summarize the position we have reached. What I have been doing essentially is trying to look at American democracy from the vantage point of a general conception of human nature not usually accepted by Americans. This perspective seems to disclose a state of mind among Americans in which all reality is viewed purely as a field of action. This state of mind, which may be called "omnisecularism," is implicitly antagonistic to democracy because, in denying the sphere of the sacred, it necessarily denies the central tenet of democracy, the sacredness of the person. Omnisecularism arises from great natural wealth and uninhibited industrialism—not as an effect, however, but as a moral response. The crisis of democracy, then, is moral; it is chosen. But according to the basic postulate of this paper the moral perversity which is manifest in the depersonalization challenging democracy is a strong and enduring human trait. Thus we are compelled to recognize that democracy is not to be saved merely through appropriate programs of action, through spontaneous historical progress, or through respecting traditions and established institutions. The crisis of democracy is not a problem in the sense in which a matter like developing a silent jet airplane is a problem. It does not fall within the field of action but within the field of freedom in which action originates. It represents, so to speak, a crisis of man himself. This is the position—one lacking all of the assurances which have been associated with liberalism, Marxism, and conservatism—in which the question of hope is presented.

I suggest a paradoxical answer to the question: that only when we have experienced the kind of hopelessness that arises from being divested of every objective assurance, can the kind of hope befitting a mature people begin to emerge. The ground of this suggestion, I must acknowledge, is faith, but not a faith that is tied to any particular church or dogma and not a faith which is lacking in rational support. According both to Judaism and to Christianity history moves in a direction that corresponds with the deepest and most ineradicable striving of man. This does not mean that man can enjoy all that happens. The meaning of history is sometimes enacted through tragedy rather than the satisfaction of desires. Thus man must live in history without assured comprehension or control of the course of events—but not without hope. To resign all claims to historical sovereignty, if it is not done from despair, is to open up the possibility of participating in a course of events far more promising in their ultimate bearing than any that self-confident man could envision or effect. A mature hope, according to this faith, depends altogether on humility. In our time, one of the most moving expressions of this outlook is Boris Pasternak's *Doctor Zhivago*.

This suggestion will be totally misunderstood, however, if it is construed as recommending inaction or calling for acquiescence in the status quo. I suggest that just as hope emerges from hopelessness, effective action paradoxically originates in passivity. Fruitful action is not decided upon at a sovereign post from which all possibilities can be rationally surveyed, but is rather in the nature of a gift. This corresponds with an old and widespread intuition. Lao Tse calls for a style of government which moves the world by doing nothing. The *Bhagavad-Gita* demands that man strive and act in a spirit of detachment and inaction. According to Isaiah, "In returning and rest shall ye be saved; in quietness and in confidence shall be your strength."[3] St. Paul writes, "When I am weak, then am I strong."[4] Even for Nietzsche, with his faith in the *Uebermensch*, the thoughts that guide all things come on "dove's feet." The self-confidence and activism of Americans render such ironies exceedingly unpalatable. Is there not, however, a certain look of sense in the notion that if America ever fulfills its image of itself as the hope of the world it will not be through what is willed and imposed but through a wise and expectant repose?

Faith, of course, does not come easily today, and thus it seems particularly appropriate to note that these suggestions have an underpinning in natural reason. The omnisecularism which blots out the sacredness of persons is rooted in pride, in the confidence that everything is manageable; the objectification of persons is a logical expression of this confidence. This implies that the defeat of omnisecularism, and the reconsecration of persons, requires an admission of historical powerlessness and vulnerability. Through humility we become accessible to the mystery of being. The key error in America's recent past has been the denial of man's unreliability, a quality deriving both from his freedom and from his imperfection. This denial was not a benevolent and healthy emphasis on the good side of things. It placed man in a false position, one of universal sovereignty, and from this position being was obscured. The sacredness of persons became undiscernible. Only a fundamental change of position, one brought about by an acknowledgement of moral insecurity, can bring the dignity of individuals again within the scope of vision.

The idea that out of acceptance of inaction may come a capacity for action likewise has an underpinning in natural reason. Our insensibility to persons is what has paralyzed our political imagination and, in turn, our political will. Since we do not clearly perceive the needs and sufferings of persons we cannot avoid being politically disabled. So long as we are merely troubled, but not despairing, government is becalmed; when circumstances become alarming, we are susceptible to the hysteria and senseless activism exemplified by Fascism. Thus it seems that the only way to gain the historical composure in which we can wisely decide and act is through a humility which must be, at least momentarily, resignation to inaction. In this resignation we may begin to discern the dignity, and the requirements, of persons.

I would not like to bring these reflections to a close without acknowledging that I am suggesting what amounts to a radical change in national attitudes and that my basis for doing so is no more than an undemonstrable postulate concerning man. It seems to me, however, that one cannot contemplate the tragedies and perplexities of recent history without feeling that the postulate I have adopted is plausible and that the path of American progress may now lead through a spiritual change.

According to the Book of Proverbs, "Where there is no vision, the people perish."[5] We may understand vision to consist in a due sense of the distinction between things that are sacred and things that are to be used. I think the challenges to American democracy are owing to the fact that vision has been lost and consequently the American people, as a compassionate and communicating political entity, has perished. Thus everything depends on the restoration of vision. This, however, depends on a power little cultivated in the American past —the power to wait.

NOTES

1. Luke 23:34.
2. Reinhold Niebuhr, *The Irony of American History* (New York: Charles Scribner's Sons, 1952), p. viii.
3. Isa. 30:15.
4. 2 Cor. 12:10.
5. Prov. 29:18.

5: THE CHANGING ROLE OF THE COMMUNIST PARTY IN ITALY
Robert H. Evans

Since the fall of 1969, Italy has been wrought by strikes and latent political conflicts have come into the open. Foreign newspaper correspondents wonder if the *vide de pouvoir*, as in the France of the fifties, will not be met by a presidential republic or a *repubblica conciliare* inspired by the right or the left. According to their ideological inspirations the commentators express doubts as to the system being able to resist the pressures cast upon it during the last decade by the extremes of the political spectrum.[1]

The Italian newspapers, though trying not to present too drab a picture exhort the political parties to refuse the delights of the system. For the young democracy to survive the political class must face its responsibilities, act autonomously and reject outside influences, reform bureaucratic and financial structures of the nineteenth century used to administer the country, and cooperate with the economic class that has created the Italian "miracle." Giovanni Sartori writes, "The overwhelming power of the parties has become impotence and atomization. Anarchy does not stem from the country. Before and above all anarchy permeates the political class."[2]

Pessimism is rampant. But we cannot and must not overlook the fact that only one century ago did Rome become the capital and that the generational process of socialization and politicization has been hindered by a series of hurdles, none of which are prone to foster stability. To wit, the rapid turnover of regimes ending in the republican period; an unbalanced economy—rocked by rapid expansion and prosperity but unable to bridge the abysmal differences between North and South, rich and poor;[3] large movements of population which have swept the peninsula, concentrating the population in the north and the coastal plains, while the Apennines, traditionally a seat of conservatism, resemble more and more a desert. The inordinate and rapid process of urbanization—with all the conflicts it breeds—has developed a new electorate (among those who left and also those who remained), a new political consciousness[4] that all the parties have sought to exploit, the extremist and demagogic more successfully than the advocates of change without disorder. Simultaneously, the political structure has not risen to the challenge: the Constitution was only halfheartedly enforced by the leading party, all the groups struggling for power seemed more intent on dividing than on integrating.[5]

Today the Italian state is confronted by a general crisis of authority and credibility, part of a larger whole which invests the major governments of the world as well as the Catholic church. Political scientists, sociologists, psychologists have offered a variety of terms, descriptions and explanations, the richness and imaginativeness of which is only surpassed by the nuances of the Italian political vocabulary.[6] Polarized pluralism vies with imperfect bipartisanship; pro and antisystem parties struggle for the limelight. In terms of the integrative or disintegrative role played by the parties, in a perspective of development and search for greater legitimacy and political maturity (equated with democracy) convincing explanations have been offered at the level of society. Edward Banfield indicates that amoral familism, the moral basis of a backward society, inhibits the growth of democratic institutions;[7] La Palombara makes it clear that Italians are

> not meaningful participant citizens . . . nor even subject in the sense of accepting as legitimate or justifiable the institutions and outputs of the political system . . . [their] attitudes and behavior therefore do not generally contribute to the maintenance and growth of stable democracy.[8]

It is the irony of a system

> in which the formal democratic constitution is supported in large part by traditional clerical elements who are not democratic at all and not even political in the specialized sense of the term. Opposed to the Constitution is a left wing which, at least in part and at the rank and file voter level rather than among the party elite, manifests a form of open partisanship which is consistent with a democratic system.[9]

The changing role of the Italian Communist Party (PCI) must be examined at the level of politics and society. In the somewhat broader perspective of change and development some considerations with regard to the ideological variations in the party and the influence of the environment will be offered; its integrative potential will be assessed; some prospects for the future will be suggested.

At a national level changes have occurred in the PCI, particularly with regards to ideology and parliamentary behavior. Accusations of deceitfulness, insincerity, falseness, hypocrisy are expressed more frequently than not.[10] This is the connotation given to *doppiezza*, which in the mind of its author, Togliatti, was understood as duality, a contradiction to be superseded by the party.

> The duality of the PCI consists essentially in that Communist political culture has exhumed the medieval theory of dual-truths, the truth of faith and the truth of reason. . . . It is exact; the party loyally accepts the rules of parliamentary representativeness. But it is also true the party is a Marxist-Leninist party, which rests its beliefs on an ideology, on a view of society that considered democracy on its death-bed in 1917.[11]

Has faith prevailed over reason? No analysis, however thorough of the intellectual wanderings of the PCI can provide a definite answer, while a study of the politics the party has pursued only affords a fragmentary description. The question itself was outlined and left unresolved by Togliatti. "There is no experience regarding the way in which the battle for socialism can or must be waged in a regime of advanced monopolistic capitalism. . . . There do not even exist explicit prescriptions in the classics of our doctrine."[12] The doctrinal itinerary of the PCI is too well known to be developed in the present context.[13] Suffice it to say the Russian party never materialized in Italy. Togliatti in 1944 proposed the "creation of a democratic and progressive regime;"[14] in 1946 a state "governed by a representative parliamentary regime;"[15] in 1948 he explored "the Italian road to socialism, the road dictated by the particularities, the traditions, and the conditions of our country,"[16] a theory which after the 1948–1956 crisis would become the official party line at the national and international level, a line that would be sanctified and elevated to the rank of doctrinal principle by the followers of the so-called Yalta memorial.[17]

In 1963, Togliatti once again stressed that "the forces that follow the PCI must enter the government area."[18] The question is more actual than ever in view of the breaking down of the center-left coalition and the positions of the PCI in its twelfth Congress held in Bologna in February 1969. Longo in the opening speech did not call for open participation in the government (Berlinguer excluded it), but stressed:

> We are open to all confrontations. We are ready to discuss with all. . . . We must continuously search for possible convergences and agreements, movements for unity, social and political alliances. All exclusivisms and preconceptions must be banished. . . . With the disappearance of the anticonstitutional principle of preestablished majorities . . . the pressing and important questions of society can be met and resolved in Parliament.[19]

Debate was free, opinions expressed. Factions appeared to be emerging and being officially recognized. The newly elected vice-secretary, Enrico Berlinguer while acknowledging the PCI was not the only group to represent the working class, pointed out shortcomings, proposed reforms and in particular mentioned "the *intrinsic* democratic potential" of party life which will permit development of a "*non-metaphysical* concept of democratic centralism."[20] Giorgio Amendola, in polemic with Lelio Basso developed the arguments:

> To recognize that an alternative [to the present system] is not ready means to work concretely in view of its formation. . . . [Our objective] is to reach the point of forming a democratic government of the working classes, which, without being a socialist government and operating within the framework of the republican constitution, while performing the reforms that the country's situation requires, will open the road for a democratic and socialist transformation.[21]

The Christian Democrats (DC) were correct in noting that little had changed since Togliatti's days (is more change possible without the party ceasing to exist?), but Mr. Piccoli's conclusion "that the PCI cannot be considered as an opposition in the State as we conceive it," and "our 'NO' is interpretative of all Italian society" appears far too drastic.[22] Mr. Moro seemed to interpret the mood of society in reproposing his strategy of attention: We must be attentive, he declared,

> to the presence of that party [PCI] in political and social life . . . to its capacity of effectively representing (though in our opinion in a distorted fashion) large segments of the country. . . . In such a way one avoids rigid and opaque contrapositions, a policy which rests exclusively on drastic and emotional 'NO's.' "[23]

The left wing would go further, the *Sinistra di Base* declaring: "If in Parliament we were about to vote a just law [and saboteurs, i.e., Social Democrats were around] then let the communist votes be welcomed."[24]

By its tactics in Congress and in the streets the PCI has helped fracture the center-left coalition: nowhere is it evident the *doppiezza* has been resolved, but neither can it be said that numerous tokens of good faith have not been offered. No tears were shed when the extremists in the party founded a pro-Chinese movement at Leghorn. The more recent quarrel of the *Manifesto* can also be looked at as evidence of a change. The protagonists of the review who had expressed their views publicly in Congress have been removed for having continued to publish their opinions. The accusation is the traditional one of factionalism.[25] This episode might be better understood in terms of practical politics rather than if one casts a machiavellian and Stalinist light upon it. The right wing has defeated the extreme, revolutionary elements, the *only* revolutionary elements that still existed in the party. That the operation was poorly conducted and took over six months is evident. The PCI could not tolerate open and hostile criticism of the Soviet Union in the party ranks that went beyond its own views on the Czechoslovak invasion, because, above all, it wishes to avoid a direct intervention of the CPSU in its own internal affairs, all the more so as this intervention could be in the form of support to the Stalinist lines still present in the party.[26] Furthermore, by excluding the defenders of internal, violent revolutions, the PCI not only preserves its unity—a somewhat fictitious concept in view of the struggles between left and right—but also indicates it does not intend to foment revolution.

The heart of the matter lies in the revolutionary myth of the PCI, a myth it is incapable of sustaining. While officially part and parcel of an international movement, it seeks to avoid its support; nevertheless it has to project an image and yet not act accordingly. Today its strength stems from organization and no longer from ideology: the cement that holds it together is the organization per se and the unfortunate state of present day Italian society. As Galli puts it:

> [Nowhere can its strength] be associated with its position of Marxist-Leninist party and Italian interpreter of the Communist revolution which it proclaims is taking place in the world. The power the PCI wields in Italy is only specifically Communist in its authoritarian methodology of Stalinist derivation.[27]

Only historical and moral reservations separate it from participating in the national administration and explicate its formal position of not sharing in governmental responsibilities. The Marxist-Leninist myth of revolution being on the wane, new myths have to be created to justify the party's stance. A Communist author states:

> Many roads lead to socialism today: a rigorous and logical Christian conscience (Tenth Congress); a strong exigency of freedom (P. Gobetti, P. Calamandrei); an integral opening towards men, life and peace (D. Dolci).

> [In the creation of the socialist society] one must give serious consideration to the contributions of the Christian, E. Mounier, of the rationalist, A. Einstein, tending towards a cosmic religion, of Ghandi believing in a religion of life.[28]

The Communist party might well be available to act and serve as a responsible opposition. It is because of this very availability which is emerging that it has to struggle—and is struggling—with the remnants of a doctrine which makes it reticent to share in the formal responsibilities of government.

An examination of the party's practical policies of opposition, taking into account certain sterile approaches due to the doctrinal hangover, make it clear the PCI has not acted as irresponsibly as it is taxed with having done. Sartori states the dilemma: "Party leaders—even if realistic or skeptical—remain entangled in their outspoken ideological nets, thereby creating for themselves more problems than they can solve."[29]

The PCI is a legal party but its legitimacy is constantly questioned by the leaders of the system; nevertheless one quarter of the electorate recognizes it as legitimate in granting it its vote and only one of its opponents, the DC, ranks higher in the people's sympathy. In fact, the PCI represents the aspirations of a large share of the Italians for a more just world and projects an image of the party of the poor where it is not in power, or of the party that governs through the people whenever it has gained local power.[30] For the government parties the PCI is a sterile and antisystem opposition—and only in the late forties and today are fringes of the leading group reconsidering their position. The PCI which for many years felt and expressed a vocation of government, a vocation it is rediscovering today, was refused all credit for its attempts to integrate into the system on the grounds of mutually exclusive goals of foreign policy between it and the other parties, because of the antireligious dimensions of its doctrines in a state dominated by the Church, and finally because of evident differences in the meaning the opponents gave to the word "republic." Unfortunately, "while the Communists were taking on stronger reformist positions, the conservatives identified this reformism with Stalinist-authoritarian communism; they believed they were preserving the system by labeling as Communist measures that would have reinforced it."[31] Only recently have groups realized that when the boat is about to sink the captain's main task is to keep his vessel afloat. To be prosystem without understanding the rules of the game is not too different from being antisystem while playing the democratic game according to the rules. With regards to the PCI, once the season of revolutionary hopes had faded away from the minds of the leaders and supporters alike, its differences with the other parties were less contrasting than appearances revealed. From the outside, the opposition is peremptory and global; in terms of the substance of the regime it is hardly preoccupying.

At the end of the summer of 1948, following the attempt on Togliatti's life, for evident international and internal reasons, the PCI no longer considered overcoming the democratic government of Italy. It was not necessary: it exercised power at the local levels, controlled parapolitical organizations acting as pressure groups, it was near to enjoying most of the delights of *sottogoverno*. While it sent its troops into the streets to be faithful to its evanescent revolutionary myth, it also exploited the roads that would legitimize it in Parliament.[32]

More often than not the Communist parliamentarians, following an implicit or explicit agreement with the majority parties have voted in favor of the government. They have been rewarded with conditions nearly equal to those of the majority at all levels. Specifically, and from a parliamentary point of view, 75 percent of all legislation is dealt with in committee where the PCI represents 20 percent of the membership, the exact figure necessary to transfer debate from committee to the floor of the House. In the third parliament, 90 percent of all the projects of law that went into committee were approved unanimously. There are no indications that the trend is declining. The idea of collaboration (albeit indirect) may be pushed a step further: a current of the DC can only overthrow the government if it is ready to accept Communist votes! These have also been essential in the election of the president of the Republic in 1955 and 1964; collaboration has also been necessary in all deliberations and elections that take place on the basis of a qualified majority (revision of the Constitution and constitutional laws, election of the judges to the Constitutional Court and members of the Supreme Council of the Judiciary). It is true, nevertheless, that the political significance of this act loses some validity in that a denial of agreement would paralyze the system.

In the midst of the anarchoid explosions that have rocked Italy and the social unrest of the *autunno caldo* the role played by the PCI can be judged harshly. Two elements however should temper this assertion. The strikes were seeking redress for an unfortunate economic situation acknowledged by all the parties. While the Italian General Confederation of Labor (CGIL) was the most adamant negotiator, the strikes were largely economically and socially motivated, and not exclusively political as has often been construed. In the words of Lipset:

> The increase in economic strikes as distinct from political ones, though often resulting in an overall increase in the strike rate, has been interpreted . . . as reflecting the integration of workers into the industrial system; an economic strike is part of a normal bargaining relationship with one's employer. Some have suggested that the Italian strike wave of 1961–1962 [and we add the present one] was perhaps the first of their type since the war in that country.[33]

With regard to the anarchoid tendencies in the country, of which the student-movements assaulting the universities are but a reflection, the Communist party after a period of hesitation (or was it reflection?) disassociated itself from the movement. The delegates to the twelfth Congress repetitiously censured the adventurism of the student vanguards; the party refused to take a revolutionary stand (though it exploited the situation to its benefit,)[34] both because of its ideological position and because it was prompt to realize the adult backlash building up in the lower classes.[35]

In opposition, following a strategy that is no longer revolutionary, the PCI is considered irresponsible. To a degree this is true. But only by forcing the issue, by choosing a program which offers all to all can it attain better electoral returns. This is well expressed by a commentator of the Twelfth Congress:

> To ask the PCI to formulate a program of government if it wants to be recognized seems to escape the rules of logic. . . . At the present point of its development, i.e. of its effective influence and political power, the PCI's program can logically NOT be a program of government, but of opposition at a representative level and of creation of new socialist forces that will radicate the party always more realistically in the Italian social reality. In brief, it is not yet the season of a government with a Communist presence, not only because the moderates will not come to agreements . . . but because the passage from the present type of society to a socialist society cannot be played like a bet, where the loser goes home, exactly like the winner.[36]

In point of fact, the Communist party is evolving towards what Otto Kirchheimer called a catch-all party,[37] if we survey its attitudes vis-à-vis the electorate. It is true that, in a fragmented population and having an ideological image to bear, the PCI cannot hope to capture all categories of workers; but it is also true that the economic disparities that breed conflict are less than they were and that the party may have a reasonable expectation of capturing more voters in those categories whose interests do not adamantly conflict. It seems the party has chosen "the transfer of ideology from partnership in a clearly visible political goal structure into one of many sufficient but by no means necessary motivational forces operative in the voters' choice."[38] The cumbersome political ideology, less and less adapted to the society in which the PCI operates, is being discarded; the number of votes counts, not the beliefs they express.

Following a decade of internal strife the right wing of the central leadership appears to dominate and its actions and omissions are being judged from the viewpoint of their contribution to the entire social system rather than with any exclusive identification with the goals of their particular organization. In part this coincides with the psychological image of the Communist M.P., more open-minded and less dogmatic than his Christian democratic colleagues.[39] While the party presents itself as the party of the working class, it has also indicated it did not claim to be its sole representative. Furthermore, attempting to recruit at all levels, its stand on the religious issue makes it more and more palatable to the marginal Italian Catholic.

These developments fill all of Kircheimer's criteria for a catch-all party except for that of downgrading the individual party member which has not been fulfilled; but even here, due to a decline in party membership, compromises are in the making. Kircheimer, in the mid-sixties, noted that while the PCI excluded itself from the catch-all category it was under considerable pressure to join the club. Today "the primordial need for sweeping political change . . . has been carefully eliminated from the expectations, calculations and symbols of the catch-all party."[40] The PCI is near to fulfilling these conditions at the level of national politics. At the regional and local levels it has already done so.

Since 1946 the PCI has expanded regularly in absolute numbers, above all to the detriment of its socialist allies and the left in general. But only in the South has it truly made inroads passing from 13 percent of the parliamentary electorate in 1946 to 24 percent in 1968, nearly reaching its national average.[41] It has been compensating for its relative decline in the North by increased gains in the South. But this progression follows a most peculiar pattern and one can wonder if the role the PCI has chosen for itself in the South is not erroneous.

> While the migration movement pushed northward, Communism shifted southward; while the country became more and more urban, Communism became more and more rural; while Italy became more and more industrialized, Communism became increasingly agrarian.

Thus Communism goes against the stream. Society goes in one direction, Communism in the other. This phenomenon is best described as social ataxia, to use a biological term, which designates the pathological noncoordination of the movements of the body.[42]

Certain positive dimensions can be granted to Southern Communism. In terms of the North-South dichotomy "many of the old obstacles to political integration . . . have become weaker mainly as a result of the presence in both North and South of this militant left-wing party."[43] In an environment, a civilization based upon personalism and clientelism, where the government enjoys no legitimacy whatsoever, it has taught the people that resignation was no longer a virtue and that when it gave way to frustration, ambition could be fulfilled. Here, the PCI plays a powerful and exotic role, but has not been able to escape the contradictions and peculiar circumstances of the South. It is paradoxical that the PCI expands while the benefits of its social and educational efforts are reaped by the DC. "If the postwar period began with protest marches and the struggle for the land, it has finished in the arena of day to day southern politics, where the Christian Democrats, with the resources of the Church and the State at their command have been as inventive as the Communists."[44]

Because the party sought to apply a strategy elaborated for the North it has failed to exploit the frustrations it was the first to expose. It appears to undermine its own efforts; as a Communist said: "The *via Italiana al Socialismo* halted what the party really needed in the South—the consolidation of the peasant movement begun in the struggle for the land. When [this] . . . strategy began, the peasant movement was somewhat crippled."[45] The revolutionary goals of southern communism, which correspond to an objective social situation, are no longer compatible with the overall positions evolved in the Central Committee. This will not lead to a decline in strength: the frustrations are numerous[46] and urbanization, conducive to radicalism, is taking on gigantic and disordinate proportions. It is nevertheless an indication that the PCI is not seeking violent change. The strategy is based on a successful experience of local government in the North—without due consideration being given to the historical antecedents that favored it—while the past of the South plays more in the direction and the methods of the Christian Democrats, more experienced with clientelism, patronage and corruption, elements the southerner is more apt to sympathize with.

In the North, particularly in Emilia, the PCI, for two decades, and the left, for over half a century, have reigned supreme. This power beyond the organizational dimension is based on a phenomenon of osmosis. The party has managed to gain the sympathies of the entire population, striving, (or being incited) to achieve a harmonious balance between the social, economic, religious, and political segments, leading to a state of coexistence.[47] The party has been able to fulfill its integrative role all the more in that local politics have been rather carefully divorced from national ones, as they are in practice divorced in the minds of many Italians. More than *campanilismo*—in a surrounding of deideologization—it might be more proper to consider this as a simple reflection of well-conceived interest and getting the best out of the present circumstances; it is particularly well evidenced in the business world. Significantly, in Bologna, Cardinal Lercaro invited the Japanese architect Tange to discuss sacred architecture, the Communist administration commissioned him to draw up the town plan, a group of local entrepreneurs gave most of the guildlines and most of the money.

> [The PCI] . . . is the greatest political employer in the country for all those posts which are below the level of national government; it is solidly in power in about 1,200 municipalities, including many of the large cities. In this sense it is hardly a party confined to sterile opposition. Quite on the contrary, it has the best group of civic administrators in the country, and one could say the PCI has all the power it needs below the threshold at which power corrupts.[48]

The last member of the sentence can be rephrased: the PCI is not immune from corruption. Faced by an antiquated system of administration, dealing with men and being itself of human flesh, it accepts the amount of corruption necessary to make for competent and efficient administration. Efficiency is undoubtedly a secret of success; in the case of the PCI, while it claims all the merits, all the merits are not its own. It is well documented that, at the level of local government, the PCI is not more efficient, though it might possess better technical skills than the Christian Democrats.[49] But it has done a formidable job in creating, projecting, and maintaining an image of successful achievement, which, in its words, would be greater still were it not hindered by the government in Rome.

Of necessity, continuous bargaining takes place between the central government and the provinces. More significant are the bargains, gentlemen's agreements, reached between the PCI and the government parties in an attempt to prevent blocking the mechanisms of local government, the alternative being the appointment of a commissioner and new elections which—if one looks at the past—have never adequately solved the problem. In the town of Bologna the Communist minority government only survived with outside Socialist support; the local DC never called for a radical break between the two partners. Today the latter have rejoined forces and, in the words of the mayor, "Bologna . . . has built and proposes to the country the vision of an original and autonomous model of relationship between State and society corresponding to the very principles outlined in the Constitution."[50] The Christian Democrats, while regretting the new leftist coalition which ends the center-left collaboration, note that "the points of agreement of the parties correspond to real political and social, local and national exigencies."[51] At a higher level the DC administers the province, the PCI the town; harmony and good will has characterized this relationship since 1958. Other significant attempts at harmonious relationships have been made, particularly in Ravenna, that qualify the PCI as a responsible opposition. Since April, 1969 the experiment of *giunte bilanciate* (balanced town councils) has proceeded relatively smoothly: the center-left parties have reached a tacit agreement with the PCI, whatever the policies prevailing in Rome. With no majority in the local and provincial councils, the center-left offered the PCI the province in exchange for the town hall. The agreement proved satisfactory until January 1970 when the Unified Socialists (PSU) felt compelled to withdraw, forcing the Nenni Socialists (PSI) into an agreement with the PCI and leaving the DC out in the cold.[52]

The question of autonomous majority does not plague Emilian local politics as it does national ones. The "metaphysical" parties have given indications of political maturity and attempt to divorce practical policies from sterile ideological quarrels. It is not possible to pronounce a formal indictment of the PCI at the national level and even less at the local level.

Political parties have an integrative task to perform. The contribution of the PCI can be examined by considering the value-systems that have led 27 percent of those Italians voting in parliamentary elections to give it their votes and contrasting these values with the ones more commonly accepted by society at large. Ninety-one percent of the Communist electorate falls into the lower economic bracket, 90 percent has received an elementary education or is illiterate,[53] 55 percent consists of urban proletarians and industrial workers, 35 percent of agricultural workers, 10 percent of salaried petty bourgeois, middle and upper bourgeois.[54] Undoubtedly it is the Italy of the poor—not necessarily the destitute—an electorate that is no longer resigned, men and women who to a large extent are expressing their frustration against a system they perceive as unjust, a system that appears paralyzed, unable to bring about change at a fast enough pace, more interested in order and stability than what they consider social justice. Change partakes more of a mental attitude than of an objective economic situation. In terms of the socioeconomic class outlined above, the relationship between voting behavior and social class perception will be far more important than the relationship between voting and objective class composition. In other words the analysis must proceed at a subjective level, focusing on the level of perception of conditions and the subjective image of the party, not at the level of objective social conditions and party organization per se.[55]

The values that permeate the Italy of the miracle are easy to identify in the North.[56] The observer is struck by the pervasion of society by material values hardly visible some fifteen years ago: money has a primacy over other elements and is translated into a continuous quest for consumer goods, while profit is more and more rationally calculated. A cursory glance at the Italian papers and magazines of left or right inspiration leave little doubt as to the changes which have occurred. What counts is success, not necessarily rapid, as it is still combined with a quest for security.[57] Material progress has taken on an ethical value and has combined with an unlimited faith in technical progress—elements which were long rejected by the dominant system—to transform the peninsula. However, the change in mental attitudes has not divorced itself from the past. If religion is less and less a collective spiritual act and more and more a personal phenomenon corresponding to the intimate tranquillity of the individual, certain values of nineteenth century Catholicism still dominate social thought: social order is the paramount value of society—which is quite acceptable—but charity is still considered as the most adequate corrective to disorder of or in the system. This group of values is not recognized by large strata of the population and at this level the PCI has played a preeminent role in the reconstruction of personality and the creation of new social identification. Nowhere is this more evident than in Emilia where the party has been active at the political, economic, and social levels. In fact voting PCI does not imply a political attitude or judgment, no more than it is intended to express a refusal of the existing political system.

The changes in values that have taken place within the Communist electorate can be considered at two levels: in terms of the militant (a peculiar phenomenon in a society where political participation is very low; the PCI only counts 80,000 activists as opposed to triple that number twenty years ago) and in terms of the marginal voter. With regard to the militant the picture is far less drastic than the one described by Almond in his *Appeals of Communism*.[58] Confronted by a society in a rapid state of change, the PCI has been obliged to submit to some of its dictates and to make its own the idea of modernization. The image of the militant is undergoing a continuous process of transformation and a new model is emerging. While originally the party brings the militant into society, helps him to climb the social ladder—in brief, integrates him—society has accepted the challenge and accepted the militant. Consequently the party has been compelled to deemphasize the political commitment, the political pledge dimension of militancy, all the more so as the PCI felt less adamant in stressing its own ideological matrix. In turn this is translated into less proselytism, a lower degree of participation in party activities but a higher degree of participation in societal activities, forcing the PCI, for instance, to reorganize at the level of the section rather than stressing the cell. Comparing the militant of today with the militant of the fifties it appears he is less confident in his capacity for changing social reality. The party, in an effort to associate him more with political life, has put more stress in his participation in local activities which are less susceptible to the ideological contrasts characterizing national politics. The leadership is still unhindered in its freedom of maneuver at the national level but the base is now free to devote its energies to those local tasks the outcome of which affects it directly.

Changes in society and in the social orientation of the government parties have forced the militant to less intransigence in his evaluation of the social situation; his faith is less absolute, violence and themes of violence are more contained, "zones of neutrality"[59] seem to be expanding. The militant is less alienated by his environment and disposed to accept some imperfections; only in electoral periods and when recruiting new members does he feel compelled to insist upon the themes of exploitation and revolution which characterized him in the fifties. The militant is partially integrated into society; he now seeks total integration which the party cannot afford him. There is a desire to be accepted for what he is—not an ideologue, but simply a defender of peace and social justice, hostile to any form of aggression. Simultaneously the forms of his participation have evolved; the main emphasis is put on the electoral role of the party, where propaganda and responsibility rests with the central organization, while mobilization and agitation on a continuous level are no longer consistent with the party's ambitions. The new activist is

> . . . an open participant . . . neither dogmatic nor dichotomous, centered on the party which makes a distinction between the sphere of political engagement and his cultural, professional and family life. In a sense we are witnessing the gradual passage from a totalitarian and missionary militancy to a professionalized and specialized one; from a militancy based on "faith" . . . to a more rational measured form which operates through dialogue, conciliation and consensus.[60]

The picture that holds for the marginal Communist is entirely different. While certain elements that pertain to the militant remain valid (e.g., the party image), they are enhanced by the alienation from the system of this segment of population. At this level the tendencies towards violence are easy to uncover and it is possible to use the term "modern *jacquerie*."[61] This is the sector that sees the reins of the state in the hands of men with whom they have nothing in common: in their view the problem is not freedom but change in their economic condition and their status in society. This is the humble man, the uprooted peasant who has seen his traditional values crumble and be trampled by modern society. He perceives himself at the very bottom of the social scale. His system of values is antithetic to the values defended by society, but not necessarily less valid.

The marginal Communist has acquired a strong sense of his own personality and wishes to participate in the life of the country. Above all he is beginning to view himself as a free man with a dignity of his own. Thus he wants to work under equal conditions, and because he is often oppressed or discriminated against, he feels solidarity with all those whom he perceives as victims of social injustice: whenever necessary this will lead him to demonstrate in the streets. His vision of progress and only a partial understanding of it increase his frustration as he believes that technical progress can be applied in the field of social accomplishments if those who control the means so desire. Religion in the past had provided at least a superficial framework for order: today the priest is viewed as useful for the future, the PCI is far more effective in the present. The vote cast by the marginal Communist can be interpreted as a protest vote, but it is less and less the politics of despair. A hope is materializing, a process of democratic formation is taking place. The marginal Communist has opened to new ideals and feels committed to better his own social condition and that of his fellowmen.

By choice and because of circumstances the PCI has evolved considerably during the last twenty years. Its ideology has not resisted the challenge of change in the Italian society, its politics have been forced to adapt to new conditions, its social appeals have been modified. Socially and politically the PCI is a party that cannot be ignored, no more than it can be isolated or left to die or to change. It is possible it has not given sufficient guarantees of democracy, it is true that presently it does not provide for an alternative and responsible opposition.

Change—at the political, social and economic level—should be dependent on the political class that guides the country. One wishes the DC could provide the leadership so necessary for Italy: unfortunately it appears congenitally unable to do so. Only marginal groups in its left have offered a challenge—not a contrast—to a party that represents one Italian out of four. While some dialogue has taken place at the lowest levels, ideological preconceptions have limited the contacts at the summit.

Because of the present situation it becomes necessary for the parties, and in particular the DC, to reconsider the role the PCI can play in the system. The party which appears more and more like its socialist predecessors, the revolutionaries of the nineteenth century, does not request partnership but is ready to provide outside support to a political system accepted by all, while all denounce its ailing conditions.

The only remaining solution might be a test, a *pari démocratique* on the future evolution of the PCI. This will undoubtedly call for major realignments in Italian politics, but in the final analysis might provide for a better, more stable and democratic society. Ten years ago the center-left appeared as a faint possibility. In a country that has evolved *trasformismo* to an art, the association of the PCI to government might not be as remote as it seems.

NOTES

1. *Espresso*, no. 1, January 1970; P.J. Franceschini, "Correspondance de Rome," *Le Monde Diplomatique*, 17, no. 190, January 1970.

2. G. Sartori, "I sotto partiti," *Corriere della Sera*, 24 February 1970.

3. See Vera Lutz, *Italy, A Study in Economic Development* (New York: Oxford University Press, 1962). Lloyd Saville, *Regional Economic Development* (Durham: Duke University Press, 1967).

4. " . . . the movement from the rural to the urban center should make the individual . . . engage in more meaningful participation in the political process." Joseph La Palombara, "Italy: Fragmentation, Isolation, and Alienation," in L.W. Pye and S. Verba, *Political Culture and Political Development* (Princeton: Princeton University Press, 1965), p. 325. See also S.M. Lipset, "The Changing Class Structure and Contemporary Politics," *Daedalus* 93, no. 1 (Winter 1964), 271–296. And Joseph Lopreato, *Peasants No More* (San Francisco: Chandler, 1967).

5. Norman Kogan, *A Political History of Postwar Italy* (London: Pall Mall, 1966).

6. Giovanni Sartori, *Il Parlamento Italiano* (Naples: Edizioni Scientifiche, 1963). Giorgio Galli, *Il Bipartismo Imperfetto* (Bologna: Il Mulino, 1966). G. Braga, *Il Comunismo fra gli Italiani* (Milan: Comunita, 1956).

7. Edward Banfield, *The Moral Basis of a Backward Society* (New York: Free Press, 1958). It should be stressed that the author was concerned with southern Italy. Too often his concept has been extended, maybe too generously, to northern Italy.

8. La Palombara, "Italy," in Pye and Verba, *Political Culture*, p. 252.

9. G. Almond and S. Verba, *The Civic Culture* (Princeton: Princeton University Press, 1963), p. 160.

10. See editorial "Il PCI nello stato della doppiezza," Nord e Sud., no. 119, (November 1969), 50–52 for a good example.
11. Giorgio Galli, Bipartismo, p. 85. Chapter three is significantly entitled "DC and PCI, Metaphysics at the Service of Opportunism."
12. Quoted in La Palombara, "Decline of Ideology, Dissent and Interpretation," APSR 60 (March 1966).
13. See Dante Germino and Stefano Passigli, The Government and Politics of Contemporary Italy (New York: Harper and Row, 1968).
14. Vent' anni di vitae lotta del PCI (Rome: Rinascita, 1952), p. 598.
15. Ibid., p. 203.
16. Due anni di lotta dei comunisti Italiani (Roma: Riuniti, 1947), p. 37.
17. For a convenient location of documents, see P. Togliatti, La via Italiana al socialismo (Roma: Riuniti, 1964).
18. Unità, 5 March 1963.
19. "Il Congresso del PCI" in Civitàs 20, no. 3, 4 (March–April), 79–81. For a more recent statement: L. Longo in Corriere, 16 October 1969.
20. In Questitalia 12, no. 130–131 (February 1969), 114.
21. G. Amendola, "La Questione della Nuova Maggioranza e del Governo," Critica Marxista 7, no. 4–5 (July–October 1969), 182–194.
22. Civiltà Cattolica 120, no. 2858 (July 19, 1969), 170.
23. Ibid., p. 179.
24. Gonella in Corriere, 19 February 1970.
25. See "Il PCI-Manifesto- Un brutto affare," Questitalia 12, no. 139 (October 1969), 7–9; and Corriere, December 7, 10, 11, 12, 16, 23, 1969; January 9, 23; February 20, 1970.
26. "Communist parties without a Moscow centered world party would be like national Roman Catholics without a pope. . . . And many observers predict that the individual parties will follow the road of protestantism. . . . Those parties which operate within democratic societies will be under constant pressure to modify their totalitarian structures, as in fact the PCI seems to be beginning to do." S. M. Lipsett, "Changing Class Structure," in Daedalus, p. 295.
27. Galli, op. cit. p. 248. For an excellent study of the relationship of PCI-CPSU and the role of international communism in the PCI, see Donald L.M. Blackmer, Unity in Diversity, Italian Communism and the Communist World (Cambridge: MIT Press, 1968), in particular pp. 383–394.
28. Lombardo Radice, Socialismo e Libertà (Roma: Riuniti, 1968).
29. G. Sartori, "The Case of Polarized Pluralism," in La Palombara and Weiner, Political Parties and Political Developments (Princeton: Princeton University Press, 1966), p. 159.

30. Galli, *Bipartismo,* p. 355.
31. *Ibid.,* p. 206.
32. Leopoldo Elia, *Opposition et Contrôle en Italie (1944–1966)* (Grenoble: IAPS, 1965), p. 6.
33. Lipset. "Changing Class Structure," in *Daedalus,* p. 380.
34. *Corriere* 9 December 1969.
35. Federico Mancini, "From Reform to Adventure," *Encounter* (November 1969), pp. 413–422.
36. Umberto Segre, "Da Bologna, le vie del PCI," *Il Ponte* 25, no. 2, 198.
37. Otto Kirchheimer, "Transformation of the Western European Party System," in La Palombara and Weiner, *Political Parties and Political Development,* p. 190.
38. *Ibid.,* p. 187.
39. See Gordon Di Renzo, *Personality, Power and Politics* (Notre Dame, Ind.: University of Notre Dame Press, 1967).
40. Kirchheimer, "Transformation," in La Palombara and Weiner, *Political Parties and Political Development.*
41. Galli, *Bipartismo,* pp. 121–127.
42. Mattei Dogan, "Political Cleavage and Social Stratification in France and Italy," in Lipset and Rokkan, *Party Systems and Voter Alignments* (New York: Free Press, 1967), p. 192.
43. Sidney Tarrow, *Peasant Communism in Southern Italy* (New Haven: Yale University Press, 1967), p. 4.
44. *Ibid.,* p. 342.
45. *Ibid.,* p. 366.
46. Ann Cornelisen, *Torregreca* (Boston: Little and Brown, 1969). This book provides some excellent examples.
47. Robert Evans, *Coexistence: Communism and its Practice in Bologna, 1945–1965* (Notre Dame, Ind.: University of Notre Dame Press, 1967).
48. G. Sartori, *Il Parlamento Italiano,* p. 147.
49. S. I. Tozzi et al., *Il PCI e la DC nella amministrazioni locali e in parlamento* (Bologna: Il Mulino, 1968).
50. Comune di Bologna, *Notiziario* 9, no. 39–40, 1.
51. *Ibid.,* p. 17.
52. See *Corriere,* 14 January 1970.
53. Mattei Dogan, "La stratificazione sociale dei suffragi," in La Palombara, *Elezioni e Comportamemto politico* (Milan: Comunità, 1961), pp. 458–470.
54. Mattei Dogan, "Political cleavage etc.," in Lipset and Rokkan. *Party Systems and Voter Alignments,* p. 151.

55. *Ibid.*, pp. 172–176.
56. Arnaldo Nesti, *I Communisti l'altra Italia* (Bologna: Dehoniane, 1969), pp. 75 ff.
57. La Palombara, "Le aspirazioni della gioventu" in La Palombara, *Elezioni*.
58. See in particular Alberoni, et al., *L'Attivista di Partito* (Bologna: Il Mulino, 1967).
59. *Ibid.*, p. 519.
60. *Ibid.*, p. 520.
61. Nesti, *I Communisti*, p. 46.

6: THE CRISIS OF PARLIAMENTARY GOVERNMENT IN ITALY
Giovanni Bognetti

There is little doubt that the Italian political system is going through a period of crisis. Since roughly 1960 the government has not been able to solve many important problems originated by Italy's tumultuous economic growth and deep internal transformation. This is not a judgment prompted by any partisan political evaluation. Problems posed by the structural changes of society certainly exist.

Today nobody would deny the urgent need for a reform—to mention only a few examples—of Italian public administration and civil service, of the school and university system, of the fiscal system, of the law concerning urban development, and of the regulations affecting companies and stockmarkets. The government might have brought about the needed reforms, shaping them either on predominantly conservative principles or on predominantly progressive or liberal principles, according to its own political orientation. The fact is that the government seems unable to make a decision; it usually defers all decision and action. In some cases the government *has* acted, but instead of basing its action upon a definite and coherent program, it has yielded to sectional pressures. The effects of these haphazard interventions have therefore often been contradictory and self-defeating. Consequently, the country, left without leadership, appears to be drifting. All social groups, feeling the bonds of political unity and legal discipline loosening, have begun trying to draw as much profit as they can out of a situation where the state has almost ceased acting as an umpire among them. This process of increasing government paralysis and effacement has recently become so generalized and accelerated that one is at times under the impression the Italian state must be on the verge of collapse.[1]

Some Italian political scientists and political observers have explained this crisis of the political system in terms of a theory tracing its origin to an illegitimate usurpation of state powers by predatory political parties. Italy should no longer be considered a *democrazia*, a democracy, but rather a *partitocrazia*, a "party-cracy." The state organs (Parliament, the cabinet) to which the definition of the state's public policy is constitutionally entrusted, have been deprived of all power of independent decision. They act at the dictation of irresponsible party oligarchs. According to this theory, the most important Italian political parties are organized as mass parties in the sense given the word by Duverger. They are dominated by professional politicians who have made themselves masters of the state machine and exercise the state power only to foster their own interests, or, at best, their ideological prejudices. Instead of acting as mediators between society and the state, parties and party bureaucrats have gradually interposed as a screen between them, preventing social demands from getting adequate response in terms of effective state action.[2]

The theory of *partitocrazia* seems to move from the implied premise of an assumed incompatibility of the modern mass political party with the correct functioning of a true democratic regime and depicts Italian political parties as very strong organisms of this kind. The theory, in the first place, does not seem to point out a sufficient cause for the present crisis of the political system. Italian parties could be dedicated to pursuing their own group interests even more savagely than the theory maintains and nevertheless be able to promote and sustain vigorous, consistent state action. However, just the lack of such action is apparently the peculiar feature of the present crisis of the Italian political system. Indeed what is lamented is not so much oppression at the hands of a crudely partisan leadership as the absence of any leadership at all. In the second place, recent sociological research has revealed that Italian political parties, far from being powerful and robust organisms (as alleged by some), have in a certain sense become increasingly feeble in the last twenty years. Today they seem no longer able to mobilize the passions of large social strata and to interpret and translate them into organic political programs. Of course they are still able to develop activities aimed at the canvassing of votes at election time and at providing the personnel to operate the state and all its agencies. But their internal weakness prevents them from developing another activity, quite normal for political parties; namely the aggregation and transmission of political demands.

Actually, Italian political parties, according to a second theory based on the above-mentioned sociological studies—a theory that we may for certain purposes consider the direct opposite of the theory of partitocrazia—have long since ceased being mass parties. They are now organisms ready to accept and transmit all sorts of sectional social demands, without seeking to make them fit into a coherent and systematic scheme. They operate simply in view of the possible advantage to be reaped thereby in the struggle for the conquest of power positions: parties that may be properly labeled "catch-all parties." Their internal weakness should be primarily imputed to the very low level of interest and participation of the citizens in political life and political matters.[3]

Although resting on carefully ascertained factual data, this second theoretical model for the explanation of the crisis of the Italian political system seems to me no more adequate and satisfactory than the first. According to the logic of the partitocrazia theory, in order to cure the crisis mass parties as such should be wiped out of the Italian scene; according to the other theory they should be revitalized by raising the level of political interest and participation. But I see no necessary correlation between high political participation and a vigorous, consistent line in governmental action. Mass mobilization of the citizens' political feelings might perhaps be necessary to push through a program of reforms inspired by progressive ideals in a contemporary democratic system. But limited participation should not by itself be able to prevent the effective realization of a policy line shaped on conservative ideas, but willing to face, on that basis, the new problems emerging from the flux of a changing society and to offer a solution. The trouble with the Italian government today, I must repeat, seems to be not so much that it acts with a systematic intent of favoring, let us say, capital over labor. The trouble is that the government either does not act or that it acts at random. Sometimes it even acts at cross-purposes.

Both the above-mentioned theories tend to explain the crisis of the Italian regime against the backdrop of analyses about structures and functions of political parties that transcend the Italian case. More sensitive to the need of sticking closely to a careful examination of the peculiar features of the Italian political world in order to give a valid explanation of the crisis, is a third theory which has obtained wide currency in Italy. From the viewpoint of this last theory the key to understanding the mechanism of the crisis lies in a special characteristic of the Italian party system.

It is usually said that a multiparty system operates in Italy. (Indeed, nine parties are represented in Parliament.) But according to this theory, the distinctive trait of this party pluralism is that there are two major parties functioning as poles around which all others revolve as satellites. Moreover, one of the two major parties is radically opposed to the existing economic, social, and political order, which it is its final aim to reverse and completely reconstruct. Christian Democracy and the Communist Party are the two pivots of the Italian party system: a system which, because of this absolutely prominent role of theirs, could be dubbed, in a certain sense, a two-party system. An "imperfect two-party system," though; for contrary to what happens in the classic systems of this kind (one thinks of the English and of the American instances), the minority party, being institutionally opposed to the established fundamental order of society, does not have a real chance to oust the majority party. The majority of the Italian people do not want the subversion of the basic structures of their community. Therefore, they know they could not vote Christian Democracy out of power and the Communists in. The theory maintains that this circumstance has actually been a determinant for all postwar Italian political life. As a result, the Christian Democratic Party has become the irreplaceable master of the state, the party controlling the government by institutional necessity. But the rise of the Christian Democrats to the status of the party institutionally in government has in turn deeply affected the whole political system.

To begin with, Christian Democracy, free from fear of ever being removed from power by popular vote, has lost all interest in the realization of any definite political program. Besides, all interest groups (with no exception) have naturally tended to seek permanent communication channels with the party in government and permanent representation within it. Consequently, this party has tended to become the melting pot of all sorts of different social and political demands. It would be hopeless to look for a consistent, vigorous policy line in the action of a government controlled by such a party.[4]

It is the merit of the theory of the "imperfect two-party system" to emphasize the importance of the ideological fracture that by a tragic destiny has for long years divided Italian society into two parts, thereby rendering, among other things, the foundations of Italian democracy particularly weak.[5] The fracture has deep roots in Italian history and culture and the present crisis of the system must be explained against its background. Much of the present inaction and inefficiency of the government can be imputed to two facts: the political system offers no real chance of an alternation in power of a majority and an opposition party, and the party permanently in power has long been immune to any serious outside control by popular vote. Yet the theory fails to take into consideration (or at least it does not sufficiently stress) another factor which, although in some way connected with the deep ideological split that divides Italian society, must not be confused with it. It is a factor that cannot be overlooked in an analysis of the causes of the crisis without omitting from the picture an element that is essential and, probably, also decisive.[6]

In 1948, with the vote cast in the election for the first Parliament of the Republic, the Italian people showed clearly that they rejected the model of a Communist economic, social, and political system. The choice made then was tacitly confirmed at subsequent polls. But in the twenty years following 1948, Italian society deeply changed. The impetuous economic growth has more than doubled the gross national product. In northern Italy social structures today are in many respects similar to the structures of the most fully developed among contemporary European societies. In the South, the first impact of industrialization has shaken institutions and customs that were a legacy of the Middle Ages and still thrived at the end of World War II. This rapid social change has had consequences in the political attitudes of the people. Election returns between 1948 and 1968 indicate a slow but continuous shift of the popular vote to the left.

The shift can first be noticed within the very group of parties that had originally denounced the "Communist menace." The voters have gradually reduced the support given to the small parties located to the right of the Christian Democrats. Those parties used to poll about 15 percent of the vote until 1958. Today they poll, more or less, 10 percent.[7] On the other hand, the Christian Democratic Party has not suffered substantial losses since 1953. But one cannot ignore the changes that took place in the internal fabric of the party. The party was originally led by groups of notables, all of prevalently conservative and moderate political leanings. Afterwards, the party was given the structure of a mass party and within it regularly organized factions or *correnti* gradually emerged. Left-wing factions have meanwhile increased their strength and are today a real force within the party, though still limited.[8]

But the more important aspect of the vote shift concerns the size of the political forces that, grouping around the Communist Party, had originally declared their radical aversion to the "system." The parties that united to form a popular front in 1948 have, as a whole, constantly progressed in popular support. While in 1948 they reaped about 32 percent of the vote, twenty years later the sum total of the votes they obtained would have been well above 40 percent.[9] In particular, the Communist Party has increased its share of the vote from about 20 percent in 1948 to almost 28 percent in 1968.

From a certain point of view it was both inevitable and healthy that the vote for the left should increase. As the country developed economically and socially, new expectations arose, requiring reforms to be introduced by law. It was quite natural for the voters to look for new leaders to meet this need. But, because of the peculiar makeup of Italian politics and the very low level of Italian civic culture,[10] this tendency was not able to manifest itself in a vote for an opposition dedicated to reforms, but at the same time firmly loyal to democracy and conscious that reforms must in all cases be based on a realistic and pragmatic appraisal of the situation. Most of the new "progressive" vote in the last twenty years has gone to the Communist Party and its appendices.

There is an opinion that the relatively good fortune of the Communist Party in postwar Italy is due primarily to the unenlightened attitude of the political class in power, which did not show enough courage and vision to immediately bring about a program of incisive social reforms so as to win the full support of the working classes. This opinion is especially widespread among foreign observers.[11] But one may entertain some doubts as to its being entirely grounded. For one thing, in order to foster rapid economic growth the government had probably, at least for a period, to adopt a policy wholly acceptable to the privileged classes. In the second place, it would in any case have been difficult to pass reforms apt to meet fully the demands of the dissatisfied social strata. The economic resources of the country that could be used for the purpose were limited. Finally, one must take into account the easy tendency of politically immature social groups to turn to radical beliefs and to put faith in radical political movements when they are freed from ancient patterns of life by an accelerated process of economic growth and are subjected to the pains of a difficult adaptation to new patterns. The Communists were there, managing adroitly to profit by this tendency.

But the shift of the popular vote to the left is the factor that created the conditions out of which the recent paralysis and effacement of the government have emerged. Up to 1960 there had been a relatively clear and consistent line in the action of the government: it was a conservative line aiming primarily at backing the driving forces of a young, neocapitalistic economic system.[12] But by the late fifties, it had become clear that in the next decade the coalition that had held the government until then would probably not be able to command a majority in Parliament. Unless the ruling class chose to give a general, sharp shake-up to the political situation by adopting a stronger and more authoritarian attitude toward the opposition, a new coalition had to be found as a basis for government. This might have involved, at the end if not at first, the dissolution of the democratic regime itself. The Christian Democratic leaders then adopted a strategy that had already been tried fifty years before by Giolitti when he was first confronted with the newly born Socialist movement. They endeavored to attract out of the bloc of the left-wing opposition those forces that appeared ready to join the government on the basis of a compromise. The move was made easier by the evolution that the Socialist Party—at the beginning a loyal partner of the Communists—had meanwhile undergone. As is well known, the compromise between Christian Democracy and the Socialist Party gave birth to the new coalition that supported the center-left governments throughout the sixties. But while that very compromise probably secured a peaceful continuation of democracy in Italy, it was pregnant with germs that quickly made the government passive, inefficient, and without a clear political orientation and policy line of its own.

Indeed, the Socialists, although by now converted not only to democracy and to the acceptance of Italy's position in the Western world but to political gradualism, were obviously still in favor of a strong line of social reforms which might bring immediate benefits to the working class and put checks on the powers of capital. In this they were supported by the left-wing Christian Democrats. However, their joined forces were not enough to compel the bulk of the Christian Democratic Party to deflect from their prevalently moderate and cautious attitudes. The "conservative" Christian Democrats did not deny, in general, the necessity to face the new problems created by the economic and social growth of the country and to pass adequate reforms, but they would have liked to have reforms inspired by more orthodox ideas as to the just evolution of society. On the other hand, if the "progressive" forces could not impose upon the government a program to their liking, they had sufficient power to oppose, in turn, the adoption of a clearly conservative program aiming at a modernization and a rationalization of institutions chiefly with a view to the prevalent, immediate interests of the Establishment.

So, out of a balance of contrasting tendencies and powers followed the main characteristic feature of all the governments of the decade. Each time a new cabinet was formed, government programs were agreed upon only after long, exhausting negotiations. At times they contained contradictions. Consent was given to them with the implied reservation that they would not be acted upon. In fact they were seldom carried into execution.[13] If a too clearly defined measure (of a conservative or a progressive trend) was about to be enacted, that was sometimes the pretext to cause the cabinet to fall, so everything would have to be negotiated all over again. As the decade drew to a close, this frustrating impotence of government reached its peak.

In the sixties, the new balance between conservative and progressive forces, created by the shift to the left of the popular vote, brought the political situation almost to a stalemate: only this notion can offer, I think, an adequate explanation of the crisis. Other factors provide necessary elements for the setting of the crisis; but they could not constitute a sufficient cause by themselves.

The structures of the "imperfect two-party system" had not prevented the government from operating in a relatively efficient way during the fifties, when Christian Democracy was firmly dominated by conservatives and the so-called center coalition could muster a comfortable majority. There is no reason for doubting that had there been a shift of the vote to the right instead of to the left, the political system would have been able to produce in the sixties more or less homogeneous governments as it had in the fifties: governments endowed with a much more consistent political will than it was actually able to produce, and this despite the persistent existence of a Communist Party practically out of the political game. They would have been governments furthering a conservative political orientation and policy line; but a line, a clear line, would have at least existed.

Feuds between parties and between factions within parties and savage personal rivalries between political leaders increased in number and asperity after 1960, and they account for much of the recent instability of cabinets.[14] But the instability of cabinets is ordinarily a chronic disease of parliamentary government combined with party pluralism. Periodical alternation of cabinets also characterized the fifties in Italy. The fact had not then generated a public impression that the government did not have a clear position regarding all the fundamental problems of the period. When the ultimate political values that the government is willing to promote and, if necessary, to defend, are clear and do not change, it matters less whether or not the state rudder remains always in the same hands and minor affairs are administered in the same way. But in the sixties the government was not able to decide even what had to be done as to matters of first importance and of a pressing nature. It has rightly been said that the result of this government uncertainty and inactivity was indirectly the perpetuation of old institutions and of old patterns of state action so that, to all practical effects, the period can be considered one in which conservatism largely prevailed. This conclusion is to a certain extent correct, if we confine the word "conservatism" to mean merely mechanical, passive continuation of old practices in new and different situations. But even in that case it should be remembered that whatever in fact prevailed in the period was not a deliberate choice of the government, giving the citizens the sense that leadership existed and that there were precise values that would consistently guide and control governmental action for at least some of the time. Governmental uncertainty, arising out of an unresolved clash of conservative and progressive trends, has given the citizens the growing feeling that the country is living in a political vacuum.

The proliferation of pressure groups, corresponding to the liberation of social forces caused by the recent development of the Italian economy, has certainly contributed to making the mediating task of the government more difficult.[15] But it would not have had the explosive effects it has had, it would not have put governmental decisions many a time at the complete mercy of sectional, egocentric interests as it has, had not the political class in power been so internally divided as to the political goals that should be achieved.

Finally, what of the alleged decline of the interest and participation of the citizens in political life? One is almost tempted to say that if that decline had been sharper, the efficiency of the political system might even have improved, in a paradoxical way.

The above-mentioned shift to the left of the popular vote is at least due in part to reactions to events canalized by clever ideological propaganda and conditioned by unwarranted hopes in the potentialities of political action. A more marked disinterest of the citizens in political life, caused by a growing skepticism as to the effects of participation, might have reduced the size of the shift. This would have limited the power of the progressive trends, thereby preventing or attenuating the balancing of opposite, competing political forces, that has brought government to the present stalemate.

Suppose the hypothesis I have set forth correctly identifies the proximate cause of the present crisis of the Italian political system. The knowledge of that cause should help us also in the formulation of some tentative prediction as to its outcome.

First, we should dismiss a false belief as to some possible immediate effects of the crisis. I said at the beginning that one is at times under the impression that the Italian state is on the verge of collapse. The impression is genuine; reality is however a little more complicated. The crisis of the political system does exist. Its long-range negative repercussions cannot be calculated exactly, but one is entitled to suppose they may be serious. The image of the present protracted impotence of the state is probably working on the minds of all citizens, thereby severely damaging the little loyalty they may still feel for the body politic. However, as to the present, one should at least not be led to the hasty conclusion that the political vacuum in which the country seems to live will call forth an immediate reaction that will destroy the system. It is sometimes said that when the state does not exercise the authority it possesses, society will not long tolerate being deprived of a guide. I do not think the maxim applies without qualifications to the present Italian situation. At least in the short run,

Italy should be able to keep the economic system working at the present rate of expansion even if the government remains undecided as to the precise political orientation and policy line it wants to follow. On the other hand, although sections of public opinion may already be somewhat restless, there seems to be no sign of an impending outbreak of exasperated resentments. Despite a few contrary insinuations, there also seems to be no inclination in any sizable social or political group (including the military element) to have recourse to force to end the present political uncertainties.[16]

Once the ground has been cleared of unwarranted premonitions and unjustified fears such as the ones just mentioned, it is relatively easy to envision the basic alternatives that lie ahead of the Italian political system.

It is possible, first of all, that the center-left coalition presently controlling government, after some further quarreling, may arrive at an agreement as to what the government should do. It is possible that the coalition finally may arrive at a compromise program, some way between conservative and progressive extremes, and carry it out more or less consistently, putting through at least some of the most urgent reforms.

This would possibly bring about a gradual withering away of the crisis. And it would bring it about peacefully, within the framework of the present balance of political forces. In any case, one should not imagine that the recession of the crisis would be speedy and the reforms eventually enacted would be all enlightened and have all positive effects. On the contrary, the process of recovery could not but be slow and reforms would probably sometimes bear the marks of demagogy. But at least as a beginning, the important thing would be the government's engagement, its commitment to a positive line of action, since a most serious aspect of the crisis is precisely the present effacement of governmental authority. Time and successive adjustments would probably provide for the rest of the cure.

In a certain sense, the picture just outlined portrays the most optimistic among the possible outcomes of the crisis. It does not necessarily portray the most probable one. Its coming true depends on many conditions. We must concentrate our attention on one of them.

As a preliminary remark it is necessary to point out that the present center-left coalition is not a static system of forces. The present balance between conservative and progressive trends is a precarious one. In particular, left-wing Socialists and left-wing Christian Democrats today seem eager to see the balance altered by a further extension of that process of inclusion within the area of potential governmental coalitions of political forces originally belonging to the antisystem opposition, a move that was accepted ten years ago as a defensive strategy by the conservative Christian Democratic ruling class. Today the "progressive" wings in the coalition would like to "open" to the very stronghold of the antisystem opposition, the Communist Party, in order to overcome the resistance of the conservatives and to become the real balancing element in Italian political life. This attitude of the "progressive" groups within the center-left coalition would perhaps disappear if the shift to the left of the popular vote that has characterized past election returns should stop.[17] The question is, however, whether that shift will stop.

In general, one is inclined to think that an end to the shift is rather unlikely in the near future. Even if the government enacted vigorous measures expressly aimed at cajoling the working class, the effects would probably be limited. While reforms are necessary in Italy in order to keep the country abreast of the recent remarkable growth of society and economy, no reform, however courageous, would be able today and for a long time to offer adequate solutions to the new problems created by that growth. The resources available, both social and economic, are still limited and insufficient in comparison with the expectations aroused. These would necessarily remain at least in part unsatisfied, no matter what is done to meet them. Of course, the drift of the vote toward the left may nevertheless stop. Electoral trends are governed by mysterious laws. But it would be rather odd if at the future polls the Communist Party got no more or fewer votes than in the past.

Suppose that the tendency of the vote to shift to the left—and in particular to the opposition left—continues. One is immediately faced with a range of perspectives different from the ones we have outlined above. The tensions within the coalition would increase greatly, perhaps becoming unbearable. Certainly, overcoming the crisis would not at that point be possible as a smooth process controlled and guided without special effort by the parties of the center-left. Two alternative courses can be envisaged as possible ways out.

The thrust in favor of an "opening" to the Communist Party,

already noticeable in the center-left coalition, would become very strong in case of a further drifting of the vote to the left. But in Italy there are still powerful forces that are ready to oppose that "opening" with determination. They may also be stiffened in their determination by a possible international veto, tacit or not, barring the signature of a "foedus impium" for which the world's and Europe's balance of power may not yet be ripe.[18] These forces might still get the upper hand. However, in order to prevail, they would have either to subdue the left-wing appendages of the coalition, curbing their already clear tendencies to make common cause with the Communists, or to part company with them. In both cases the government would probably have to assume a fighting attitude toward the Communists, an attitude that has been absent since the first years after the foundation of the Republic. In both cases the atmosphere of general political relaxation that was inaugurated around 1960 would come to an end. The strategy of gradual absorption by the system of forces originally opposing it would abruptly finish, there being left no room for its extension beyond the point already reached. The government again would be in possession of a more or less clear political character, but it would have to face a stronger opposition enraged at the renewed political ostracism to which it would be subjected. The crisis would perhaps be over, but the political system would be in some danger with regard to its very survival as a parliamentary government and perhaps even as a democratic regime.

A few words ought to be dedicated to this disquieting perspective. It is not entirely unwarranted to say that if the Italian people were called upon to choose again in a clear electoral context between the horns of a sharp communism-anticommunism dilemma, they would stick to the choice they made more than twenty years ago, although not perhaps with the same overwhelming majority as then. But the fact is, the existing constitutional structures of the state and the present arrangements and composition of political parties are not made for facilitating a clear presentation of such a dilemma to the people and a subsequent undeviating execution of the people's choice. For many reasons, the Christian Democratic Party today is far from inclined to resume the strong anticommunist attitude it maintained in the early fifties[19] and would not be able to do it without, probably, a serious party split. On the other hand, parliamentary government, more than presidential government, is often tempted to collude with the opposition, especially if the majority supporting the government results from a coalition of parties and factions. This is particularly true in the Italian case, where certain peculiar features of the legislative process add to the possibility of collusion of that kind.[20] So, to try to prevent an "opening" to the Communists in the presence of a further shift of the vote in their favor might possibly (even if not necessarily) involve a general, violent shake-up of the Italian party system. Whether such a political earthquake would also stop short of shaking the constitutional structures of the state cannot be safely predicted. The earthquake might generate other earthquakes. There might ensue an attempt to set up an executive endowed institutionally with much greater power and stability than the present one. It is not unreasonable to entertain fears that the process would go even further, leading to an authoritarian regime.[21] Of course, that is not the only possible outcome of a decision to refuse Communist cooperation in the event of a further shift of the vote to the left. But it remains, nevertheless, a real possibility. Should the constitutional structures of the state suffer violent change of any kind as a consequence of such a decision, the present crisis of the political system itself would collapse either totally or partially. The same cause which brought about the impotence of government in the sixties would bring about in the seventies, by increasing its pressure and in combination with other conditioning factors, its breakdown. The crisis of the system, which has maintained itself thus far in a nonacute phase, characterized by nonlethal though damaging troubles, would have plunged to a fatal conclusion.

I referred above to a second alternative, a second possible way out of the tensions created by a hypothetical persistence of the shift of the popular vote to the left. It is—it goes without saying—the "opening" to the Communist Party.

It is not for me to say how much and in which respects the Communist Party has changed since 1948. It will be sufficient to mention the fact that the party now proclaims its final faith in an "Italian way to socialism" which should exclude even the temporary demise of the democratic methods; that it has for years worked in a democratic and orderly way at the level of local authorities and of labor unions' activities; that it has become completely "bourgeois" as far as the way of life of its bureaucrats is concerned; that for some time now it has insistently offered to collaborate with the government parties, asking, in exchange, not revolutionary changes in society, but limited reforms.

Some maintain that such a party cannot any longer be considered as operating against the system, but should be regarded as a more or less integrated element of it. Some believe that unless the Communists are admitted to governmental collaboration, it will be impossible to overcome the resistance of the conservative forces still opposing reforms vital for the development of Italian society, while, moreover, the danger would always be impending of a right-wing authoritarian development. Besides, before letting them assume direct governmental responsibilities, it would be possible to test the Communists' goodwill by making them support the government as outside partners, as with the Socialists before the birth of the center-left governments in the sixties.

Numerous obstacles stand in the way of a development along these lines in Italian politics. Were they all removed and should this new and total "opening to the left" take place, certainly a great structural change would occur in the Italian political system. That would indeed mean the end of the so-called "imperfect two-party system" which has swayed Italian politics since 1947. What would temporarily replace it might be a sort of "great coalition system," with the Christian Democrats and the Communists sharing (perhaps in different proportions) power and its benefits. The change with regard to the present situation would be vast. But one cannot be sure that it would result in an improvement as far as clearness in the political line of the government and effectiveness in state action are concerned. Improvement in that direction would chiefly depend on the degree to which the Communists would have turned (no matter what names are used) into a real social-democratic party of the traditional European type. Should they, instead, still show tendencies incompatible with the position of Italy within the western European economic and political concert, the troubles that presently affect the Italian political system would not be over; the government would certainly be divided within itself, once again (though perhaps on new and different grounds) torn between right- and left-wing trends. Furthermore, leadership and governmental effectiveness are not the only values that count in a political system. Referring before to the hypothesis of a course of action opposite to the one we are now discussing, I mentioned the danger that that course might end by causing the constitutional structures of the system to break down. It is necessary to recall that the danger also exists in connection with the other choice. No one can really predict where the Communist Party would take or try to take Italy, should it be admitted to share in governmental power. No matter how much the party may be changed, its ties with Soviet communism are far from severed and one has a right to be suspicious about the political *forma mentis* of the leaders and members of a party which has been nurtured for years on the food of a totalitarian ideology.

In outlining the actual and possible interactions of some of the factors controlling the functioning of the Italian political system, I have stressed the role of one of them: a gradual shift over the years of the electorate's political orientation. I am inclined to hold this factor as a decisive variable in the life of the system. It has determined the deterioration of leadership and effectiveness in governmental action during the sixties. If it continues in the same direction, it may determine momentous consequences affecting perhaps the system's basic structure and its identity. It is not only a decisive variable. It is also an element in the system which cannot be relevantly modified by deliberate political action within the framework of the normal functioning of the system itself and in a short period. Given the social and economic setting in which the political system operates, given the peculiar constitutional features of the system, given the choice of certain fundamental political and economic goals whose achievement is thought indispensable, and given the reasonable decision not to take steps that may seriously unbalance the system, there is little the political class in power could have done (or could do) to correct the natural course of that trend. Today the orientation of the Italian electorate is basically determined by cultural, social and psychological conditions which are rooted deeply in past Italian history and by the consequences of the present takeoff of the economic system, both factors interacting among themselves. Political action, respecting the limits imposed by the rules of a democratic regime and operating under the concrete circumstances of the Italian situation, could not and probably cannot cause the results of that interaction to change considerably in a short span of time. Only the radical modification of those conditions and the achievement of a higher general level of economic development would do. But to obtain that by democratic methods may take a very long time.

This conclusion may sound shocking and unacceptable to politicians and statesmen who believe in democracy and would like to make it stronger and more efficient. Perhaps rightly so. Their craft is action, and action must rest on an unproven yet firm confidence in its own immediate power. To political scientists, however, it provides a hypothesis which deserves to be carefully considered and tested. It may prove, after all, to be true. If so, then relevant evidence would be offered to support a theory that Italy is one of those societies whose social and economic development not only makes democracy possible, but also makes it necessarily weak. Until that stage is over, the functioning of democracy in such societies is by necessity often defective; its very survival depends less on the prudent exercise by political leaders of whatever power they hold than on the merciful will of the gods. One who believes in democracy and loves his own country can only hope the gods will be benign. Fortunately science has not yet pronounced the hope to be, in the circumstances, a forlorn one.

NOTES

1. Opinions reflecting the impression that the Italian government has been for some time in a state close to paralysis can be found not only in the Italian press, but in the foreign press as well. See (to mention only one source) the surveys of Italian affairs in the issues of *Time* throughout 1968, 1969, and 1970.

Judgments lamenting the increasing incapacity of government to cope with the fundamental problems of society and its inaction or *immobilismo* come in Italy both from the right and from the left. For instance: Maranini, *L'Italie* (Paris, 1962), p. 149 ff.; Piccardi, Bobbio, Parri, *La sinistra davanti alla crisi del Parlamento* (Milano, 1967), passim; Galli, *Il bipartitismo imperfetto* (Bologna, 1966), Ch. 1, 11; A. Pizzorno, "Elementi di uno schema teorico con riferimento ai partiti politici in Italia," in Sivini *Partiti e partecipazione politica in Italia*, ed. (Milano, 1969), pp. 5, 30 ff.

2. The classic version of the theory is to be found in Maranini's books and articles: "I partiti nella democrazia," *I partiti e lo stato*, ed. Spadolini (Bologna, 1962); *Il tiranno senza volto. Lo spirito della Costituzione e i centri occulti di potere* (Milano, 1963); *La Republica* (Firenze, 1965).

It should perhaps be recalled that (in Maranini's view) the remedy against "party-cracy" is a reorganization of the state structures. This includes a new electoral system based on the principle of the single member constituency. Something will be said later on the question of possible modifications of the state constitutional structures: See paragraph 3.

3. This interpretation is presented in the essay by A. Pizzorno mentioned in note 1. Pizzorno's interpretation is linked in many respects with the theory exposed by Kirchheimer in his essay, "The Transformation of the Western European Party Systems," *Political Parties and Political Development*, ed. La Palombara and Weiner (Princeton, 1966), p. 177.

4. The most elaborated version of this theory is the one offered by Galli in the work already cited in note 1.

5. Of course, Maranini and Pizzorno—the authors mentioned as typical representatives of the two other theories—are aware of the importance of this element and of all its consequences. They tend, however, to give a prominent place to the other factors referred to above; namely the degenerative effects of *partitocrazia* and the decline of political participation.

6. In any survey, however short and incomplete, of the main theories concerning the crisis of the Italian political system and its causes, the name of Sartori should not be omitted. (See his "Dove va il Parlamento?" in Samogyi, Lotti, Predieri, Sartori, *Il Parlamento Italiano, 1946–1963* [Napoli, 1963], p. 279; "European Political Parties: The Case of Polarized Pluralism" in La Palombara and Weiner, p. 137; "Bipartitismo imperfetto o pluralismo polarizzato?" in *Tempi moderni*, 1967, n. 31, p. 4; "I sottopartiti" in *Corriere della Sera*, February 24, 1970). But it is perhaps legitimate not to set up his theory as a fourth one side by side with the three typical ones we have briefly outlined, as his position can be considered, for the sake of classification, as straddling the ones of Maranini and of Galli. With Maranini he seems to share the opinion that the Italian party system does not allow the real will of the people to assert itself in the state's policy line and that the demise of proportional representation could bring about serious improvements in the functioning of the political system. (But he apparently does not attribute much importance to the fact that Italian parties are today no longer "parliamentary" parties along the lines of the English or the American models.) With Galli he believes that most important, as a cause of the crisis, has been the existence in Italy of a strong leftist opposition which is "antisystem." But he rejects the formula of the "imperfect two-party system" because he thinks the presence of other parties, besides the Communist Party and Christian Democracy cannot be discounted in an adequate explanation of the malfunctioning of the system. He prefers, therefore, to speak of a "polarized party pluralism." At any rate, not even Sartori seems to give *primary* relevance to the element which, in my opinion, is on the contrary the really decisive factor. Besides, the logic of this interpretation would lead one to hold that element to be the consequence of

some amendable defect of the political system. I am inclined to believe that its roots are embedded in the underlying structure of society and cannot be removed by manipulating the political system—at least not without at the same time putting in danger the very continuance of democracy in Italy.

7. To calculate these figures, the following are considered parties located to the right of Christian Democracy: "Movimento Sociale Italiano," "Partito Democratico di Unità Monarchica," "Partito Liberale Italiano." As for the elections of 1948, the votes given to "Uomo qualunque" must be reckoned in order to establish the percentage attained then by the right-wing movements.

8. On the original composition of the Christian Democratic Party, its development into a mass party, and the emergence of left-wing factions within it, see, among others, A. Cavazzani, "Organizzazione, iscritti ed elettori della Democrazia Cristiana" in *Partiti*, p. 171; G. Galli and P. Facchi, *La sinistra democraziana* (Milano, 1962).

9. The "popular front" of 1948 was basically composed of "Partito Comunista Italiano" and "Partito Socialista Italiano." The figure of over 40 percent in the 1968 elections is reckoned by also taking into account the votes given to "Partito Socialista Italiano di Unità Proletaria," a party born from a split of "Partito Socialista Italiano" in 1964.

10. A generally reliable, though at times questionable appraisal of the low level of Italian civic culture is offered in the well-known work by Almond and Verba, *The Civic Culture* (Princeton, 1963).

11. It substantially permeates, for instance, such valuable works as Jean Meynaud's *Rapport sur la classe dirigeante italienne* (Lausanne, 1964), and N. Kogan's *A Political History of Postwar Italy* (New York, 1966).

12. Critics of the Italian party system (such as, for instance, Maranini) tend to attribute a lack of consistency and vigor also to the governmental action in the late forties and in the fifties. It is my opinion that this judgment cannot be shared, if one considers the achievements of the period. The reconstruction of the state after the collapse suffered in the Second World War, was carried out in such a way as to provide at least a sufficient political framework for a vigorous takeoff of the economy. In the field of foreign policy the government pursued a firm line in favor of a strict cooperation with the Western capitalistic democracies and of the unification—both economic and political—of Europe.

13. The program of the first Moro cabinet (1963) included reforms in the fields of urban development, the fiscal system, the civil service, and the school system. In none of these fields have reforms thus far been carried out. The program also included the organization of new political

units at a local level, the "regions." The regions are being finally organized in the course of 1970.

14. Cabinet instability has been accused from different sides of being in direct causal relation with present government impotence. Besides Maranini's works, already mentioned, see: G. Sartori, "Dove va il Parlamento?" in Samogyi, Lotti, Predieri, Sartori, *Il Parlamento*, pp. 382–5; N. Bobbio, "Le istituzioni parlamentari ieri e oggi," in Piccardi, Bobbio, Parri, *La Sinistra*, p. 45; S. Galeotti, "Il potere di decisione," in *Justitia*, 1968, pp. 123, 145–8.

15. On the Italian pressure groups, J. La Palombara's *Interest Groups in Italian Politics* (Princeton, 1964) is, of course, still fundamental.

16. Hints that a military coup-d'état might take place in Italy have been made from time to time by certain sections of the Italian press. For a balanced and still valid appraisal of the role of the army in Italian politics: Meynaud, *Rapport*, p. 62 ff. of the Italian translation (Milano, 1966).

17. There may however be some doubts as to this. The tendency of the left-wing Socialists and of the left-wing Christian Democrats to seek an *entente* with the Communists, feeds on deeply ingrained ideological preferences and on the hope of playing, through the *entente*, a controlling role in Italian politics. I suspect that at this point, only a very sharp (and therefore improbable) reversal of the electoral trend would induce them to abandon their plan of bringing Communism within the area of potential governmental coalitions.

18. Conversely, it is certain that should the United States become less interested in the destiny of Western Europe and should Russia in some way extend its influence on the area, the probability of an effective resistance against the "opening" to the Communists would greatly diminish. In that case, the "opening" would become almost inevitable, even if the election returns were not to show any increase on the left. My analysis of the possible developments of Italian politics is based here, of course, on the explicit assumption that the international balance, as it exists in the spring of 1970, will not undergo basic changes.

19. One reason, among the others, is the changed attitude of the Roman Catholic church vis-à-vis the international Communist movement. It is obviously not necessary to recall here the great influence exercised by the Church on Italian political life in general and on Christian Democratic politicians in particular.

20. I am referring especially to the power given in Italy to standing parliamentary committees—in which all parties are represented in proportion to their respective parliamentary strength to legislate in matters of minor consequence. The bulk of Italian legislation comes from these

committees whose work is not public and is therefore particularly apt to foster collusion of all sorts, and not from the floor of the houses. See Predieri, "La produzione legislativa," in *Il Parlamento*, pp. 203, 228 ff.; Mortati, *Istituzioni di diritto publico* (Padova, 1970), pp. 696 ff.

21. In the past, and apart from the problem of avoiding the "opening" to the Communists, there have been quite a few proposals to correct the malfunctioning of the political system through reforms affecting some of its fundamental structures. We mentioned, in note 2, Maranini's point of view. Among the political writers already mentioned (to limit a list of citations otherwise long), Sartori was apparently in favor, in 1966, of the adoption of the single member constituency with second ballot runoff ("European Political Parties," p. 170); and, perhaps, in 1963, of the transformation of the Italian regime from parliamentary into presidential government ("Dove va il Parlamento?", p. 384); Galeotti was advocating, in 1968, the election of the prime minister directly by the people, echoing ideas sponsored in France by Duverger. Usually, writers sponsoring basic changes in the structures of the state have avoided discussing the problem of how to bring them about democratically; i.e., on the basis of the political forces prevailing in parliament and in the country (forces which have always opposed such changes). They have also failed to consider the fact that the reluctance of all the parties of the government area to promote reforms in the basic state structures has probably depended not so much on the ignorance of the fundamental principles of political engineering (as Sartori seems to insinuate) as on the existence, on the one hand, of serious legal and political obstacles, and, on the other hand, on the fear that in all cases an attempt to introduce important changes in the state fabric might have set in motion a chain of reactions apt to exasperate the political struggle and to accelerate the emergence of dangers for the very survival of the democratic system. In my opinion the fear was not unjustified.

7: CHALLENGES TO DEMOCRACY IN CANADA
Douglas V. Verney

Normally, a challenge to democracy consists of a takeover of power either by a dictator or by a junta. If this is what we mean by challenge, then there is no threat at present to democracy in Canada. Of course, Canada remained a colony after 1776—but so did seventeen of the thirty or more British possessions in the Western hemisphere. Canada did not achieve independence at the same time as the American colonies partly because there were very few settlers, and partly because the main part of Canada, or what is now the Province of Quebec, had only recently been conquered. The Quebec Act of 1774 favored the French-speaking Canadian settlers, much to the annoyance of the American colonists. Canada achieved self-government in the first half of the nineteenth century. In 1867 Canada became a dominion and has been a liberal democracy ever since. It has a federal and parliamentary political system that has never until recently been challenged.

But threats to liberal democracy can take place at a lower level than that of the federal government. In Canada, at the provincial level, there have been challenges from time to time, notably that of Maurice Duplessis who was premier of Quebec from 1936 to 1939 and from 1944 until his death in 1959.[1] Many Canadians compare Duplessis' rule to that of Huey Long in Louisiana.

In American eyes, Canada is thought of as a friendly country, if it is thought of at all. Nowadays emigration between the countries is from the United States to Canada as much as from Canada to the United States. Americans also consider it one of the "Anglo-Saxon" democracies, to use the terms adopted by Robert R. Alford[2] and Seymour M. Lipset.[3] Canada can perhaps best be described as a semi-independent country. It is only semi-independent because of the power of American business and because its trade with the United

States now exceeds 10 billion dollars a year, making it easily the United States' most important trading partner. But it is independent in the sense that Canada trades with Communist countries, it can express doubts about NATO, and in many ways separate its policies from those of its American partner. In the middle of 1970, for example, the Canadian dollar was allowed to float upwards.

Should we then, at this time, consider that there is no challenge to liberal democracy in Canada? Much depends on our sense of history. There are many who look at the history of the British Isles and regard it as one of slow, peaceful evolution. This is to ignore completely the Irish question. Similarly, with Canada, if we ignore the problems faced by the Province of Quebec and its relations with the rest of Canada, then Canada also is a stable Anglo-Saxon liberal democracy. But such an approach is surely superficial. We must begin by asking: What are some of the characteristics of liberal democracy in Canada, the United States, and Britain?

There would seem to be three attributes that each of these countries accepts.

1. The existence of private enterprise. The state is not all-powerful; it does not control all business.
2. The rule of the majority. The politics of each of these countries is assumed to be based on elections where there is a swing of the pendulum from time to time between political parties which roughly are equal. Each of the two major parties can assume that it has a chance after each election of forming a government.
3. There is an acceptance of the rules of the game or what used to be termed the rule of law. Each country has a constitution on which the political system is based, though in Britain of course, this is not written down. Each country shares a long tradition of parliamentary procedure that governs the way in which political life is conducted. In two countries, Britain and the United States, there has been civil war and the failure of a minority to determine the future of the country; there has been no civil war in Canada.

But in all three of these areas—private enterprise, majority rule, acceptance of the rules of the game—there do appear to be threats in Canada. We shall examine each of them in turn.

I. CHALLENGE TO PRIVATE ENTERPRISE

The challenge to private enterprise takes three forms in Canada: (a) the revolt of the young, (b) American control of the economy, and (c) Quebec's fears.

a) Youth in Canada is as opposed to "the military-industrial complex" as youth is in the United States. There is a distaste for the notion that the graduating student taking his first job will become a cog in a large machine. There is concern for the price that apparently must be paid for the affluence of suburban living. There is doubt about the notion of economic growth as being the raison d'etre for one's labors. There is an increasing sense that a moral purpose should underlie one's life.

b) Many Canadians oppose control of their economy by the United States. J.-J. Servan-Schreiber has written that Western Europe now has 14 billion dollars of its economy (in the form of fixed assets) owned by American citizens.[4] Melville Watkins has estimated that the United States has 15 billion dollars of direct investment in Canada.[5] In Europe 80 percent of computers are American-owned as are 95 percent of integrated circuits. But whereas in France 40 percent of the petroleum industry is American-owned, in Canada the figure is 74 percent. Ninety-seven percent of the Canadian automobile industry is American-owned. Indeed, if we take all manufacturing in Canada, 60 percent is American-owned.

One consequence of this discovery was that Lester Pearson, when prime minister, appointed Walter Gordon to look into some of these matters. He in turn invited Professor M. Watkins of the University of Toronto to produce a report on American ownership. Since then Watkins has become active politically and now leads what is known as the Waffle Group of the New Democratic party. Although at first the Canadian government soft-pedaled opposition to American ownership, it has found itself compelled in recent years to intervene increasingly to protect the Canadian economy. In 1970 there was a dramatic instance of this when the owner of Denison Mines (which produced uranium) was not allowed to sell them to an American-controlled group. There now is a policy of Canadian control of natural resources.

It is hard to argue that private enterprise is a bulwark of freedom and democracy when the private enterprise is foreign. In Canada, therefore, the defense of private enterprise has to be that it promotes a higher standard of living. But this is not a defense of the same quality as that used by Americans. We should also remember that traditional political theory has been concerned with such issues as sovereignty and the equality of the individual. In powerful countries such as Britain and the United States this theorizing seems to represent the mood of the people. In Canada, however, "sovereignty" is hard to defend. The "equality" of 20 million Canadians versus 200 million Americans is equally hard to defend. Canadians generally do not know which of the companies listed on their stock exchanges are Canadian. In some ways the existence of American corporations is debilitating to competition. Americans have a great deal of know-how and the branch plants in Canada have all the support of the large multinational corporation with its headquarters in the United States. Private enterprise seems to some people a threat to Canadian liberal democracy rather than a bulwark of freedom.

It is worth examining this phenomenon if Americans wish to understand the problems that they are facing politically in other countries. For if Americans cannot satisfy Canadians of their good intentions, then clearly their hopes of being accepted in other countries, particularly developing areas, are doomed. (One alternative of course, is for the United States to abandon its policy of a liberal democracy, friendly disposed to other liberal democracies, and to accept an imperialist role and all that this implies.)

c) In Quebec there is not only fear by the young people of the military-industrial complex, there is not only the concern of Canadians over American ownership, there is a sense that Quebec itself is dominated by what are called "anglophones" that is to say, English-speaking people, whether Canadians, Americans, or British. French-speaking people in Quebec, the Québecois, sense a threat to their culture and their language. For English is the language of large firms and if the Québecois employee wants promotion outside the province, then clearly he is going to have to speak English. (Of course we may ask whether any language today is equal to English. Even the Russian language is not equal to the English language.) There is a double disadvantage, therefore, for the people of Quebec: they are few in number, six million in all, and they also speak a different language.

However, minorities often underestimate their power. Minorities in many large countries have created trouble and have ultimately established their own autonomy. One is reminded of the Irish at the time when the British Empire stretched across the world[6] and one thinks of the American blacks today.[7] Certainly Canada itself is by no means a helpless orphan. Only twenty-four countries in the world have a larger population. Only eight countries produce more. Only the United States produces more per capita. By some reckonings Canada is the largest country in the world. It is the largest trading partner of the United States. It has had the great advantage for the most part in that it is ignored by its American neighbor.

II. RULE OF THE MAJORITY

At this point we leave economic issues and turn to issues which are perhaps better described as moral and philosophical, or even mathematical. As long ago as 1859 John Stuart Mill concerned himself with the tyranny of the majority. In politics the alternative to majority rule would seem to be rule by the minority. It is often assumed that there is no monolithic majority, merely a majority in the sense of the aggregate vote at election time and the number of seats held by those who support the government in power. Politics, the rule of the majority, as a principle, is based on the assumption that the majority does not misuse its power. To ensure this there is a very elaborate parliamentary procedure in Britain, Canada, and the United States. In the United States there is the filibuster of the American Senate. And in all countries the principle of closure, whereby debate is ended, is carefully guarded. The principle of majority rule assumes that the majority changes at election time. It assumes that there is a coalition of forces, and that even if one party forms a majority party and controls the government, there is at least a coalition of pressure groups and of interests.

This notion of majority rule has long been criticized in continental Europe where liberal democracy did not take root so easily in the nineteenth century. It has been especially criticized by sociologists in Europe who have written books about elites, the ruling class, and the iron law of oligarchy. But now we are seeing a new criticism of majority rule in the Anglo-American world where liberal democracy has for so long been taken for granted. The blacks in the United

States and the French-Canadians in Canada regard themselves as permanent minorities that require special consideration. They consider themselves opposed by permanent majorities. It is astonishing in retrospect that for so long the English majority in Canada ignored the problems of the French-Canadians who formed one-third of their population. The leading textbook in Canada, MacGregor Dawson's *The Government of Canada*, for many years did not pay much attention to Quebec.[8] Indeed some of the standard works on Quebec have been written by Americans such as Everett Hughes, Helen Taft Manning, and Mason Wade. We should also remember that the nineteenth century attitude to minorities was not as tolerant as ours is today. There does seem to have been a basic assumption in the United Kingdom that the surplus Irish population should emigrate. There was the hope that French-Canadians could be outnumbered by the immigration of British people to Canada. There was the hope by many Québecois of *la revanche du berceau* (that the cradle would provide revenge) whereby, through a higher birthrate, French-Canadians would gain predominance. Today, of course, the fear is the opposite. It is thought in Quebec itself that the low birthrate of French-Canadian families may enable English-speaking people, through immigration, to increase their minority. It is interesting to note the awareness of de Tocqueville of America's racial problems 140 years ago[9] and to compare his analysis with such a book as Seymour Lipset's *First New Nation* (1963), a book which deals with blacks of the United States.[10] I might also note that Milton Gordon's *Assimilation in American Life* does not deal by and large with the problems of the American Indians or the blacks.[11]

In Canada, majority rule is exercised in Parliament and by the cabinet. Parliamentary government may have its weaknesses for minorities. The British, despite their efforts to make parliamentary government work at Westminster were never able to secure the full cooperation of the Irish members between 1801 and 1922. Canada fortunately adopted federalism in 1867. This, however, complicated the parliamentary system as this was understood in Britain. The city of Ottawa is not bilingual. The Canadian federal parliamentary system, until very recently, depended on French-Canadian lieutenants who helped English-speaking prime ministers. (French-Canadian prime ministers did not have English-Canadian lieutenants.) The backbenchers in Ottawa are relatively powerless and this is important when one considers the role of French-Canadian MP's in the parliamentary system. They are a minority, and in addition are backbenchers. In Parliament itself, English has, until quite recently, been the dominant language.

Even cabinet government, the term which is nowadays used to describe the political system in the United Kingdom, is different in Canada from its counterparts elsewhere. Unlike the British cabinet, the cabinet in Canada has to represent the various regions of the country. Collective responsibility and secrecy, two established principles of cabinet government, make life difficult for French-Canadian cabinet ministers: they have to bow to the decisions of the majority. If that decision is contrary to French-Canadian interests, they are labeled *vendus*. The only alternative is to resign. It is interesting to note that according to Peter Newman, Jean Marchand was able to make his voice felt in Pearson's cabinet largely by threatening to resign.[12] This is not the proper way to make parliamentary and cabinet government work. French-Canadians, once they have agreed to serve in the federal cabinet or Parliament, tend to lose touch with the Province of Quebec. To many Québecois the Quebec government is the government of French-Canadians and the Ottawa government something slightly alien. They are aware that in 1917 and 1942 the Canadian cabinet voted in favor of conscription despite the hostility of the French-Canadian minority. Over fifty years ago Robert Michels wrote a famous book called *Political Parties* which dealt with what he called the iron law of oligarchy. It would be interesting to have a Canadian analysis of the iron law of majority rule in Canada. One side effect of the parliamentary cabinet system as practiced in Canada seems to be excessive casualties among those French-Canadians who try to make the system work. There is a long history of illness and sudden death of active French-Canadian politicians. Though this has never been analyzed, one may speculate on the political pressures they must bear.

The status of the Province of Quebec, which is one of the ten provinces of Canada, is not altogether clear. It is not, of course, a province like the others. But it does not have a *statut particulier*; it is not an "associate state" as many would wish. Still less is it a separate state as the separatists have hoped for. One proposal has been that Canada should be regarded as a country of two founding races. The Royal Commission on Bilingualism and Biculturalism was set up in the

1960s on this assumption.[13] Canada was assumed to be the homeland of two founding races. Unfortunately, approximately one-third of Canadians are neither British nor French in origin. And many of those who are British in origin are Scottish, Irish, or Welsh and not English. French-Canadians, of course, traditionally claim as French much of what is today North America. Only 120 years ago Francis Parkman in his travels to the West would refer to Canadians as people who normally spoke French.[14] Quebec today is one of ten provinces, though it comprises one-third of the population.

The Province of Ontario also comprises one-third of the population of Canada. This means that the other eight provinces among them have another third. But if Ontario, as the largest and richest province is only one of ten provinces, why should Quebec be so concerned about its status? The explanation is that Ontario is the heartland of Canada. Every other province feels that it is part of "outer Canada." The capital city, Ottawa, is in Ontario and there is some identity of interest between Ottawa and the Province of Ontario. Quebec's status is very different.

Some have seen a new role for French-Canadians in recent years. It is clear that the government of Quebec is firmly in French-Canadian hands and that government administration is carried on largely in the French language. But since Mr. Trudeau has become prime minister, French-Canadians for the first time have held leading portfolios in Ottawa. The French-Canadian members of the cabinet are very able men and very much in command of the situation. It remains to be seen, however, whether this trend implies that Canada shall henceforth be controlled by an elite able to converse in both languages and to move easily between two cultures.[15]

One can see the changes in Canada quite clearly by an examination of some of the books written about the country. The early editions of Dawson's *Government of Canada*, as we have seen, said little about Quebec. Recent books by Ramsay Cook[16] and Pierre Trudeau[17] on the federal government of Canada stress the role of French-Canadians. Writings by such men as Daniel Johnson,[18] former premier of Quebec and René Lévesque,[19] the leader of the *Parti Québecois*, the separatist party, point to the possibility of a distinct and separate Quebec.

Sectionalism is a fascinating and worrying matter. As long ago as 1886 there were many in England who thought that the separatist movement in Ireland was overrated.[20] In 1968 at a panel of the American Political Science Association, I was assured that sectionalism in the United States was dead.

What then is to be our conclusion? It would seem that majority rule is defensible if the alternative is to be ruled by the minority, if the majority obeys the rules of the game, if there is shifting popular allegiance at election time, and if the most important forces such as pressure groups do not comprise a monolithic majority. But majority rule is inadequate if it ignores sectional feelings. For a minority can become a majority if its own section becomes independent. Canadians remember attempts by the American Confederacy to establish an independent government in 1861. They are not sure what would happen if French-Canadians were to decide at some point during the present decade that they wished also to become independent. Majority rule is also inadequate if the rules have been set by a conquering majority without reference to the minority. Who set the rules in Canada? Moreover, popular support in subcultures may go first to local representatives. It is important that we study Canada, and for that matter other countries, with an understanding of the different points of view of subcultures. Nationalism has always been a major force. But for many people today, nationalism may not mean Canadian or British nationalism, but Welsh, Scottish or French-Canadian nationalism.

Canada is fortunate at present in that it has a leading federal party in the Liberal Party. This party has support in Ontario and Quebec. The main opposition party, the Conservative Party, has very little support in the Province of Quebec, where conservatives prefer the *Union Nationale*.[21] The New Democratic Party, the party of the trade unions and of socialism, also lacks support in Quebec. In Quebec itself, there is another party called the Créditistes that seems to be something like the party of Poujade in the French Fourth Republic. In the Quebec election on 29 April 1970, the Liberals won a handsome majority. But the real significance of that election was the decline of the other main party, the *Union Nationale*. Even more significant was the success of the *Parti Québecois* which attracted 23 percent of the vote. If one considers that this 23 percent was probably 30 percent of the total French-Canadian vote and if, on the whole, this was a vote by young people, then clearly we may have to face the possibility of a two-party Quebec divided between a federalist and a separatist party. Traditionally, in the parliamentary system, through the give and take between parties, the revolutionary party (e.g. the early British Labour Party) modifies its stand. It remains to be seen whether this will happen with the *Parti Québecois*, and whether, if it attains power, it will abandon separatism. (If Irish history is to be our guide, it will not.)

It is however necessary to go beyond the economic problems faced by Canadians in the control of the economy by American corporations and to go beyond the political problems of an anglophone majority government. The question of the Constitution itself is now being raised.

III. CHALLENGE TO THE CONSTITUTION

It is arguable that Canada has no constitution, that it has only the British North America Act of 1867 passed by the British Parliament. There is disagreement over the "repatriation of the Constitution" which some people urge. Strictly speaking Canada does not have a constitution and since the British North America Act was never a Canadian act it can hardly be repatriated. But to understand Canada's problem with the constitution, it is useful to put Canada's political development in a perspective with which Americans are familiar.

A. THE UNITED STATES: THE EXTENSION OF POLITICAL DEMOCRACY

It is taken for granted that in 1776 Americans obtained self-determination, in 1863 freedom for the slaves, in 1920 votes for women, and since 1957 votes for an increasing number of blacks. At the same time there has been an extension of the two-party system to all states of the union; no longer are northern states generally Republican and southern states solidly Democratic. Today in most states there is a party contest. The American dream has been one of extending the franchise and of encouraging competition between two political parties. It is sometimes assumed that everything else—and everything which is good—flows from this achievement. Government, it is assumed, responds to the popular will, and the parties adapt to this will. Third parties therefore are assimilated into the two-party mainstream.

B. Outside the United States: A New Party

Sweden and Great Britain have seen in the twentieth century the emergence of new parties, the Social Democratic Party[22] and the Labour Party. We therefore find some limitation to theories of elections popular in the United States, for example, V. O. Key's theory[23] of landslide, realigning, reinstating[24] and reaffirming elections. This American theory does not allow for the basic change in parliamentary systems, the emergence of new socialist parties. These new parties have changed the nature of politics, especially in Britain, as much as has the extension of the franchise. As Duverger pointed out some years ago, socialist parties were created outside Parliament and only later established their own parliamentary parties. They have depended upon national organizations of a permanent character which do not come alive only at election time. These parties are linked with trade unions and thus have a powerful base among the working people. They have made other parties (Conservatives, Liberals, Republicans, and Democrats), which Duverger calls caucus parties, seem archaic in organization. When Duverger first wrote about parties in the early 1950s, his view of American parties was rejected in the United States.[25] But in the last few years it has become accepted,[26] largely because of the growing concern over the adaptability of the Republican and Democratic parties.

C. New Regimes

In some countries, the most notable feature of modern political life has been the exchange of one regime for another. In France there have been the Third, Fourth, and Fifth Republics, in addition to the wartime government of Marshal Pétain.[27] In Germany the Weimar Republic was succeeded by Hitler's tyranny and then by the Bonn Republic. In Italy, the early monarchical constitutional democracy was replaced by Mussolini's Fascist regime and then by the postwar democratic republic. If we omit the periods during which Pétain, Hitler, and Mussolini were in power, we find that there has been a new constitution, often within the same liberal democratic framework. In other words, in France, in Italy, and in Germany, there has been not only the extension of the franchise and the emergence of new political parties but also the introduction of new regimes.

D. NEW SOCIETIES

In some countries, particularly after revolution, a new society has been created. France is assumed to be very different since the end of the *ancien régime* in 1789. Soviet Russia is assumed to be very different from the Russia of the Czars before 1917. In the United States there is argument over the implications of 1776 and of the Constitution which followed the revolution. Some think there was a new society but an old polity. Certainly it is assumed that insofar as "feudalism" in a loose sense was extended to America through British colonialism, it ended with the Revolution. The United States became a "bourgeois democracy" (in a loose sense).

If we accept the notion that modern political life consists of the extension of the franchise, the growth of parties, the possible emergence of new parties, the transition of one regime to another, always with the possibility of a revolution and the creation of a new society, how does Canada fit into this historical analysis? Clearly, the nineteenth century saw in Canada, as elsewhere, the extension of liberal democracy through the extension of the franchise and the growth of political parties.[28] Canada, like Britain and Sweden, has seen the development of a new party on a socialist base. The old Cooperative Commonwealth Federation or CCF gave way in 1960 to the New Democratic Party, the equivalent of the British Labour Party of Canada. But Canada has also experienced new regimes. In 1763 the English conquered Quebec. In 1774 the Quebec Act established a peculiar form of government for Quebec different from that of the English-speaking colonies of North America. There followed constitutional acts in 1791 and 1840 regulating the political organization of Canada. In 1867 of course, there was the establishment of the present Dominion of Canada.

But since 1867, Canada has not had a new regime. As for a new society, it is arguable that there has been no great watershed since the Conquest of 1763 (if only because 1774 preserved the system of Quebec). However, there have been many changes. Canada today is an advanced industrial society. It would seem that Canada has demonstrated the possibility of changing without a revolution of a sort that was apparently necessary in the United States, in France, and continental Europe, or even since 1869 without requiring a new regime.

But when we turn from Canada as such to the Province of Quebec in 1970 and note the demands for change that have been made, a different perspective emerges. Anglophones in Canada are puzzled by the *Parti Québecois*. Do the French-Canadians want a new party, such as the *Parti Québecois*, rather than a transformation of the old parties? If the *Parti Québecois* becomes a powerful party, will it demand a new regime rather like the new regime characterized by France? Or is there a demand not only for a new party and for a new regime, but for a new society at least for the Province of Quebec, a society separate from that of Canada and which is French, republican, presidential and socialist—perhaps different in its presidential and socialist form from other societies. Canada by definition, has had to be a somewhat conservative country reacting against the United States. Presumably Quebec could be original in both its political attitudes and political organization because it is so different in its history from both English Canada and the United States. Perhaps some schematic Cartesians in Quebec discern the "end of feudalism" in 1763, and the end of "bourgeois colonial domination" in the 1970s.

The reaction of anglophones in Canada to this development varies enormously. The conservatives tend to regard 1867 as the final act when Canada was set up much as the United States was established in 1787–1789. However, few conservatives are against change entirely. This makes Canada very different from the United States where the Constitution is sacrosanct and opposition can be called un-American. The advantage of a parliamentary monarchical and evolutionary system is that there are no watersheds and much greater flexibility.

The moderates of English Canada tend to regard the British North America Act as a useful document but one which can be amended, perhaps drastically. They support the monarchy but do not regard it as an essential feature of the system. If Quebec insists, there may have to be wholesale overhaul of the British North America Act, particularly its archaic language, which is apparent from the first page.[29]

A few anglophones are radical enough to consider a complete overhaul as essential. But many people outside the French-Canadian community are not sure what the *Parti Québecois* really wants. And of course the people in Quebec are unwilling to spell out their demands too carefully because of a possible hostile reaction.

It needs to be realized that the French-speaking Canadians also are not united. The conservatives merely want a radical overhaul of the Constitution and a greater role for the provinces, especially the Province of Quebec. The moderates might well opt for a new regime. Daniel Johnson, former premier for Quebec, argued that if changes were possible in 1763, 1774, 1791, 1840, and 1867, further changes should be conceivable. After all, "Canada" has changed a lot since 1763. At one time it comprised French-speaking North America. Later, from 1791 to 1867, it comprised "Upper and Lower Canada," the present provinces of Quebec and Ontario. Since 1867 it has comprised the Dominion of Canada from sea to sea (and, since 1949, Newfoundland). There are some people in Quebec who believe the term "Canada" should comprise everything except the Province of Quebec! The radicals in Quebec are, of course, suspected of wanting a new society which is not only independent but will go its separate way. For some, a separate state, rather like Finland (1918) or Norway (1905), is what is desired. For some, Quebec would be an associate state, part of a Canadian or possibly North American common market. Such persons argue that nobody really has complete sovereignty today. But for many the situation is unclear. When General de Gaulle shouted "*Québec libre*," it meant different things to different people. Who in their right mind would oppose the notion of Quebec as a free society?

It is questionable whether all these challenges are really threats to liberal democracy. They may mean greater democracy in the form of domestic controls over the economy, or some restriction on the majority which rules the country, or possibly a new constitution. We need to consider the possibility that the American northern states were perhaps misguided in not letting the South obtain its independence in the Confederacy. We realize that it was probably wrong to try to assimilate Ireland throughout the centuries. Sweden was probably sensible to let Finland in 1809, and then Norway in 1905 become independent. Today the Scandinavian countries seem more capable of cooperation than ever before; while the Irish are not considered foreigners in England. Perhaps one can take unity too seriously.

IV. CONCLUSION

a) Is American economic imperialism a threat to Canadian democracy? American economic imperialism, if we must use such a term, is no more a threat to Canadian democracy than it is to American democracy. However, it may be a threat to Canadian independence. But complaints about the power of big businesses often ignore the extraordinary powers that governments wield, particularly if they have the support of the voters. American policies in the last two or three years have indicated that the American voter concerned about pollution or about the war in Vietnam has much greater power than many people believed possible a few years ago. Canada, for its part, is more powerful than many Canadians realize. Ontario alone has a gross domestic product greater than that of half of the members of the United Nations. The United States is hardly going to absorb 20 million unwilling people into the Union on top of its own pressing problems. Canadian independence therefore depends on the determination of the Canadian people. So far the advantages of American investment in Canada have seemed to outweigh the advantages of nationalism. The governments are increasingly watchful, and much of the former liberalism which characterized Canadian economic policies is being eroded.

b) Is majority rule a satisfactory principle? Majority rule is a necessary, but not a sufficient principle. All men are not equal. The majority may be a permanent majority. Politics is a forum enabling the weak to protect themselves against the strong. Thus voters in politics, like employees in business, have to stand up against those who have economic power. Where a minority feels a grave injustice it may incline toward separation. Quebec, of course, is not like Ireland but in some ways finds itself in the position of Norway before the separation of 1905 because of the different attitude to external powers. "Majority rule" in Quebec seems to mean rule by the dominant anglophone culture of the rest of Canada. Hence the need to protect the minority. It is arguable that perhaps this could be best preserved if Quebec had its own state and its own control over radio, TV, etc. The arguments for Canadian independence from the United States (and the United Kingdom) could be applied to Quebec itself.

Where there is a minority, one solution is to give it overrepresentation and to allow special representation by its own organization. In the United States the Senate does tend to protect the smaller states of the Union. There is nothing quite comparable in the Canadian parliamentary system. The counterpoise to the authority of the federal government tends to lie with the government of Quebec. This is as though, instead of southern senators defending southern politics in the United States federal system, the defense of the southern way of life lay with the governors of the states and their legislatures. The aim of minorities everywhere is of course to avoid assimilation by the majority. Perhaps the Canadian political system requires modification.

c) Would a new constitution destroy Canada? According to Mr. Pearson the cry of "Québec libre" would mean the destruction of Canada. Canada, as we know it today, would presumably be destroyed if it were replaced by something else. We need to go back to the nineteenth century to note the similar fears, particularly in the British Empire. There was the fear that if Ireland had its own home rule then the empire would be destroyed. Yet countries have survived despite even greater changes than are contemplated in Quebec. Canada could, it is feared, become like the Indian subcontinent divided between India and Pakistan. However, the possibility that Quebec would hold the rest of Canada to ransom is increasingly remote not only because of the movement of the economy westward, Japan taking the place of Britain, not only through the use of the aircraft, not only because the Northwest Passage has been opened, but also because the St. Lawrence Seaway is used not only by English Canada but by the United States. Quebec is hardly in a position to prevent the use of the St. Lawrence by English Canadians. And indeed, Quebec might have less bargaining power it it were separate. Moreover, a separate Quebec would mean that the new state would inherit the problem of a minority, as 20 percent or more of its people are English-speaking. It is doubtful whether the assimilation of the English people into Quebec life would be more successful than the assimilation of French-Canadians to the English.

d) How unique is Canada? Provinces in Canada are not like the American states; they are fewer in number and more powerful. The conferences between the federal and provincial governments are now part of the political system. (Mr. Pearson made the mistake of trying to mediate between the federal government, which he represented, and the provincial governments!)

Ottawa is not like Washington: it is in Ontario. There are plans for a federal capital district which would cover part of Quebec. The French-Canadian migration into Ontario and into Ottawa is not really comparable to the black migration to Washington. There is a greater tradition in Canada of an elite public service. Parliamentary government in Canada is not a copy of British parliamentarianism. There is no Establishment. There is no London. Party leaders are elected by conventions, somewhat more comparable to American conventions than British party elections. Canada's system is a continental polity which must satisfy all the regions. The two main cultures are very different, more different in fact than the difference between parts of Scandinavia, between Ireland and England, between the South and North of the United States. It is possible that Canada can compare itself with the European Economic Community. Indeed the French-Canadians talk of the need for integration of communities as distinct from the assimilation of individuals. This point of view is worth greater examination. It needs to be remembered that communities everywhere are concerned about assimilation. The Welsh have talked recently about their own fears of cultural genocide. Many articles imported into Canada have the words "made in Scotland" stamped on them. If the Scots can do this, why not allow the Québecois to say "made in Quebec"?

Canada is not in quite as serious a situation as many Canadians fear. It may well be a semisovereign state, but then so are a number of other countries. It may be that the Province of Quebec is quasi-sovereign, but it is also possible that the whole notion of sovereignty is outmoded. It is worth remembering that in the 1680s after the painful civil war in England, John Locke in his *Second Treatise on Civil Government* did not use the term "sovereignty" at all and was somewhat vague in his determination of where ultimate power lay. It may well be that we can go back to John Locke—not to read into his work what the Americans have read into it about liberalism and individualism, but to discover the plain fact that sovereignty is not as simple and as important as many of us troubled about the unity of our countries have been tempted to believe.

NOTES

1. Herbert F. Quinn, *The Union Nationale; a Study in Quebec Nationalism* (Toronto: University of Toronto, 1963).
2. Robert R. Alford, *Party and Society: The Anglo-American Democracies* (Chicago: Rand McNally, 1963).
3. Seymour Martin Lipset, "Anglo-American Society," *International Encyclopedia of Social Sciences*, 1 (New York: Crowell, 1968).
4. Jean-Jacques Servan-Schreiber, *The American Challenge* (New York: Atheneum, 1968).
5. Melville H. Watkins, *Foreign Ownership and the Structure of Canadian Industry* (Ottawa: Queen's Printer, 1968).
6. J. L. Hammond, *Gladstone and the Irish Nation* (Hamden, Conn.; Archon, 1964).
7. Donald R. Matthews, J. M. Prothro, *Negroes and the New Southern Politics* (New York: Harcourt, Brace and World, 1966).
8. R. McGregor Dawson, *The Government of Canada* (Toronto: University of Toronto, 1947). Most recent edition is 1964.
9. Alexis de Tocqueville, "The Present and Probable Future Condition of the Three Races that Inhabit the Territory of the United States," *Democracy in America*.
10. Seymour M. Lipset, "Epilogue: Some Personal Views on Equality, Inequality and Comparative Social Science," *The First New Nation* (New York: Basic Books, 1963).
11. Milton M. Gordon, *Assimilation in American Life* (New York: Oxford, 1964).
12. Peter Newman, *The Distemper of Our Times* (Toronto: McClelland & Stewart, 1968).
13. Royal Commission on Bilingualism and Biculturalism: Preliminary Report, 1965; Book I. General Introduction; The Official Languages, 1967; Book II. Education, 1968; Book III. The Work World, 1969 (Ottawa: Queen's Printer).
14. Francis Parkman, *The California and Oregan Trail* (1849).
15. "Canadian Culture in the 1960's," *Times Literary Supplement*, 28 August, 1969.
16. Ramsay Cook, *Canada and the French Canadian Question* (Toronto, Macmillan, 1966).
17. Pierre Elliott Trudeau, *Federalism and the French Canadians* (Toronto: Macmillan, 1968).
18. Daniel Johnson, *Egalité ou Indépendance* (Montréal: Éditions de l'Homme, 1965).

19. René Lévesque, *An Option for Quebec* (Toronto: McClelland and Stewart, 1968).

20. J. L. Hammond, *Gladstone and the Irish Nation*.

21. Herbert F. Quinn, *The Union Nationale*.

22. Douglas V. Verney, *Parliamentary Reform in Sweden 1866–1921* (Oxford: Clarendon, 1957).

23. V. O. Key, *Parties, Politics and Pressure Groups*, 5th ed. (New York: Crowell, 1964).

24. Philip Converse, et al., "Stability and Change in 1960: a Reinstating Election," *American Political Science Review* 55, (June 1961), 269–280.

25. Maurice Duverger, *Les Partis Politiques*, reviewed by Alfred De Grazia in *American Political Science Review* 46 (June 1952), 563–564; *Political Parties* (New York: Wiley, 1954).

26. Samuel P. Huntington, *Political Order in Changing Societies* (New Haven & London: Yale, 1968).

27. D. W. S. Lidderdale, *The Parliament of France* (New York: Praeger, 1952).

28. Leon Epstein, "A Comparative Study of Canadian Parties," *American Political Science Review* 58, 1 (March 1964), 46–59.

29. British North America Act. See R. M. Dawson, *The Government of Canada*, Appendix.

8: THE WITHERING AWAY OF WESTERN LIBERAL DEMOCRACY
Anthony Hartley

This really is a somewhat pessimistic title. On the other hand, we may console ourselves with the thought that, like the withering away of the state in Marxist terminology, it may never come to pass. It is always dangerous to extrapolate what is happening now, to believe that present trends will continue—only more so. This seems to me to be the trouble with all the futurism that makes our flesh creep so nowadays. We have been told so much about the terrors of the year 2000 that it never occurs to us that things will change. I was recently reading an article in which it was predicted that when there were forty or fifty nuclear power stations along the Mississippi the waters of the river would be heated to such an extent that the entire climate of the Midwest would be changed—something of great significance, I should imagine, to many people here. But the point is that there are so many variables in this kind of prediction that it is very unlikely to be realized. We wait for the year 2000 in much the same state of mind as men in the tenth century waited for the year 1000. The futurists predict the second coming to us and point to rains of blood and dragons flying over various parts of the world—much as the Anglo-Saxon chroniclers did in their time. But I suspect we may all wake up in the year 2000 and find that nothing so very much has happened. I think that the climate of the Middle West is going to be with us for some centuries to come.

So that when I talk today about the withering away of Western liberal democracy, I do not want you to think that I am predicting something which will inevitably take place. I am simply pointing out a number of things which make democracy as liberal westerners have conceived of it more difficult to carry on.

Now what do we mean when we talk of democracy? There are

definitions ranging from Aristotle to Disraeli and onwards, but I am not going to discuss those—it would be imprudent to do so in a university setting! What I should say that we mean by democracy is the ability of every citizen to play some kind of institutionalized political role in the society in which he lives. Institutionalized because a totally anarchic society is not exactly a democracy, and, equally, a political role can be assumed by the ordinary citizen who takes a weapon and assassinates a tyrant, but this does not mean that the society in which he lives is a political democracy; it means the reverse. No, what is meant by a political democracy is a society whose institutions are so arranged that they afford to each citizen the maximum amount of control over his own destiny through political action.

At this point, of course, we come to a difficulty. Who is to decide whether in fact a citizen exerts some influence on his own destiny? It is one of the charges made by Marxists and by members of what is called the New Left (but is really something a good deal more traditional) that the democratic system in the United States deprives the citizen of such influence. There is, so it is said, a "power structure" which really rules and is only veiled by what might be called a pretense at democratic institutions. People do not control their futures through their votes. They only think they do. In reality, men in bedrooms filled with cigar smoke or in the boardrooms of corporations decide what will become of the average American.

Now, history is rarely conspiratorial, and the paranoid intellectual style of the New Left has done it a great deal of harm—amongst other things it has made most of its arguments circular, apt to prove anything or nothing. But the fact that such opinions about the character of Western democracy should be prevalent is of great significance in itself. And it is also true that whether or not liberal democracy is in a healthy state depends to a large extent on how its citizens imagine it to be functioning. If they believe their own views and opinions to be expressed satisfactorily through democratic institutions, then those institutions are probably working not too badly. If not, then we have some grounds for criticism and even alarm.

One of the striking facts of the present era is that there is a good deal of dissatisfaction with the workings of liberal democracy. It is criticized by both right-wing and left-wing political groups. I have mentioned the New Left but the dislike of the centralized state which we find in their writings is curiously similar to the attitude adopted by the New Right. Opposition to a gun law, for instance, comes from both groups in the name of a conception of personal freedom which sometimes seems to anyone who has been at all concerned with administration asocial, if not antisocial. Then there is the slogan "community power" which can equally be used on the right or on the left, though for very different purposes. In the one case the objective is to give the poor of the city slums some control over their own local government and thereby raise their conditions of living—it is, of course, very uncertain that "community power" would have any such effect. In the case of the right, "community power" is put forward as a slogan to prevent interference on the part of central government—interference to force through such measures as redistributive taxation, social services, and integration of black and white in the school systems.

On the other hand, there are also some signs in imaginative literature of dissatisfaction with the liberal democratic state as it has evolved over the last decades. Here I refer to a form of writing which can directly reflect criticism of political and social systems since much of it is Utopian: this is science fiction, the popularity of which should make us attach some importance to it as a symptom of social change. Let me summarize for you one typical plot which recurs again and again in different variants. The society of the earth (or of a planet or a galaxy) has been thoroughly organized by social controllers. Every detail of men's lives—even of their sex lives—I might say, above all of their sex lives—has been controlled. They work, play, sleep, and eat to order. Of course, they also think to order. All except one—the hero of the novel. He begins to have doubts about the system. He no longer loves Big Brother or believes in the myth on which the social system is based. He is pursued by the thought police; he frequently has a girl along with him, but eventually succeeds in undermining the rigid social system and bringing it down. There is in all this, you will see, a longing for exemplary heroic political action (I would remind you that Hannah Arendt has defined political action as exemplary public action) as well as a profound distrust of bureaucracy, of the "social engineering" and manipulation of which we are told so much nowadays by sociologists. In other science fiction stories can be found a similar longing for political action tailored to the scale of the individual—action in a setting that recalls the Greek city state, where a speech can turn the tide, a personality cause an audience to follow him.

And you will notice in all this the resemblance to campus politics as they have developed over recent years. I would simply ask the question: Has not campus political activity developed on the scale it has because it affords these satisfactions of the urge towards exemplary political activity while real politics no longer does? In any case, in itself it can be treated as another example of dissatisfaction with the way in which Western liberal democratic systems are organized—a dissatisfaction betrayed unconsciously in the utopian literature of science fiction.

What are the causes obscurely felt behind this dissatisfaction? The obvious one is the bureaucratization of politics and of the administrative decision-making which affects the lives of citizens. The complicated questions that governments have to decide these days are not responsive to the purely moralistic opinions which are the way in which the political views of most of us tend to express themselves. For example, one may dislike the pollution of the Great Lakes, one may say that it is bad—people are constantly saying that it is bad—but then one will not have got very far. A technical decision has then to be taken about what to do. That technical decision may well affect individual citizens, but it is very unlikely that they will understand the reasons for it. It is unlikely that it can even be explained to them. So they will be required to pay more taxes or to install different systems of sewage collection or pay more for their electricity—all without much comprehension of why this should be. Now it may be said that the whole question should be discussed with the "community" in such a way that everyone fully appreciates what is being done, why it is being done, and how it will affect himself. This is very easy to say, but it is also very easy to reply, "Do you want the pollution cleared within the next decade or not?" If you do, you cannot possibly give a sort of power of veto to any group of all the inhabitants of the area around the lakes. Even local discussions, if thoroughly carried on, would take far too much time. So the most that can be done is to decide through Congress and state assemblies and so forth that the officials (the much-abused bureaucrats without whom nothing would get done) should work out a scheme to carry out the general political intention. That scheme will have as its general aim the cleansing of the lakes, but its technical details do have to be left to experts. No other course is possible when an administrative operation on this scale is to be undertaken.

There are, of course, a whole range of decisions in which "participation" by the individual citizen is equally impossible and lack of participation is equally unsatisfactory. People wanting to buy houses naturally complain about high mortgage rates, but then they also object to an inflationary rise in prices. Since they are not necessarily economists, they are not aware that the one is intended to act as a brake upon the other. Here, of course, the connecting link ought to be political leadership. In broad questions of this nature which touch upon the lives of most citizens, there is no substitute for the political leader—prime minister or president or chancellor—explaining the measures taken and the reasons for them. Where such explanations are reasonably presented, they will be accepted. Unfortunately, it has not always been the case that democratic political leaders have spoken out to their electorates. Then we come up against the so-called credibility gap. The less such leaders tell their peoples the truth the less they will be believed in the future. It would be banal here to quote Abraham Lincoln.

Clashes between the citizen and bureaucracy in which the latter acts in an arbitrary or tyrannical fashion are a contributing factor to the resentment of the individual, to his feeling of separation from the government which he is meant to control. In my own country, Great Britain, government and local authorities have powers to make compulsory purchases of land required for various public purposes—widening of roads, building of municipal housing, and so on. These are measures justifiable in view of a greater general good, but which have also given rise in their operation to injustice or a well-founded sense of grievance in specific cases. In democracies there should always be a remedy for the arbitrary decisions of officials, an appeal to some higher and more impartial instance. It is thoroughly unsatisfactory and ultimately damaging to democratic government when officials are judges in their own cause. One of the things that Western liberal societies badly need is some cognizance taken of administrative law—a process in which the French Conseil d'Etat might serve for a model.

Basically, however, the difficulties of applied democracy in the process of government of advanced industrial societies remain difficulties of communication: rapidity of communication as well as possibility of communication. Take a case such as the measures introduced by the French government to meet the run on the franc in November 1968. There was no time to consult even political opinion —let alone the various categories of people vitally interested in the fate of the national currency. Any delay would have increased the amount of money going out of France to a catastrophic figure—it was nearly catastrophic as it was. And there is a whole range of subjects of which as much could be said. It is unlikely that the opinions of the average citizens on defense matters will be given much weight by any government. The government's view of these matters will be dictated by knowledge which is necessarily kept secret and by calculations which have been growing in complication yearly. Such a question as the pros and cons of the SALT negotiations can never be totally debated in public. It would be a delusion in the case of either party to imagine that they can. Anyone who has been the least bit involved in the world of defense thinking will realize that there is a vast area of knowledge (the underside of the iceberg) which never gets into the daily press at all, though some of it is referred to in specialized publications such as *Survival*, the journal of the London Institute for Strategic Studies.

All this makes it very hard to have an informed public opinion on questions such as the desirability of constructing antiballistic missile systems (ABM). Basically, the debate between the present administration and its critics on this subject has not been an open debate at all. Each side has got its experts. Each side has presented its own case without any regard for the points made by the other. You pay your penny and you take your choice. The idea of an educated citizenry deciding an important question of international relations with a full knowledge of the issues has somehow got lost.

But I think that the point has been made. It is quite clear that even parliaments or congresses now find it extremely difficult to do much in the way of real criticism of a government in areas where that government has access to better information, and that area usually includes defense and certain aspects of foreign affairs. Between the democratic political process and the realization in practice of governmental policies there intervenes more and more a corps of technicians without whom decisions cannot be translated into action and by whom they are sometimes changed before they become action. This is the dilemma. It is easy enough to see why it causes dissatisfaction among those who mistrust the processes of bureaucracy, and it is harder to understand the necessity for those processes than to distrust them. But, of course, it is almost impossible to see how one would replace a professional body of civil servants or skip the administrative stage in the realization of political decisions.

This is one problem which leads to the separation of people from government in Western liberal democracies (of course, the whole thing is worse in totalitarian regimes, whether Communist or right-wing). But there is an additional factor which comes into play. This is what I should call the increasing Bonapartism which is making itself felt in democratic countries. Modern publicity, television and the tendency of party organizations to try to back a winning figurehead all lead to a concentration of attention and power on the person of the party leader. He is the one who will carry the banner during the electoral period. He is the one who, if he and his party succeed, will be so identified with its fate in the public mind that no one can get rid of him without risking the destruction of the party itself. This is the so-called charismatic style of leadership, and it may range from the widely publicized and irrelevant fact that Mr. X has a happy family life to all the nonsense about getting countries moving (as if they were trains) which we hear at election time. The style has its disadvantages which might be summarized in the phrase "up like a rocket and down like the stick," but it does lead to a concentration of power. The national leaders in question can appeal over the heads of elected assemblies by television. Their parties are unlikely to revolt against them since their means of manipulation and patronage give them powerful means of pressure within the party machine. They can be removed by any means only with great difficulty. It is they who, through the TV screen, are known to the country. Their mere presence at the head of affairs gives them an enormous political advantage over any rival.

But if there has been a concentration of political power in the head of the executive in Western liberal democracies, there has also been an increasing concentration of administrative power. In the United States, to take one example, the president is constitutionally bound to get a declaration of war approved by Congress. But does anyone any longer believe this to be possible in the case of a full-scale "total" war? If enemy missiles were sighted coming towards the United States, the decision on how to respond would rest with the president and the president alone. Even in the Cuban crisis of 1962, there was little attempt to formally consult Congress, though congressional leaders were told something. The president of the United States, the president of France and the prime minister of England all have far greater powers than their opposite numbers of the past—their democratic opposite numbers I should say, since clearly Napoleon III in France was not comparable. And there is a serious problem here—one aspect is emphasized by the momentous nature of decisions concerning nuclear war and the impossibility of spreading responsibility for them. This however may not be the most serious aspect of the evolution of the head of a winning party in a democracy.

For what has been taking place is the substitution for parliamentary government as the nineteenth century knew it of government by an executive advised by civil servants and only dimly affected by an elected assembly. The tightening of party organization, the technical complication of the questions government has to decide and the charisma imposed on the head of the party by the habitual techniques of public relations have all combined to make government less responsive to the fears and desires of the average citizen; to make it, if you like, more paternalistic and technocratic. In the nineteenth century, Bagehot could describe the British cabinet as a committee of the House of Commons, Bryce could talk of the Speaker of the House of Representatives as the second most important man in America. Neither of these statements would be true today, and taken together the change adds up to a downgrading of the elective assembly in each case. More recently it was a specific objective of Gaullists in 1958 to end the "government by assembly," which was their term of reproach for the Fourth Republic. As everyone knows, the French National Assembly has done very little governing or even influencing of governments since 1958.

It is therefore possible to say that the political structures of countries have responded to modern administrative needs by becoming more and more self-sufficient and that the process of political decision or choice has more and more been pushed to the top where elections are simplified to a choice between two policies on one particular issue, if they are not decided purely on the personal characteristics of the two contestant leaders. It is undeniable that popularity polls and public relations techniques have done Western liberal democracy some damage.

For naturally, a democratic government that becomes irresponsive to political pressures and insensitive to dissatisfaction on the part of its citizens casts discredit on democracy as such. The causes—the remote causes—of the student disorders of May 1968 in Paris still remain somewhat unclear, but it is probably not too far off the mark to associate them with a certain stiffening of the joints on the part of the Gaullist regime, a certain lack of appreciation of the state of opinion and a tendency to treat even justified criticism as lèse-majesté. In such cases, the result is a violent outbreak which sooner or later disintegrates the minimum of common ground needed to operate democratic institutions at all. In fact, one need not be favorable to the insensitivity of government or the lofty indifference of certain types of political leadership to believe that minorities who resort to violent protest are probably contributing to give the coup de grace to democratic systems which may be insufficiently in touch with those whom they are meant to serve, but which are probably better than anything that is likely to replace them.

Anarchic behavior on the part of small extremist factions is both traditionally ineffective in political terms and destructive of liberal institutions. If those factions are what is called "progressive" (progressive "splinter-groups" like the various factions of the SDS here or in Germany), then it is especially unlikely that, in any situation where the democratic rule of law has broken down, they will be gainers. Significantly, in France recently the result of left-wing factional violence within the faculties of the University of Paris has been the emergence of genuine Fascist groups—Occident and the like—for the first time since World War II. It is, in fact, usually the left that is the loser from the disappearance of a viable liberal democracy. To remain viable, democracies must be able to combat the threat of such small groups in their midst, but they must also try to remove the conditions in which widespread dissatisfaction with the workings of government provides an atmosphere in which such groups can work.

This problem is very difficult. As I have pointed out above, the conditions in which modern administrative techniques can operate are hardly likely to be changed. Administratively, we cannot abandon the computer for the abacus simply because the calculations of the latter are more easily explained to onlookers. There are occasions on which the abacus is more efficient, on which administration of rather small units may produce the best results. We should not choose size for the sake of size. But the fact must be faced that if economies of scale are to be effected and the costs per head of local government and national government reduced, then big administrative units—units far removed from the New England town—will be necessary. It is all very well to have your own police chief in your own local community, but to have forty-three different police forces in Westchester County costs more and is more inefficient than a unified force would be. If "community power" were seriously introduced—apart from making New York a bit like G. K. Chesterton's London of *The Napoleon of Notting Hill*—it would also lower the standards of city services in the poorer areas and raise them in the richer ones. Is that what is wanted? Part of the point of city-wide or state-wide administration, of the kind of connurbation authority that exists in the Greater London Council, is to redistribute the yield of taxation and also the skills of administration so that poorer areas are brought up to the level of richer ones. That is the objective, even if it is not always carried out. "Community power," on the other hand, seems intended to let everyone stew in his own juice regardless of whether that juice is particularly nourishing or not.

It is therefore very hard to suggest ways in which the citizen can really be consulted about the processes of administration once the general political decision to go in a certain direction has been taken. In cases of individual injustice when decisions bear hardly on one individual or another, then redress can come from the courts or, in Europe, from a special administrative court. But, ultimately, it is only the explanations furnished by political leaders which can justify the administrative measures that affect the lives of citizens. That is why it is important that such measures should be brought forward at the time of elections as public issues and debated as such. For the public, having willed the ends, must will the means. That is also why I think one may have grave doubts as to whether judicial and administrative action is really the right way to introduce sweeping social reforms, just as the blocking of social reform by judicial rulings was also wrong. If people have voted on a question, they will usually accept the result of that vote even if it goes against them. Speaking purely as an observer, I am not at all sure whether the omission of the political process from racial reforms such as desegregation of schools and so forth is not rather a bad thing. Political questions should be decided politically and not judicially, in my view. A nonelective body taking political action can produce the contrary effect to that intended. This is something that has been seen again and again in history.

Another point which might be made in this connection is that it would be no bad thing if the expectations of citizens of democratic states were somewhat reduced. It is unfortunate that the style of leadership apparently needed to get elected tends to put a premium on a false air of dynamism presented with all the skills of the media, but with little connection with the real situation which the politician will find when he comes to power. They come in with their new societies and new frontiers, huffing and puffing and going to blow away all the troubles of the country—whose citizens naturally expect to go on getting better and better off without any particular effort on their part. Then when the promises are not fulfilled, when something unexpected happens, there is disillusionment: not merely with a particular political leader which might be reasonable, but with the political system which is less reasonable. The first requirement for a sound democratic system is that politicians should not behave like confidence tricksters and citizens should not behave like idiots. Dr. Johnson's reply when someone asked him "So you laugh at schemes of political improvement" was "Why, Sir, most schemes of political improvement are very laughable things." This reply, it seems to me, represents the healthy skepticism of a citizen in a democracy listening to its political leaders. What is called "charismatic leadership" is to some extent a confidence trick. It begins with the promise of a new dynamism and ends with the reality of a credibility gap. A more modest style of leadership, or one which genuinely springs from the personality of the leader concerned and not from the drawing boards of Madison Avenue is better for democratic institutions.

9: THE EUROPEAN COMMUNITY AND CONSTITUTIONAL DEMOCRACY

Bastiaan van der Esch

Preceding papers dealt with challenges to democracy on the national level. These challenges are a direct result of a variety of interrelated social, economic, technological, and psychological factors which in a more or less autonomous way generate changes in our pattern of living, working, and thinking. These primary and largely involuntary factors put ever increasing pressure on constitutional democracy as the only mechanism for conscious, deliberate and organized change which we consider, rightly or wrongly, acceptable in our type of society. Often we find these challenges difficult to meet. The reasons for this are manifold and can be traced to ignorance, indifference, and lack of foresight as well as to a widespread and deliberate refusal to give up privileged positions and the antiquated concepts that support them.

The subject of the present paper is different and yet related. Under the impact of the creation and the development of the European Community, the political landscape in western Europe has changed considerably in the last twenty years.[1] As such, this development is one of the more encouraging examples of democracy's capacity to bring about fairly fundamental changes. At the same time the emergence of the European Community in its turn creates its own demands on constitutional democracy.

The challenge in this respect is double. In the first place and to the extent that the Community qualifies as a new political entity, it is an obvious necessity to give democracy a proper role and place in its construction and management. Of course, only the future can tell what the Community is ultimately going to be. Little doubt is possible however for the political forces which support the Community; these forces are working to make it a political unit in its own right, fully structured politically, economically, and socially and designed to offer western Europe the political, administrative and psychological dimensions best suited to its intrinsic possibilities. The implementation of democratic principles within such a unit is for obvious reasons one of the most vital tasks before us.

The second challenge is of a different nature. It arises from the need to reconcile the emergence of the Community with the exercise of those retained powers on the national level upon which social and economic progress in the member states still depends.

A discussion of the first challenge has to begin with a few words about the Community as it stands today, at the end of the transitional period.

The customs union as defined in the EEC Treaty is operating satisfactorily. The free flow of industrial goods is no longer hampered by customs duties, quantitative restrictions, or fiscal barriers. Technical barriers to trade resulting from regulations concerning quality, composition, technical specifications, etc., remain of considerable importance for certain categories of goods. Machinery exists, however, to deal with this.[2] Furthermore a constant check is being kept on privately induced restraints on intracommunity trade as well as on restrictions which result from such public interventions as subsidies or discriminatory public purchasing policies.

In the agricultural field, the unity of the market has been largely achieved through the system of single prices for the basic agricultural commodities.[3]

Furthermore constant progress is made on the road to freedom of movement of workers, freedom of establishment, and freedom of capital movement, although much remains to be done.

A common commercial policy, embodying the unity of the Community in its trade relations with the rest of the world, is being actively pursued.

Of course not everything is bliss and perfect harmony. Introduction of the added value tax had to be postponed in Italy and Belgium.[4] Not all state trading monopolies have yet been fully adapted to the requirements of the Common Market. A number of internal obstacles to trade remain in force for goods imported from outside the Common Market but which, due to differences in national commercial policies, cannot yet be given the right to free circulation within the market. In particularly complex areas such as transport and energy, the achievement of conditions identical to those of a domestic market is extremely slow.

More important still, the customs union is only a halfway house anyway; beyond it, by implication as well as by design, a certain degree of economic union is necessary. The treaty recognizes this and stipulates certain rather timid steps in that direction. Practical experience of the first twenty years points with great insistence to the same objective. In modern circumstances a common market cannot exist and be operated completely severed from the economy as a whole; that is to say, the social, economic, industrial, financial, and monetary environment in which the goods traded within such a market are produced.

Opinions may vary (and indeed they do) as to the necessary degree of economic union and the best methods to achieve it; but the need as such is not seriously in doubt. In fact, a large part of the Community's activity is devoted to designing and building both the conceptual and procedural framework for more economic union than exists at present.[5]

Finally, to round off this quick stock-taking of the Community today, a few words about the institutions which carry it; i.e., the Commission, the Council, the Court of Justice and the European Parliament. Over the years these have been thoroughly run in. Together they have coped with several major political crises such as the French refusals to negotiate British entry, the French claim that majority voting as provided for in the treaties should not be applied, the French internal economic crisis and the monetary upheavals linked with French devaluation and German revaluation. Similarly, the institutions have handled an enormous work load both in size and variety; in short, whatever their inevitable shortcomings may be, they have successfully matured and gained widespread acceptance.

To support this last point, I may quote a few sentences from a ruling given several years ago by the German Federal Constitutional Court in a case where the nature of the legislative powers vested in the Communities was under discussion. More specifically, the constitutionality of regulations issued by the Council or the Commission of the Community were challenged, on the grounds that these did not conform to certain fundamental constitutional rights to which German citizens are entitled under the German Basic Law, notably in respect to legal protection and remedies. In other words, the constitutionality of Community regulations was challenged on the basis of alleged conflicts with the German Federal Basic Law. This plea was held inadmissible because regulations of the Council or the Commission were not acts of German public authority. In reaching this conclusion the German Federal Constitutional Court defined such regulations as follows:

> The regulations of the Council and the Commission are acts of special supranational public authority created by the Treaty and clearly distinguishable from the state authority of the Member States. The institutions of the EEC exercise sovereign rights of which the Member States have divested themselves in favour of the Community set up by them. The Community itself is neither a state, nor a federal state. It is a gradually integrating Community of a special nature "an interstate institution" in the sense of Article 24 #1 of the Grundgesetz to which the Federal Republic of Germany—like the other Member States—has "transferred" certain sovereign rights. A new public authority was thus created which is autonomous and independant with regard to the state authority of the separate member states.[6]

Similar pronouncements have been made by the European Court,[7] but statements such as these are all the more convincing when they come from sources whose daily responsibilities do not lie with the Community and its activity. What is noteworthy is the emphatic recognition of a political process which is distinct from the one which takes place on the national level within the member states and which pertain to the exercise of the retained national powers. The German Federal Constitutional Court also underlines the prefederal stage in which the Community finds itself, leaving it to the future to unveil when and how the transition to a truly federal construction will be made.

At this point we must return to the challenge this emergence of a new and separate political process on the European level presents to democracy. Basically two observations are sufficient.

A certain degree of parliamentary control over the Community is already exercised by the European Parliament even though by constitutional criteria the role of the Parliament is mainly advisory.[8] It is widely held for that very reason that the role of Parliament does not live up to the minimum requirements of democratic control in keeping with Western European traditions and ambitions.

Let me elaborate both these points.

The European Parliament is not elected directly by the citizens of the Community. It is composed of delegates appointed by the six national parliaments from amongst their members. Germany, France, and Italy each have thirty-six members. Belgium and the Netherlands fourteen, while Luxembourg has six members.

Thus composed, the Assembly is master of its own internal organization and procedure. Supported by a fairly large staff, including research and political liaison officers, it meets on an average of six times a year for a week, mostly in Strasbourg. Whenever an urgent decision has to be made, a number of shorter sessions lasting one or two days are also held, often in Luxembourg. In between, numerous committee meetings take place, mostly in Brussels, preparing the reports to be submitted to the plenary sessions. With such a program, being an active member of the European Parliament is practically a full-time job.

The main task of the European Parliament consists in a close public scrutiny of everything that goes on within the European Community. It discusses the annual general report submitted to it by the Commission. Furthermore, it pronounces itself on the draft proposals that the Commission submits to the Council for adoption and on important acts of a legislative nature which the Commission is entitled to perform in its own right. Finally, the members of Parliament have the right to put written parliamentary questions to the Commission. In 1969, nearly 500 questions were asked, including a number addressed to the Council.

As a result of these various devices, very little of what goes on within the Community escapes public notice and debate. Yet this is not enough. The European Parliament lacks one very basic element of effectiveness and indeed credibility: it does not have the right to vote a motion of censure concerning the activities of the Council. Article 144 of the Treaty gives Parliament such a right against the Commission, but as long as the bulk of the legislative authority is vested in the Council, the power to force the Commission to resign is as effective as whipping the wrong boy. It is small wonder that under such circumstances a motion of censure has rarely been envisaged and never been voted.

The scope of this structural defect in the institutional balance of power is amplified by the fact that the national parliaments, for different reasons, are equally powerless against the individual national ministers who sit on the Council.

Whenever these ministers are interrogated in their respective national parliaments about their actions in the Council, they can explain the most glaring differences between their intentions or convictions and the specific decision reached by the Council by being outvoted or by the need to make concessions in order to gain the day in another matter.

The net result of these arrangements is that the Council as a body escapes parliamentary control on the Community level, while the ministers composing the Council elude control on the national level.

From the beginning, everyone was aware that such a situation could not be allowed to exist forever. Already the ECSC-Treaty and again the EEC-Treaty expressly charged the European Parliament to draw up proposals for election of its members by direct universal suffrage.[9] Such proposals were duly made, but the member states never reached agreement on the subject.[10]

The Commission also threw its weight behind the issue and proposed to strengthen the powers of the European Parliament as early as 1965, notably in budgetary matters.[11] All these efforts were of no avail, mainly because France under General de Gaulle started to combat the Community idea as it was embodied in the treaties which it had signed. France refused to help create what was only the natural adaptation of the initial construction to the system of common financing of certain agricultural measures which had meanwhile been instituted, mainly to take account of French weakness in the industrial sector. As neither the European Parliament and the Commission nor the other member states were willing to abandon their support for modest improvements in the system of democratic control, a temporary stalemate resulted which was broken only recently. On 21 April 1970 the Council adopted a decision which is mainly significant because of the principle which has been vindicated and secured, and much less so because of the policy area to which this principle is being applied.

In order to understand this decision a few words have to be said about the Community arrangements pertaining to agriculture and the way these are financed.

The freedom of movement of agricultural produce within the Community is achieved for the most important commodities by means of a simple support price valid for the whole Common Market. The price of imported agricultural produce is brought up to this level by a system of variable levels at the Community's border. In addition, a system of financial solidarity between the member states has been adopted, covering the cost of exporting surpluses at the lower world market prices. In 1969 the Community fund paid over 2 billion dollars to support these export subsidies. The necessary funds were raised by contributions from the member states in accordance with a fixed scale.

It is this system of shared financial responsibility which provided the political leverage necessary for an extension of democratic control. Contrary to the initial European Coal and Steel Community, the European Economic Community was not given the right to raise its own revenue.[12] Article 201 of the EEC Treaty stipulates, however, that ways and means should be studied to replace the national contributions to the Community budget by resources of the Community itself, in particular by allotting revenue from the common customs tariff to the Community. It is clear that such a step, which implies a partial transfer of the power to raise revenue from the national level to the Community level, would make the already glaring defects of the system of democratic control even more unacceptable. National parliaments would no longer be required to vote the funds necessary to fulfill their countries' obligations under the system of common agricultural financing and would lose even this last possibility to put pressure on their respective governments to keep such expenditure within certain limits.

The link between financial autonomy of the Community and adequate democratic control over its income and expenditure is therefore inescapable, as the Commission had already concluded in 1965. Five years later the evident was accepted by all partners in a carefully balanced and not overly ambitious compromise.[13] As a result, from 1 January 1975 total receipts from the border levies, total receipts from the common external tariff, and receipts equivalent to one point at a maximum of the percentage of the uniform added value tax will flow into the Community budget, less a 10 percent retainer on the first two items to cover the cost of raising this revenue. Furthermore, beginning with the budget for the year 1975, the European Parliament can, with a majority of its members forming three-fifths of the votes expressed, amend the draft budget as approved by the Council. From 1974 onwards, it will thus be possible for the European Parliament to prevail over the Council in budgetary matters.

The policy-area to which this applies is unfortunately singularly reduced. In the first place the European Parliament will not have the final say in fixing the common agricultural prices which are the main legislative decisions determining in a broad way the spending side of the Community's budget. These decisions cause approximately 97 percent of the Community's expenditure.

Secondly, even for those items of expenditure which do not result automatically from the Community's agricultural legislation—covering, by present standards, the remaining 3 percent of expenditure—the door to what some obviously consider parliamentary follies is safely bolted. To this effect the Commission has been given the task of calculating a rate of maximum increase on the basis of the development of gross national product volume in the Community, the mean variation in the budget of the member states, and the trend in the cost of living over the previous financial year. This maximum rate of increase will be binding on all institutions, including the European Parliament.

Thirdly, the level of income available to the Community can only be influenced in a minor way. Revenues from border levies and customs duties are variable in amount, but their calculatory basis is fixed and cannot be altered by the European Parliament. Only revenue from the added value tax can be influenced by modifying, within the maximum of one point, the basis of calculating the amounts to be transferred to the Community budget from this source.

The European Parliament has criticized this arrangement, and the Commission has not associated itself with it. As a result of these pressures, the Council has agreed to review the matter in 1973 in the light of circumstances prevailing at that time, also taking into account the likelihood of British adhesion in the meantime.

Clearly, a true and lasting solution can only be found within some system of more direct elections to the European Parliament. The representative character of the Parliament has to be improved considerably before its right of ultimate decision-making can be validly instituted and asserted.[14] The logical complement of such a development would be to vest legislative power chiefly in the Commission, the Council playing the role of a senate, but a senate with a very big voice in matters of importance and especially when reductions in the scope of nationally retained powers is under discussion. Such steps signify, however, leaving the present prefederal stage and moving onward to a more federal type of construction.

We now come to the second challenge I mentioned. As I pointed out in my introductory remarks, improving democratic control over the decision-making process of the Community is not the only problem area of our subject. The growth of the Community, the steadily increasing influence of Community powers or activities over the powers still remaining on the national level, create the risk that the political process within the member states loses substance. Parliamentary control of the use made of the new powers allocated to, or created on, the Community level is one thing. The true significance of the political potentialities remaining on the national level is another matter. Youth especially is wondering whether the existence of the Community does not unduly limit the development of the progressive and democratic content of national social and economic structures.

In order to understand this doubt, we have to stop for a moment at the notion of partial integration. It is a fact that while a number of national powers are now extinct[15] and while others are embedded in Community criteria and procedures,[16] the bulk of the governmental powers which shape our existence and which determine the type of society we live in, remain intact on the national level, unfettered by supranational obligations. This is true for such wide areas as social policy, economic policy, financial policy, industrial policy and regional policy.[17] The term partial integration adequately describes this situation, which is characterized by the coexistence of areas of unlimited national sovereignty and areas where this sovereignty has been more or less severely limited by the powers vested in the Community. Such a situation understandably raises the question whether the remaining areas of national sovereignty can, will, or should preserve their reformatory potential.

Indeed, hardly anybody will contest that our various national societies still have to undergo many fundamental changes before they can be considered just and humane. It is also clear that for the moment such changes can only be brought about by an efficient use of the various retained powers I just mentioned. Hence the need to reconcile further national reforms with the parallel presence and development of the European Community; that is to say, an effective union, widened wherever necessary into an effective economic union.

I already mentioned one method to achieve this reconciliation.[18] It consists of efforts to harmonize as much as possible the exercise on the national level of the retained powers, through the definition and application of common policies.

Another approach being advocated consists of a broader application of the principle of federal good faith, which requires that members of a federation in the exercise of their retained powers heed the effects of their measures both on the coherence of the federal entity and on the retained powers of the other members. Federal good faith in this way acts as a limit on the retained powers, which prevents and inhibits the export of national economic difficulties or the achievement of national social and economic change at the expense of other members. Hampering such changes either deliberately or unintentionally but avoidably would equally be out of bounds. Specific applications of such a doctrine are of course hard to construe, but the basic idea is clear: a restraint is put on the disintegrating effects which the exercise of nonintegrated powers can possibly have on the integrated sectors.

Whatever the solutions adopted, the issue as such is far from theoretical. The British Labour Party's initial doubt about joining the Common Market was based on fears that their program for national social and economic reform would be incompatible with membership. Since then it became clear that the EEC Treaty as it stands is politically neutral.[19] Presently, the emphasis shifts from the rules as initially agreed upon to certain extrapolations which appear necessary or desirable to give these rules the required durability and permanence under changing social and economic circumstances, but the same question still arises. With strong socialist parties either in office or forming the main opposition in a number of Member States, it is vital for the Community to establish a clear and unequivocal relationship to national programs for structural reform. The moment the Community identifies itself with a certain type of society and serves as the involuntary cement of a certain social order, it risks to be brushed aside with that same order. Clearly this cannot be in the interest of a European Community which is conceived and built to last.

I would like to leave the matter here. My aim has been to show the European Community—and in this respect it is like any other human endeavor—as a continuous creation. For this endeavor to remain in keeping with our ethical and political traditions, it has to be coupled with the struggle for more democracy not only on the political, but also on the economic and social level. I hope I have made it clear that the challenge here is a double one. Within the Community itself more government by consent is vitally needed. At the same time it is equally vital for the Community not to stand in the way whenever, within the member states, more change by consent is decided upon.

NOTES

1. Technically we should use the plural and speak of the European Communities as long as the European Community for Coal and Steel, the European Economic Community, and the European Community for Atomic Energy (Euratom) still are legally distinct entities. As the principle of their ultimate merger has been accepted, the singular used here is not unduly anticipatory.

2. See articles 30 and 100 of the Treaty of Rome (EEC).

3. The restrictions imposed on this unity as a result of the French devaluation and the German revaluation are temporary.

4. The harmonized turnover tax which the member states are obliged to introduce in accordance with two directives adopted by the Council on April 11, 1967, *Official Journal*, no. 71, April 14, 1967. Harmonization is essential to ensure the nondiscriminatory character of the refunds of turnover tax on exported goods.

5. See passim, *First, Second*, and *Third General Reports* of the EEC Commission (Brussels, 1968, 1969, 1970).

6. See L. J. Brinkhorst and H. G. Schermers, *Judicial Remedies in the European Communities*, (London and So. Hackensack, N.J., 1969), p. 152.

7. *Ibid.*, pp. 106–107.

8. The Treaty of Rome (see articles 4 and 137–143) only uses the name "Assembly." The title "European Parliament" was adopted by an autonomous decision of the same. This title was recognized by the totality of the member states for the first time in the communiqué of the conference of heads of state and government held in the Hague, December 1–2, 1969. See EEC Commission, *Third General Report* (Brussels, 1970), appendix 3.

9. Article 138 §3, Treaty of Rome for EEC, and see article 21 of the Treaty of Paris for ECSC.

10. See Document of the European Parliamentary Assembly no. 22 of 30 April 1960. See also W. N. Hogan, *Representative Government and*

European Integration (Lincoln, 1967), p. 215; Richard Mayne, *The Institutions of the European Community* (London, 1968), p. 70.

11. See EEC Commission, *Eighth General Report* (Brussels, 1965), §214, §344.

12. Article 49, Treaty of Paris.

13. The complex transitional arrangement covering the period between January 1971 to January 1975 are not essential to the issue here under discussion. For the full text of the Council decision on the Communities' own resources see *Official Journal*, no. L 94 of April 24, 1970, pp. 19ff. The main aspects of the draft Treaty concerning the strengthening of the powers of the European Parliament are set out in the press release issued after the Council meeting 7 February 1970.

For the full text see the Collection of Documents, *Les ressources propres aux Communautés Européennes et les pouvoirs budgétaires du Parlement européen*, published by the Secretariat of the European Parliament, with a foreword by Mario Scelba, Luxembourg, June 1970. All the past efforts of the European Parliament as well as of the national parliaments in the matter are systematically recorded there. For a commentary on the Council decision see G. Olmi, "Les décisions du 21 avril 1970 sur le financement de la politique agricole commune," *Revue du Marché Commun*, April 1970, pp. 202 ff.

14. Although we should not forget that on the national level full parliamentary powers were instituted well before these parliaments were truly representative in our sense of the word.

15. For example, the power to determine customs duties.

16. For example, the power to give subsidies.

17. In this way the Treaty contains a few obligations but these in no way hamper national measures of structural reform. Cf. articles 103–109.

18. *Supra*, p. 4.

19. See reply of the Commission to Parliamentary Question 191/69 put by Mr. Cylinne, *Official Journal*, no. C 132, 15 October 1969, p. 5.

10: EPIMETHEUS
E. A. Goerner

I was having dinner at the Parthenon with some friends and I mentioned that I was going to take part in a conference entitled "New Challenges to Constitutional Democracy in the Atlantic Community." That spark seemed to set fire to our spirits quite as effectively as the waiter's cigarette lighter set off the blazing flames on the Saganaki, and the ensuing conversation illumined more of the subject of our conference than would have the remarks I had earlier thought of making. So I decided to recount to you our dialogue rather than read you the ordinary sort of paper. Furthermore, some of you may arrive at the conclusion that, in a certain way, the dialectic mode of discourse may be radically more appropriate to the situation in which we find ourselves (and which generates conferences with such titles) than the didactic mode of discourse which is that of the ordinary paper.

Well, I had no sooner got the title of our conference out of my mouth than Pandora, as is her way, snapped at the last words out of my mouth and used them to pry my mouth back open so as to find out what I might have hidden in my mind behind such a formidably opaque title as "New Challenges to Constitutional Democracy in the Atlantic Community."

"Why are you going to talk only about the Atlantic Community? Doesn't that seem a bit parochial? There seem to be interesting enough challenges and responses, new and old, to constitutional democracy in Japan and India and the Philippines, just to mention three countries outside of the Atlantic Community and one could easily mention a lot of other ones, not to speak of such places as Australia and New Zealand which, though physically in the Pacific, are spiritually European marchlands."

"Well," I said, "there does seem to be something parochial about that. But that may just be the result of there being something intrinsically parochial about human speech. One can't talk about everything at once, not even in three days. One has to talk about this or that and while one is talking about this one is not simultaneously talking about that. The only alternative would seem to be for all of us to get together and pretend to constitute an absolute moment by pronouncing together the all-englobing 'Om' and nothing else. I say pretend since sensitive men have already noted that 'Om' itself is discursive, moves from the 'O' to the 'm' and even if one were to drop one or the other of the sounds, there would still be a beginning, a middle, and an end, and other divisions beyond our counting. And so we have decided to recognize the inherent limitedness of all human discourse and, rather than try to talk about the whole world in three days, we are only going to talk about the Atlantic Community."

"What you've just told my wife is still not a very convincing explanation," put in Epimetheus in his slow and reflective way. "The fact that you can't talk about every place in the whole world but have to choose what places you're going to talk about doesn't mean that you must talk about the countries of western Europe and North America."

"No, but then we have a grant to talk about Europe and North America and not about Asia or the Pacific, for example, and you surely know that one only talks about things one has a grant to talk about...."

"Just a minute," broke in Prometheus with mock surprise. "Don't think you will get away with that stunt. We're not going to pick up the check for your dinner just because you talk about the things we propose. On the contrary we are going to force you to be free, as Rousseau put it, by making you pay your own check. So talk or not as you please but don't think you're going to get us to be accomplices in one way or another with the sort of servility that goes with submitting to the power of the Olympian foundations, not to speak of dinner companions."

Though Prometheus said all of this with a mischievous grin that deflected his lunge from my vital organs, nevertheless he nicked me and drew a drop of blood for I replied rather hotly: "We really thought there was some sort of special cohesion to the Atlantic Community that made it a suitable unit for study when we asked for our grant and I still think so."

At this point Socrates saved us from ourselves by wondering aloud as to whether he had sinned in some way as to merit having dinner with a group of argumentative geographers.

"What is that crack supposed to mean?" asked Pandora.

Epimetheus who, as her husband, has developed the virtue of patience to a singular excellence, answered: "He only means, dear, than it is boring, because senseless, to dispute at great length about the material object of the conference's investigations without reference to its formal and final objects."

"It's always so nice to talk with you," said Socrates. "You have such neat formulae for things that I have the impression that you know what I am thinking more clearly, more surely, more distinctly that I do. In fact I sometimes wonder if I wouldn't be better off being altogether silent and devoting my time just to listening to you. Then I would have the double pleasure of both knowing my own thoughts and knowing them better than I had originally thought them."

Epimetheus just grinned at him and so Socrates turned to me and asked: "But tell me, what sort of a conference is it that you are going to join in? Am I right in thinking it's some sort of party meeting?"

"A party meeting?" I asked. "Why that?"

"Well, from the title it sounds as if you are going to gather a group of partisans—in this case partisans of constitutional democracy—in order to discuss how to defend your constitutional democracy party against other parties, such as communist and fascist parties, not to speak of Maoists and Trotskyists."

"Don't be absurd, Socrates," I said. "It is going to be an academic conference at which we will, within the limits of the humanly possible, aim at scholarly objectivity and impartiality."

"And will the program include Maoists, for example, or Nazis, or some cross section of gnostic illuminées?"

"Well, no . . . all the names are of academically respectable people."

"Furthermore," shot in Epimetheus with unaccustomed heat, "you can't have a conference with such people. They are precisely the ones who turn everything into a party rally and want to break up any kind of orderly rational process."

"There is something to what you say," said Socrates. "But it is true, then, that there are people going about who don't think that 'orderly rational process' is the highest good?"

"Prometheus, for one," I said.

"And all of your respectable academics do think that 'orderly rational process' is the highest good?"

"Not at all, Socrates," I said. "Some of them do think that and some don't. But those who don't think that orderly rational process is the highest good nevertheless think it is a sine qua non."

"That certainly seems to be something like a party. You are going to assemble a group of men who are united in holding a common principle. They won't, to be sure, agree on *all* principles and they may even disagree about the status of the principle they do share but they agree that 'orderly rational procedure' is important enough to serve as a criterion for admission to or exclusion from the party, since there are people who do not agree that 'orderly rational procedure' is even the sine qua non of common life. And you are not coming together to discuss some purely speculative issue but to discuss a grave political issue that is a focus of current deliberation and action; namely, what sort of fundamental character ought the common life of the citizens have? that of constitutional democracy? of participatory democracy? of revolutionary dictatorship? or what? Your meeting, under the circumstances, cannot but appear as an informal caucus of the establishment parties that currently share power in the countries in question."

"Well, Socrates," I said, "it may seem that way if you put such a tortured interpretation on it, but we have no such intention. We are going to discuss not only 'constitutional democracy' but the 'challenges' to it and not in any spirit of partisanship but rather in a spirit of scholarly and scientific objectivity. We will give equal time, so to speak, to the 'challenges' and we will discuss trends and try to project them so that policy decisions can be made by statesmen in the light of the best available evidence."

"Have you ever read anything in the sociology of knowledge?" asked Socrates.

"Well, yes, I have read some Mannheim, for example."

I was about to ask what that had to do with the issue, but Socrates beat me to the punch with his next question.

"And have you ever studied rhetoric?"

"Yes, when I was a very young man I was fascinated by the power of rhetoric to sway men and I practiced the art assiduously, winning medals in contests and imagining myself winning the world. But what has all that got to do with the conference?"

Socrates answered me in a way that dodged the overall question by saying: "I asked you about rhetoric because it seems to me that rhetoricians have known for a long time what the sociologists of knowledge have recently discovered; namely, that the way in which a question is put or the subject of a discussion is posed has a great deal to do with determining the sort of answers that can be given or the sort of discussion that can follow. Let me be specific. You are going to talk about new challenges to constitutional democracy, right?"

"Obviously."

"And, leaving out the 'new' whose rhetorical function in such matters is well enough known, what would you say is the focus of such a discussion?"

"The challenges. And, now that I think of it, a review of the titles of the talks would show that the challenges get more than equal time in our discussion."

"And what is a challenge?"

"Well, something like a defiant protest against something, a claiming of something by right against somebody else's claim to that thing. So one challenges the right of somebody to have or do something. A sentry, for example, is said to challenge when he says: 'Halt!' And a man who regards himself as injured by another challenges him to a duel which is to say a trial of right by battle and one is supposed to fight until one has got 'satisfaction,' as the saying goes. And in law one challenges someone's right to some property, an inheritance, for example, and lawyers challenge prospective jurors and testimony and so on. So a challenge is some sort of dispute in which one party accuses the other of unrightful conduct and claims the right for himself in one way or another."

"It is a relative term then?"

"Yes."

"And a challenge would seem to be of such a sort that the challenger need only come into view in the measure that he wants to stop the one who has established himself in having or doing something from having or doing it, so as to leave the challenger free to have or do whatever it is—perhaps in some different way from that of the established haver or doer?"

"Yes, I suppose so."

"If one studies a challenge, then, one would not study the challenger in the round, so to speak, one would not look at him from all angles nor for his own sake but only insofar as he threatened the established one, in this case those who have power and govern after the fashion of constitutional democrats?"

"Yes."

"Which is to say that other kinds of government besides constitutional democracy will not be considered unless they are current threats to constitutional democracy and those kinds of government that do currently pose a threat to constitutional democracy will not be considered in themselves but only in relation to constitutional democracy insofar as they pose a threat to it. That the discussion will be kept in such bounds is secured by the fact that the challengers themselves will not be present and so their challenge will have to be presented through the words of the challenged—the Establishment, as the saying goes. And that surely looks like a party meeting both externally and in terms of the substance of the discussion."

"I was just thinking," added Prometheus, "'challenge' is etymologically derived from *calumniari* which means to accuse falsely and so, etymologically speaking, a challenger would be a false accuser. Naturally, I don't add that to your discussion in any spirit of partisanship but only with the most pure and innocent scientific intentions, desiring nothing other than that all the available evidence be brought to bear."

Prometheus' irony always tends to slip over into such heavy-handed sarcasm and this time, as it almost always does, it provoked his brother to break into the discussion and take on Socrates' challenge in place of myself, a task I was glad to leave to him for I was obviously a tired and cornered defender.

"Oh, stop rubbing it in!" exclaimed Epimetheus. "It is obvious that he made a mistake in pretending that a scientific inquiry has nothing to do with values. The moment you mentioned Mannheim and your rhetoricians you knew perfectly well you had him on the ropes. A conference on challenges to constitutional democracy is obviously an expression of a set of values, and the values are shared, in a general way, by most professional political scientists, if not all, as well as by most professional academics and intellectuals. And everybody knows what they are. They generally go under such other names as parliamentary democracy, liberal democracy, representative democracy, and the like. And the difference of names, as almost everybody also knows, indicates that there isn't full agreement about all the details of organization appropriate to the shared values. Nevertheless, the substance is clear enough: those who hold this view of things are radically opposed to the state's being understood as an expression of some structure of absolute value that is supposed to rule the life of the citizens. Such a state is always authoritarian in principle and is authoritarian in fact whenever any citizen disagrees with the supposedly absolute value structure of the state and lives his life in a way that doesn't conform to that value structure. But liberal democrats see clearly that value preferences are not subject to rational scientific verification. The essentials of that position were clearly developed by a line of thinkers, principally Hobbes, Locke, and Hume who overthrew the Aristotelian and Platonic pretensions to having constructed a science of the good; i.e., a scientific ethics. The empiricist critique of such pretensions remains essentially valid today and is accepted by the overwhelming majority of academics, occasional Marxists excepted.

"Crudely put, Socrates, nobody—except for peripheral gnostic illuminées and some of the college kids they manage to work up to hysteria—is prepared to say that his value preferences are objectively superior to anybody else's, nor that there is a generally acceptable procedure for verifying any assertions to that effect. That being the case, the only sane sort of regime is one that does not impose the values of some one, or some few, or even the majority for that matter, on anyone else. Oh yes, Socrates, I know there are differences among liberal democrats about those matters but you won't get anywhere quibbling about them. Sure enough, some liberal democrats want to prevent value domination especially by way of formal, legal constitutional prohibitions and procedures—and that is an especially American view, though it has spread to Europe. And others, emphasizing the parliamentary tradition, are more likely to focus on the importance of various countervailing powers of groups and parties and also the importance of the conditioning influence of habitual frameworks of behavior and of recruitment of political elites; you might say 'the education and acceptable manners of public men,' I suppose, Socrates. And again others, rebutting the charge that the numerical equality involved in the one-man—one-vote aspect of democracy is a rather stupidly mechanical way to conduct public affairs, point out that because there are multiple avenues of access to decision-making and because democracy does not force participation, and because elected decision makers make their decisions at least in part in terms of a marginal utility sort of analysis of voter intensity of feeling on given issues—because of all these reasons appropriately representative democracy is the guarantee against authoritarian domination even by the majority.

"And it is true, Socrates, that people who take such positions are sometimes charged with various crimes—with elitism, for example, on the grounds that well-organized minorities with high intensity of feeling often gain better access to and exert disproportionate pressure on decision makers and rich minorities are better placed, and so on. But all of those discussions take place within a broad and widely accepted framework that can be called a set of values but only if it is understood that the freedom and equality that are valued are not taken as the absolute values of life but as proximate values, as the inescapable means of assuring ourselves the psychic, social, and economic space to live our lives as we think best; i.e., each in accordance with his own value preferences. That sort of view of things, and the regimes that more or less correspond to it and that are trying to realize it somewhat more fully are characteristic of the Atlantic area. And it is precisely because the countries of the Atlantic area share such a set of proximate values, though ultimate values vary quite a bit, that there is a sort of Atlantic community. And one can perfectly legitimately conduct an academic, a serious scientific conference devoted to an objective discussion of the threats or challenges to such a framework as well as a careful, objective discussion of possible defensive strategies, the probability of their success or failure, and their consequences."

"By George," cried Socrates as Epimetheus finished, "this is the strangest boxing match I've ever been in. I've got my opponent on the ropes and Epimetheus comes up pretending to be the referee and telling me that I've won by a TKO when, just as I am naively raising my right arm to acknowledge a roar of applause, he drops his referee's disguise and showers a hundred blows on my unprotected body. But in your rush to batter me I wonder if a blow or two may not have missed the mark? You divided the world of thinking men, at least as far as politics is concerned, into two classes: the liberal democrats and the gnostic illuminées and their hysterical followers, the Marxists being included among the illuminées, am I right?"

"Well, yes."

"And presumably it is the gnostic illuminées and their hysterical followers who pose the challenges to liberal democracy?"

"All right."

"And so the conference would have to raise the general theoretical question as to whether gnostic illuminism is a superior ethic to the ethic of liberal democracy and only then decide whether it is wise to fight the challengers or join them or whether perhaps it would be better to look elsewhere?"

"Don't be ridiculous, Socrates. Obviously, I can't tell you what they will do at that conference but everybody knows you can't arrive at a rational, scientific verification of values. What a conference of that sort can do is investigate the basic causes of the weakness of the legitimizing mechanisms that support liberal democracy. One would consider such things as the deracination, and consequent alienation, produced by the demographic shifts involved in the urbanization of rural populations produced by the industrialization of both agriculture and manufacturing. One would consider such things as the deracination, and consequent alienation, produced by the high mobility of labor implicit in a high tempo of technological change such as is already evident in America and is being forced on Europe at added pressure by the Common Market.

"Similarly, one would examine the deracination and sense of alienation produced in considerable segments of youth by the step-up in the importance of more and more formal schooling coupled with a quick increase in the number of university students, many of whom do not come from milieux with a long tradition of high appreciation of formal learning, this combined with often inadequate provision of space and instructional staff. One would examine such matters in relation to the strength of traditional legitimation mechanisms. Assuming, with Max Weber, that 'the modern state is a compulsory association which organizes domination,' the basic mechanism whereby that domination is legitimated in a liberal democracy is 'the belief in the validity of legal statute and functional "competence" based on rationally created *rules*,' again quoting Weber, but it is necessary to add that liberal democracy not only legitimates itself by the belief in the validity of rational rules (as do all genuinely modern states), but liberal democracy adds legitimating mechanisms designed to produce a sense of participation in the formulation of those rational rules, a sense that the rules are *ours*. The mechanisms by which such legitimation is achieved include regular elections, widespread and unfettered public debate and the like. Naturally, one may have to sacrifice a bit of the rationality by the use of the democratic legitimation mechanisms and a bit of the democracy for the formal-legal-rational mechanism (for instance, one erects various filtering, balancing, and retarding devices, constitutional or otherwise, to prevent excessively short-term swings of public excitement from overturning all the rational rules), but the precise details of adjustment, while open to dispute, are not the really major issue.

"The point is that under certain circumstances a considerable body of citizens, overwhelmed, uprooted, tossed about, made to feel alien by vast social and economic forces, of whose exact nature they are only dimly aware, do not see the formal legal framework and its administrative application as being particularly rational but rather as being actually absurd, as being either the cause of, or at least an ineffective barrier against the chaos that is gripping them and overturning every calculable pattern, that is to say every rational pattern, of behavior. And in such a situation they, not unsurprisingly, tend to employ the mechanisms that liberal democracy envisages as its peculiar legitimating mechanisms in order to demand a radical remedy to what they see as a radical breakdown of the sociopolitical structure. And so they use such things as elections, freedom of speech and assembly, freedom to strike, etc.—not in ways that tend to legitimate the existing liberal democracies but in ways that threaten the whole fabric not only of liberal democracy but of the modern, rational state itself because in their distress they are often beside themselves in such a way that they easily become subject to the appeals of a charismatic leader who promises one or another, essentially magical salvation, which is why I earlier called such men gnostic illuminées.

"Well, whatever the conference will actually do, one can say in a general way what a rationally organized conference *would* do in such a context. It would direct itself to an investigation of possible techniques whereby large-scale unrest could be creatively channeled through the democratic process so as to produce a more rational realignment of the formal legal structure and its administrative application in terms of current real problems of social change (whereas the formal-legal rules that structure present governmental action are often empirically irrational in that they do not operate in terms of categories that are now applicable—though perhaps once they were—to the sort of socioeconomic developments that society is undergoing). Secondly, one would investigate possible techniques whereby a more effective and systematic legal and administrative control could be obtained over the unfolding of the basic socioeconomic changes that modern technologically advanced societies are undergoing so that the necessary changes could be experienced by those subject to them as understandable, as rationally desirable, as controlled, and as undergone with such aid and support from the organized machinery of the society as to be not only bearable but even as an exhilarating adventure for some, at least. If careful scientific investigation were to aid in the development of such techniques, one would have gone a long way toward reestablishing the legitimacy of liberal democracy among large segments of those presently disaffected by reestablishing a belief in the validity of government by rational norms and by allowing the participatory mechanisms of liberal democracy to function again as legitimating the regime by active appropriation rather than as levers of protest."

"I must say," said Socrates, "that if it weren't for the fact that you speak so lucidly, I would hesitate to speak a word in your presence since the least little word on my part is enough to set you off on what in anyone else's less limpid prose would seem an interminable tirade. But you've quite convinced me, with the exception of one minor point that perhaps you could clear up. It seemed to me that you, like Max Weber, prejudiced your case a bit by your terminology. Central to your whole argument was the notion of legitimation, was it not?"

"Yes."

"And *legitimation* is derived from *legitimus*?"

"Yes."

"And *legitimus* or *legitimate* has the sense of 'according to law' in general and sometimes the sense of "according to a higher, more comprehensive and permanently valid, law?' and it is in this latter sense that you and Max Weber used it?"

"Yes, that's so, Socrates. But Weber and I use the term *legitimate* or *legitimation* a *little* bit differently. *Legitimate* can have, as you say, a sense indistinguishable from 'legal' in the broad sense of 'according to law' and it also has, as you say, the sense of 'according to a higher, comprehensive, permanently valid law.' But since neither Weber nor myself nor social scientists in general think that one can arrive at such a higher, comprehensive, permanently valid, i.e. natural, law by any rational processes, and since people who think there is such a law differ about the content, therefore when we use *legiti-*

mate we mean 'that which is regarded by somebody as according to a higher, comprehensive, permanently valid norm or source of norms.' Since we have no way of knowing rationally or scientifically about the existence and content of such a norm, we must accept whatever people regard as being of that sort as the datum with which we must deal scientifically."

"All right, and both the popular senses of the terms and your sense rest, in turn, upon the fact that *legitimus* or *legitimate* are ultimately derived from *lex* or *law*?"

"Yes."

"And what is a law?"

"Are we really going to get into that vast field, Socrates? Law means all sorts of related things, such as the binding customs of a people and so on; a great many things connected by some such analogy or other are called laws."

"Yes indeed, Epimetheus, but you like formal definitions very much and didn't hesitate to tell Pandora exactly what I meant in terms of formal objects and the like. Surely you won't hang back now and pretend that you don't have some clear and distinct definition of a law by analogy to which you would employ other usages of the word?"

"All right, all right then, let's see: a law is a general proposition or body of propositions enjoining or forbidding certain definite future behavior, communicated to a social group and accompanied directly or indirectly with threats of punishment for noncompliance. How's that?"

"Would it be fair to say it is some sort of rational standard?"

"Yes, in the sense that it involves a hypothetical prediction in terms of which one under the law can rationally calculate certain consequences of certain behavior patterns. The law says: 'if you do such and such, or if you do not do such and such, you will suffer the following penalty.'"

"And would it be fair to say that the hypothetical character of law as you have explained it indicates what might be called its conventional character? Or, to put it another way, law as you understand it, would not be seen as a specification of some natural law?"

"You are right about that," said Epimetheus.

"And neither would law, as you understand it, be some sort of proximate reflection not of another, natural law but of some sort of ultimate rightness or justice, or fittingness, or appropriateness, as natural right theorists might say, distinguishing natural right theorists from natural law theorists and both from natural rights thinkers?"

"Right on, Socrates. You aren't doing a bad job yourself of making someone else's thought clearer than he had thought it."

"Well, then I have surely learned it from you. But tell me, law would also not be the holy, the divine command, nor a covenant between God or some gods and men?"

"Well, not really; although lots of laws present themselves that way. What I mean is: legislators can't always bring to bear against those for whom they are legislating all the force that might be necessary to produce perfect compliance or even some satisfactory minimum of compliance. And so they say that the rule of behavior they have laid down was in some way or other dictated by a god who will punish breakers of the rule. By getting people to imagine to themselves such punishments, the legislator conditions the subject population in such a way that, to a surprising degree, the police can be replaced by a great cop in the sky that everyone carries about in his head. But that is a very dangerous business. Old-fashioned liberals, or republicans as they often called themselves, were usually prepared to play with that sort of thing, as you can see from the French Revolution, the writings of many of our founding fathers, and the early constitutions of most of our states. But nowadays liberal democrats don't do that for the most part because it almost inevitably encourages authoritarians and fanatics of all sorts, and secondly, because there has been a general decline in superstition and religiousity such that it is possible for the modern state to be itself more fully by publicly allowing that the basis of the validity of its actions is precisely the formal, rational character of its processes; i.e., only punishing, and by a clearly defined punishment, future deviations from a clearly defined general norm of behavior in the articulation of which everyone can have participated on some footing of equality.

"And if you were to turn to the term *lex*, Socrates, you would, in fact find a similar shift from ancient Roman to later Roman usage. By Cicero's time, lex had been 'laicized' as Ernout and Meillet point out in their *Dictionaire Étymologique*. Lex referred then both to a convention agreed to by two parties and, similarly, to a rule expressly accepted by the assembly of the citizens who were consulted by the magistrate. But there are ancient expressions that have survived. They show that *lex* originally had the sense of a religious law, and naturally enough, since primitive peoples generally so view their laws."

"But there are other Latin terms referring to rules as to how a man ought to act that retained something more of a religious character or, at least, appeared to refer not to some mere convention but to some standard of the naturally just?"

"Of course, Socrates, *jus* and *fas* are the most obvious ones, *jus* meaning 'right' and carrying with it the sense of being just, fitting, appropriate and *fas* meaning something like divine law, that which was permitted by or ordered by the gods."

"And there are modern equivalents of such terms, are there not?"

"That's obvious for English, Socrates, from what I said a moment ago. There are terms like *divine law* or *just, justice, right*, and so forth. And similarly, in German and French terms like *Recht* and *droit* are of that sort in everyday usage and carry with them the sense of what is just or fitting or right simply and by nature and unalterably. But that is in vulgar usage and most scholars do not delude themselves as to the absolute character of the *Recht* or *Droit* or Justice of the conventional frameworks taught in law schools."

"Well, that is rather like what I suspected you would say, Epimetheus. And that is why I wondered whether a conference of the sort you say ought to be held might properly be called a party meeting."

Well, I can tell you that Epimetheus didn't take that remark too well, and you could see him make an heroic effort to retain his professorial calm as he replied: "Really, Socrates, you're absolutely addicted to the charge about such affairs being party meetings. But aside from the offensiveness of the charge, what evidence is there in what I said that supports it?"

"If I were to tell you that a good part of the Chicago Police Force were about to storm into this restaurant in fifteen minutes and arrest us on a conspiracy charge; and if you, having heard me say it, only laughed and went on talking and drinking retsina, then one might not be too far from the truth if one were to say you didn't believe me?"

"Oh, here we go again; more of Socrates' fishing expeditions," groaned Epimetheus.

"Are you going to take the Fifth Amendment, Epimetheus? After all, I listened quietly during your long lectures and now when it's my turn and I want to do things my way—asking questions—you want to quit the game. Given the fact that I am not violently threatening you but only talking, that's no way for a liberal democrat to act."

"All right, all right, I'll answer. Yes, if I behaved as you say under such circumstances one might say I didn't believe you."

"And if I told you that I knew a way by which you could achieve your heart's deepest desire and you went right on talking about something else, one might also not be too far from the truth if one were to say you didn't think I knew what I was talking about?"

"Yes."

"Well, but that is the sort of thing the natural law theorists and the theorists of natural right are saying: that there may be a way in which you can avoid prison, in this case a prison of your own making, and in which you can, furthermore, achieve your heart's deepest desire and not only in a private sense but for whole cities, countries, bodies politic, maybe even the world. And your not talking at all about their suggestion suggests clearly that you don't believe them and don't take them seriously."

"I suppose so."

"And your definition of *legitimate* as what anyone *regards* as such involves, subtly, the same thing?"

"In a way, I suppose."

"Moreover, you would use the term *legitimation* or *legitimation mechanism* for any arrangement that led a people to accept government whether the government be charismatic or traditional or according to the formal-rational procedure of law?"

"Yes."

"And since you use *legitimation* as the general term, rather than *charismation* or *traditionalization* or some such neologism, and, more importantly, rather than a more impartial term like *just* or *justification*, would not a rhetorician say that, whatever may be your formal, logical definitions, on the level of rhetoric you have given the precedence to the last kind of legitimation, the formal-legal, because the same term *lex* or *law* serves as a base for both the general and the specific terms, thereby suggesting that the idea of the specific term was more in accordance with the general principle governing true science about these matters than the other specific terms?"

"Oh, I suppose one might say there was such a rhetorical leaning, but that doesn't make a meeting conducted in such terms into a party meeting, Socrates."

"Before we get to that, Epimetheus, there is something else I wanted to ask you: according to your usage, the term *law* and *legitimate* refer to certain formal-logical characteristics and not to the content?"

"Yes."

"And it would be fair to say of *law* (and *legitimation* so understood) that they were terms that referred to frameworks within which men sought to realize each one his own values, or the good as he privately saw it, but that the legal or legitimation frameworks could not be scientifically regarded as being expressions of and pointers to the good life for men in general?"

"Obviously, that's been made clear before, Socrates."

"Well, what hasn't been made clear so far is whether such a point of view isn't the point of view of a party, and a party in the most fundamental sense."

"What exactly do you mean?"

"Just this: the whole of your discussion so far has clearly been repeating to us in a host of subtle ways that the human mind can clearly and distinctly view human life in only one way and that way is such that no ultimately shareable object of human activity comes into view. That being the case, values or the good must be viewed as a private affair and beyond the competence of any public organs since the only thing we can rationally share is a framework; i.e., a neutral means, within which each must pursue his private values or aims or good. And it seemed to me that such a view of things was an ethic and that there might well be a party that adhered to such an ethic. Also, the subtle rhetoric by which such an ethic was promoted (suggesting, though not always saying, that that ethic was the one that conformed to man's reason) might not unfairly be called party-political propaganda. And a meeting set up to make such rhetoric might be called a party meeting."

At this point Prometheus, who had begun to take a greater and greater interest in the conversation and who had already tried to break in a number of times, burst in with such agitation that he nearly knocked over the table.

"Beautiful! Socrates, Beautiful! You have got him to put *himself* into the very spot I have been trying to get him to admit he's been in but that he's always weasled out of. Of course it's a party he's part of behind all that social scientistic facade which is nothing but an Establishment trick to fill up the heads of bright kids with bourgeois ideology. But the jig is up. The kids have begun to see that the supposedly value-neutral character of Epimetheus' kind of social science is just an ideological smoke screen to cover the fact that, because the governmental-military-industrial complex controls the financial resources necessary to employ social science techniques, the whole scientific university Establishment is actually tied in the most servile way to the big Establishment. And the few kids on the intellectual avant-garde have begun to point out that the whole basis of value-neutral social science is, in point of fact, a bit more than what Socrates rather generously called an ethic. In fact, the basis of that supposedly value-neutral social science is the central component of bourgeois ideology, the individualistic illusion that values or goods are, finally and ultimately private.

"Well, anybody who's been listening to what's going on in the streets, in the schools, in the professional associations, knows that the facade has got gaping holes in it. There is a profoundly humanistic revolution in the making and on every front the young are getting ready to smash your bourgeois shams, to break down the whole pseudo, value-neutral facade of science on the university front and to break down the whole fabric of bourgeois hypocrisy about an impartial legal structure within which each one can live his own private little dream world protected from the crushing social reality of his neighbors' cries of distress. In place of the pious slogans behind which bourgeois liberal democracy encourages the systematic alienation of every man from his brother, the young, having smashed those shams, are set on building genuinely participatory communities, communities of deeply experienced human brotherhood. Establishment social scientists know perfectly well what they are doing setting up conferences on challenges to bourgeois liberal democracy. They are both conducting a defensive propaganda campaign for the bourgeois Establishment and watching very closely to see if they can come up with some line that will be particularly effective, and maybe even set off a round of research grants."

Then, turning to Socrates again, he said: "That was really beautiful, Socrates. When did you join the Caucus for a New Political Science?"

"I haven't; and as far as I can see, I don't think I should."

"Do you think you will get anywhere against the Establishment by standing aside from the big confrontations between us and them that are coming? Or are you just looking for a free ride? If so, aren't you also just contributing to the individualistic, ideological smoke screen of bourgeois liberal democracy?"

"Actually, Prometheus, none of those things occurred to me, but I will tell you what did occur to me while you were speaking."

"What?"

"It occurred to me that your position and that of your brother are actually quite closely tied together, indeed generate one another. And what we are experiencing is not principally a crisis of liberal or constitutional democracy but a crisis of authority regardless of the form in which it might show itself, and that the wild oscillation of regimes and of political movements that modern times have seen is the manifestation of that crisis, as is the dispute between you and your brother.

"And it occurred to me," continued Socrates, "that the crisis is not new. In the peculiar form in which we experience it, it began to manifest itself on the theoretical level already centuries ago in thinkers such as Hobbes and Descartes. What is more recent is the spread and vulgarization of some of the fundamental opinions of such thinkers such that whole segments of the educated population suppose that they cannot know in any reasonable way anything about the good; i.e., an unlimitedly shareable object toward which in diverse ways awesome eros draws us on. And so in the dark rush of our lives so understood, some men, like Epimetheus, argue that we can at least share a common framework of constructed means. But every act pretending to be an act of public authority—i.e., an act taking, in the name of the community, some new step either in setting up such a framework of pure means or within the existing framework—is subject to a revisionist critique that points out how one or more individuals or groups have managed to secure a measure whereby they get a disproportionate share of the benefits. And so politics in general comes to be regarded increasingly as just such a scramble of individuals and groups to get theirs, checked only by fear of one another.

"And others, like you Prometheus, unwilling to suffer the anguish and shame of such a life of terrible estrangement, unwilling to repeat the chilling formulae of individualistic rationalism that assure one that one's anguish and estrangement are inescapable since no shareable, intelligible good is to be caught or even glimpsed in reason's net —you join with others like you in launching assaults upon men who seem to have come to terms with the isolation at the depths of their spirit while making a success of it on the level of their material interdependence. And in the excitement of your common battle against the bourgeois Establishment you have some feeling of breaking the arctic climate of alienation; the warmth and fire of comradeship seem to sweep in and cheer your hearts. But as Sorel saw, that sort of thing requires a myth, or rather a lie, about a future state of right, a state of affairs not to be reached in fact because you can only achieve that sense of warmth, of comradeship as long as there are still bourgeois dead souls in power who can be attacked.

"But that means there can be no act of public authority for the community on your part any more than on the part of the bourgoisie because, as long as you are fighting against the bourgeois Establishment, your acts are not acts that can be attributed to the community but only to a faction. And as for that happy time you think of in your mythic dreams when you will either have thawed out all those bourgeois dead souls and brought them back to life or when you will have changed all those bourgeois with dead souls into plain dead men, then you will see that the dead souls were right when they denied you knew of a common good. You will see that you only had a common enemy and that the heat you shared and the comradeship you shared were the warmth and friendship of hate that masked your despond. And your first attempt at an act of public authority will be subject to the same old kind of critique, unmasking the private and class interests behind your ideological slogans. And as soon as you see that, you will know that it was all an illusion; that you are the new class, as Djilas called it.

"Well, that sort of transformation has already overtaken so many of our revolutions, left or right, Prometheus, that a lot of people already have seen what that means and have lapsed into a kind of desperate and cynical rejection of every least act of authority, and that seems to be the last stage of the sort of descending dialectic you and your brother and so many like you have been carrying out to its bitter end."

Prometheus drew a long and weary breath and said, "Perhaps you are right, Socrates, but what else do you suggest?"

"I don't see any possibility short of you and Epimetheus giving up, at least for the time being, your claims and beginning in modesty a common and careful search for any evidence about an object as great as your eros, an unlimitedly shareable object."

"Look, Socrates," said Epimetheus, "I don't really have the time for a long and inevitably fruitless ethical discussion. It's late. I have a meeting on a research project tomorrow. And the proprietor of this restaurant has been trying to get us out of here for the last half-hour. Everybody else is gone and almost all the lights are off."

He got up and Prometheus followed him, grumbling that Socrates didn't understand how tough and sly the Establishment was. The rest of us followed Epimetheus out of the now darkened restaurant, tripping and falling into each other over the steps at the doorway, except for Socrates who either remembered them from having come in or who, more cautious than the rest of us, slid his foot forward along the floor, feeling his way. I don't know which.

NOTES ON THE CONTRIBUTORS

JEAN BLONDEL is Professor of Government at the University of Essex, where he also served as first Chairman of that Department in 1964–68 and Dean of the School of Comparative Studies in 1967–69. He was Lecturer in Politics at the University of Keele in 1958–63, Visiting ACLS Fellow at Yale University in 1963–64, and Visiting Professor at Carleton University (Ottawa) in 1969–70. He is the author of *Voters, Parties and Leaders* and *An Introduction to Comparative Government* and co-author of *Constituency Politics, Public Administration in France,* and *The Government of France.*

GIOVANNI BOGNETTI is Professor of Law at the University of Pavia. He was Assistant Professor at the University of Milan in 1953–62, Professor at the University of Urbino in 1962–69, and Dean of the Law School in 1969–70. Among his publications are *Il pensiero filosofico-giuridico americano nel XX° secolo* and *Malapportionment, ideale democratico e potere giudiziario nell' evoluzione costitutionale degli Stati Uniti.*

BASTIAAN VAN DER ESCH is Juridical Councilor of the Commission of the European Communities chiefly responsible for the legal aspects of a European energy policy. In 1951–53 he served in the Dutch Ministry of Economic Affairs, concerned with Marshall Plan Affairs, and in 1953–55 in the Ministry of Foreign Affairs, seconded to the Netherlands Delegation to NATO, economic section. He was Secretary of the Permanent Committee on Armaments of the Western European Union in 1955–58, Personal Advisor to the Vice-President of the High Authority of the European Coal and Steel Community in 1958–59, and Juridical Councilor of the High Authority in 1960–68. Among his publications are *A Small Revision of the ECSC Treaty, The System of Legal Protection in the European Communities, Discretionary Powers of the European Executive and Judicial Control.*

ROBERT H. EVANS is Associate Professor of Government at the University of Notre Dame. He was Assistant to the Director, Johns Hopkins Bologna Center in 1962–64, Assistant Professor at the University of Notre Dame in 1966–70, Visiting Assistant Professor at the Graduate School of International Studies, University of Denver, in 1968. Among his publications are *Coexistence: Communism and Its Practice in Bologna, 1945–1965.*

E. A. GOERNER is Professor of Government at the University of Notre Dame. He has also taught at Yale University. He edited *The Constitutions of Europe* and is the author of *Peter and Caesar.*

ANTHONY HARTLEY is Editor of *Interplay* magazine. He was diplomatic correspondent of the London *Spectator* in 1953–58, and editor of the book pages of the *Manchester Guardian* during the same period; then leader writer for the *Guardian* in 1958–60, editorial assistant for the review *Encounter* in 1960–62, deputy editor of the *Spectator* in 1962–63, and foreign leader writer for the London *Economist* in 1964–67. He edited Volumes 3 and 4 of the *Penguin Book of French Verse* (covering the nineteenth and twentieth centuries), and the Penguin edition of Mallarmé and is the author of *A State of England.*

DONALD P. KOMMERS is Associate Professor of Government at the University of Notre Dame. He was Instructor and Assistant Professor of Political Science at Los Angeles State College in 1959–63, and Assistant Professor at Notre Dame in 1963–68. He has published in the field of American and European constitutional law and is the author of the forthcoming *The Federal Constitutional Court in the West German Political System.*

GERHART NIEMEYER is Professor of Government at the University of Notre Dame. He taught at Princeton University in 1937–44 and at Oglethorpe University in 1944–50. He was a Foreign Affairs Officer, U.S. Department of State, in 1950–53 and engaged in research at the Council on Foreign Relations, New York, in 1953–55. He has been Visiting Professor at various times at Yale University, Columbia University, Vanderbilt University and the National War College. He was Fulbright Professor at the University of Munich in 1962–63. Among his publications are *Law Without Force, An Inquiry into Soviet Mentality, The Communist Ideology, Communists in Coalition Governments, Outline of Communism, Deceitful Peace, Between Nothingness and Paradise.*

GLENN TINDER is Professor of Politics at the University of Massachusetts, Boston. He has taught at Lake Forest College, Mount Holyoke College, and the University of Massachusetts at Amherst. Among his publications are *The Crisis of Political Imagination* and *Political Thinking—The Perennial Question.*

DOUGLAS V. VERNEY is Professor of Political Science at York University, Toronto. Previously he taught at the University of Liverpool, England. He has been Visiting Professor at the University of Florida and at Columbia University. Professor Verney's books include *Parliamentary Reform in Sweden 1866–1921, Public Enterprise in Sweden, The Analysis of Political Systems, British Government and Politics,* and *Political Patterns in Today's World* (with D. W. Brogan). He was president of the Canadian Political Science Association in 1969–70 and since 1970 has been editor of *Canadian Public Administration*.

LIBRARY OF DAVIDSON COLLEGE